The Death and Life of Philosophy

The Death and Life of Philosophy

Robert Greene

ST. AUGUSTINE'S PRESS
South Bend, Indiana
1999

Manufactured in the United States of America.

Library of Congress Cataloging in Publication Data
Greene, Robert, 1937–
   The death and life of philosophy / Robert Greene
     p.   cm.
   Includes bibliographical references and index.
   ISBN 1-890318-19-1 (cloth : alk. paper)
   1. Philosophy—Study and teaching. 2. Aristotle. I. Title.
   B52.G74 1999
   101—dc21   99-19015
                                                                 CIP

Table of Contents

Preface

In approaching this book, one might well wonder what kind of work it is and to whom it is directed. To some it might seem to be a popular work meant to introduce general readers to the subject of philosophy. While it can serve in part as an introduction, a closer look will quickly reveal a larger purpose: the book has a revolutionary thesis. It recommends a series of radical changes in the way philosophy is conceived and studied.

To whom, then, am I proposing these changes? Certainly to all members of the general public interested in higher education and its problems. I have written in a style that, I hope, will make the book accessible to people who are not professors of philosophy and indeed who are not professors at all. However, merely by scrutinizing the Table of Contents, readers will see that part of the work, particularly Chapters 5 and 8 and the Appendix, consists of a scholarly discussion of various texts in the philosophical tradition, from which passages have been carefully chosen to support the argument. While some topics are covered thoroughly, at many places I resisted the temptation to go into more detail, being content to deal only with the most fundamental points. A further discussion is implied. Those with a background in the subject will recognize the implications and their full force.

The book can be used as a narrative in introductory philosophy courses to accompany basic texts, as well as in courses in the history of Western civilization or the history of ideas. It also is suitable for students of the history of philosophy and specialists in Aristotle. Since it deals with the relationship of philosophy to other disciplines, it should be of interest to scholars in a wide range of fields. Finally, it proposes solutions to perennial problems in education that are of concern to the general public.

In short, this is both a scholarly and a popular work directed to experts, to students, and to a large part of the public. I have tried to make it scholarly and popular in equal measure. Readers can judge whether or not I have succeeded. One of my teachers, Justus Buchler, liked to say that "Good popularization does not oversimplify." By the same token, good scholarship ought to be expressed clearly, even if non-experts cannot follow all the details.

The essay starts off in a non-technical manner and works its way toward the more technical parts. Long before the reader reaches them, he or she will, I trust, have grasped the central argument and will be eager to pursue it to its conclusion. The notion that philosophy and science can be reunited in such a way as to preserve the central values of each is exciting, as is the possibility of doing so largely through the ideas of Aristotle.

It is not absolutely necessary to read the chapters in exactly the order they are presented. Readers with a limited background in philosophy may choose to skirt the more technical chapters, dipping into them more and more deeply as they become more comfortable with them. I hope that the narrative will stimulate readers' interest in the original texts and that it will guide them unscathed through the labyrinth of "the history of philosophy," tracing a path for them that, I dare say, cannot be found in any other work.

One does not have to go very far to see how thoroughly I question the conventional view of philosophy, and the reader may wonder how I came to such radical conclusions. Some key details of how it happened are provided in the course of the narrative. At this point, I would like to acknowledge the role that teachers, colleagues, and friends played in the shaping of the ideas contained in the essay. They are of course not to blame for any errors I have made.

My teacher, John Herman Randall, Jr., for many years F. J. E. Woodbridge Professor of Philosophy at Columbia University, deserves first mention. It was with him that I first studied the history of philosophy, and through his influence that I became immersed in it. While I have made a number of criticisms of his writings in the course of the essay, his influence on me should nevertheless be apparent. He taught me to see the grandeur of the history of ideas. In particular, he had a vision of Aristotle as a scientist with something to say to us today. As Professor Randall himself might have put it, having got that idea from him, I have "pushed" it a few steps farther.

A second influence on the development of my ideas was Paul J. W. Miller, who taught philosophy at the University of Colorado when I was a graduate student there. Professor Miller is a Thomist trained at Harvard who provided a different perspective on Aristotle and the history of philosophy from that of Randall, who read the texts from the standpoint of twentieth-century ideas. I benefited greatly from the more traditional and more literal reading of the texts that I learned to do with Paul Miller.

A third influence was Howard Smokler, who also taught philosophy at the University of Colorado and was my dissertation chairman. Subsequently I assisted him in a History of Science Program that he directed in 1976–77. Major figures in that field participated in the Program. From them and from Professor Smokler I gained a perspective on science and its history that helped me to see that there is no clear boundary between it and philosophy.

From Justus Buchler, another of my teachers at Columbia, I learned about symbolism and the psychology of language. Also, his view of the history of philosophy complemented Randall's. He helped me to see the great thinkers conducting, in Santayana's words, a dialogue in limbo, illuminating each other's ideas.

Also at Columbia, I studied Kant with Albert Hofstadter and Spinoza with Paul Oskar Kristeller. I was introduced to the ideas of Chomsky by Gerald Holien of the University of Colorado.

The last major link in the chain of ideas presented in the essay resulted from conversations I have had over the past few years with Joseph Ruthgeerts of Mount Senario College in Ladysmith, Wisconsin. Time after time I have tried to persuade Professor Ruthgeerts, who is a determined, unwavering materialist, that Aristotle's concepts of the soul and mind are capable of solving the mind-body dualism. I doubt that I ever will succeed in convincing him, but the effort to do so forced me to think my way through to a solution that at least satisfies me.

I am equally grateful to Professor Ruthgeerts for his careful reading of Chapter 8 and the section on Descartes in Chapter 5. In particular, his comments on Section H of Chapter 8 helped make the comparison of Aristotle and Darwin much more precise than it had been.

The manuscript has been read both in its early and its final form by Dean Geuras, who teaches philosophy at Southwest Texas State University. His advice and support have been invaluable. I am grateful for the observations and encouragement of Bruce Silver, professor of philosophy at the University of South Florida, who also read the entire manuscript. James Williams of the Sociology Department of the University of Wisconsin-Eau Claire read the first draft and made very helpful observations. I benefited as well from the comments of Dean Eva T. H. Brann of St. John's College in

Annapolis, who read the final chapter. Finally, I am indebted to Kenneth Maly, professor of philosophy at the University of Wisconsin-La Crosse, who read the manuscript and was especially helpful in clarifying the discussion of Heidegger.

The Death and Life of Philosophy is a radical interpretation of its subject, distinct from the views of any who inspired or advised me. Nevertheless, it would have been a lesser work without the things I learned from each of them. As noted earlier, they are not to blame for its faults.

A synergy somehow resulted from these diverse sources. Inspiration came not only from my teachers, but from the great books themselves, especially the works of Aristotle. To sum up my own role in bringing this essay into being, I am content to borrow a line from John Locke, who characterized himself as "a poor underlabourer for Mr. Newton." Since Aristotle's father's name was Nicomachus, I will simply describe myself as a poor underlaborer for Mr. Nicomacheides.

Part I
The Death of "Philosophy"

Introduction

The organization of this essay mirrors its title. Part One deals with the death of philosophy, and Part Two with its life. That is logical, simple, and clear. We must take pains to be clear in order to avoid the vagueness and the ambiguity that becloud the use of this word by the people who call themselves "philosophers." Indeed, the phrase "the death of philosophy" refers to the impending demise only of the academic discipline of "philosophy." I use quotation marks because the word does not name a real discipline. That is to say, it does not name a distinct subject-matter, but a collection of activities believed to constitute one and designated by that name. So it isn't really philosophy (without quotation marks) that is dying, but only "philosophy."

Most of the activities that constitute "philosophy" are sound, and in my account they survive, but they are – to use Hegel's word – *aufgehoben* – canceled and yet preserved in a different form, subsumed into a higher reality. Were the great tradition of writers from the pre-Socratics to the present truly merged with the sciences, the academic world would be miraculously transformed. Moreover, the pseudo-problems forming the core of the illusory discipline of "philosophy" would be cast aside.

Before this can happen, we need to understand precisely what is wrong and what can be done. For the past hundred years questions have been raised about the nature of "philosophy" and what makes it a distinct discipline. Within the past twenty years, as enrollments have declined and the role of "philosophy" in the academic world has grown ever smaller, it has been widely recognized that the discipline is ill. A careful diagnosis reveals that the illness is mortal. Not hiding the truth from the patient or from its relatives, friends, and admirers, I propose to end its moribund state and put it to rest. Euthanasia is illegal when practiced on people, but is perfectly all right or even desirable for abstract entities. While the death of mortals is sad and even tragic, the passing of "philosophy" has many elements of comedy.

Moreover, its disappearance would clear the air. Our vision of academic life and of society would be greatly improved. At present, it is as if we academics had blinders on our eyes that prevent us from looking anywhere but directly at our own narrow specialties. Up to a point, specialization is a good thing, but in the past century it has been overdone. Many people recognize that this is so, and there is a great deal of talk about being interdisciplinary. However, despite the fanfare, very little real change has occurred.

One would think that a discipline with the grand old name of "philosophy" would be helping to remove the blinders, but it is so preoccupied with its own artificial, self-inflicted difficulties that it is in no position to help anyone else. To borrow a line from Ronald Reagan, it is not part of the solution; it is part of the problem. In order to bring disciplines back together, we need a new, unifying vision, and that is the last thing the ailing "philosophy" is likely to provide. In fact, hardly anybody in any discipline currently is offering grand solutions, not even bad ones. There is hardly a false Messiah to be seen anywhere in Academe. Even political correctness seems to be running out of steam. What we see is a bureaucratic hunkering down, over-administered colleges and universities, academic leviathans desperately protecting their turf.

Take, for example, undergraduate education. With a discipline calling itself "philosophy" still teaching the works of a great tradition of writers ranging from the ancient Greeks to the present day, it can be argued that there still is such a thing as liberal education. However, the contact of undergraduates with this tradition is so limited and the presentation of it so weak and incoherent that, in the end, it contributes little to liberal education. A similar criticism can be made of English and history, the other major liberal arts disciplines. However, "philosophy" is the one most suited to playing a unifying role, and it is the biggest failure. Undergraduate education today is really pre-professional education with a smattering of liberal arts, but it is packaged and presented to the public as much more than that. The continuing existence of "philosophy" contributes to the sham. Granted that pre-professional and professional education in certain areas – medicine, engineering, and the natural sciences – is still very good, the students in these areas are only a small part of the total number. In general, students and their families pay large amounts of money, often piling up mountains of debt, and for what – a meal ticket perhaps, but not a true liberal arts education.

If liberal education fails, then higher education as a whole fails, and eventually so does the whole educational system. As declining test scores and many a critical report tell us, the slide has been occurring for at least a generation. Ultimately, if education fails, democracy fails. Thus, whether "philosophy" lives or dies is not an esoteric question. It is of the greatest consequence and goes to the center of our educational system. Far more is at stake than the fate of a seemingly obscure discipline.

If the stakes are that high, killing "philosophy" might seem to be the wrong approach. We should be trying to save it. But that is precisely the point. I am proposing to do away with it in its ailing state in order to resurrect it in a much healthier condition.

Once "philosophy" is dead, can most of its organs, still viable, be successfully transplanted into other disciplines? Some observers, less sympathetic to it than I, might seize the opportunity to kill them off too. However, I suspect this will not happen. More people would like to see it revived and healthy than wish it were gone for good. But how are we to accomplish this?

It will be revived in the same way that it is killed. We will proceed with a historical analysis that breaks the bonds of disciplines, that questions shibboleths and destroys icons. We will see that "philosophy" and "science" resemble each other far more than is commonly supposed. The full synthesis of the two will, however, be presented only in outline, with a summary of discoveries I have made in the writings of Aristotle.

In regard to Aristotle, I wish to emphasize that I am not offering a package deal. All the criticisms of the current state of Academe and the proposals for reform can be accepted without *ipso facto* accepting the claims made for Aristotle. However, the one does lead in the direction of the other. If the skepticism and dualism of "modern philosophy" can rightly be questioned, what do we replace it with? Perhaps with an updated and corrected version of what it itself replaced.

Centuries ago, modern science discarded what was mistaken in Aristotle. In the process, it rejected or ignored much that was sound. The latter turns out to be much greater than people in modern times have realized. Aristotle's ideas on the nature of living organisms, on mind, human nature, the social sciences, and language were all equal or superior to modern conceptions. These ideas can be synthesized with modern science. Hundreds of years ago, science corrected Aristotle's errors. Now he can return the favor. The synthesis of the best in modern science and the best in Aristotle will prove to be wonderful and marvelous. We will keep the benefits that specialized research has brought us, but we will overcome the excessive specialization and the narrowness of our current intellectual life. We will have truly interdisciplinary research and education. The split between the sciences and the humanities that runs through our thinking and our everyday lives will be healed. We are so accustomed to this division that we do not realize how much could be accomplished were we free of it. If only we can keep our negative and destructive impulses in check, we will experience a creative flowering like that of the Renaissance, or even realize the heavenly city of the Enlightenment philosophers, a condition similar to what Aristotle and his successors in the Hellenistic period seem to have had in mind more than 2,000 years ago.

1

Attempts to Define the Discipline

I will begin by considering the nature of the discipline in which I was trained, philosophy. In the eyes of some, to do this is to tread upon a path filled with pitfalls. Consider the comments made at the beginning of his history of philosophy by my teacher John Herman Randall Jr.:

> It is customary to begin any study of the history of philosophy by defining philosophy itself. Like most customs, this is both extremely convenient and exceedingly foolish. It is convenient, for by confining the selection of materials to one's own philosophical problems, it is easy to make the entire course of history lead up to one's own solution, and thus be freed of responsibility for considering what may well be more important ideas. It is foolish, for no really satisfactory definition of what men are agreed to call philosophy has ever been offered, beyond the literal one of "love of wisdom.". . .
>
> It is safer to admit that philosophy is like poetry or religion: every definition is the expression of a particular and limited perspective upon a domain as broad as human life itself. . . . There is no question here, then, of imparting a new one at this point. Rather, this whole volume will be gently insinuating what philosophy is by pointing to what she has been and done. . . . To the incurious many, philosophy has always seemed a subtle deceiver: promising all things, she has delivered not even truth. . . . A philosophic idea, like the words in which it is clothed, when held up by itself and contemplated with too great reiteration, soon seems but a chain of meaningless sounds. How well the academic life has made that clear! But observe it in its natural environment: there is laid bare the secret of its long career. Viewed as an imaginative vision, an ultimate expression of the judgments and aspirations of human nature, a great philosophy may touch our mind with its clarified perfection, its architectonic beauty, without stirring our heart or compelling our will. But when we grasp the climate of opinion out of which that organic structure of ideas arose, when we sense the great social and intellectual conflicts that drove men to construct it, when we see it per-

forming in the world of men that function for which it was created, then we no longer wonder at its appeal and power.[1]

At least Randall admits that ideas have played a powerful role in human history! However, his view of the nature of philosophy is highly skeptical and relativistic: there is no dominant wisdom and truth, just a succession of contending ideas. This is the prevailing contemporary view, except in religious institutions, where philosophy is still the handmaiden of theology, as it was in the middle ages. When Randall asserts that the academic life has made the meaninglessness of philosophic ideas clear, he puts his finger, perhaps unwittingly, on the heart of the problem: philosophy has become a thoroughly academic discipline, in the pejorative sense of the term, and that is exactly what is wrong.

In contradiction to this view, I will give the reader a more positive view of philosophy, while roundly criticizing it in its current state. Whatever philosophy may have in common with poetry or religion, it actually is closer to science. *Pace* Randall, that has been its true identity down through the centuries. While it is true that the literal meaning of *philosophía* in Greek is "love of wisdom," this has been taken to mean "the *pursuit* of wisdom," *i.e.*, systematic rational inquiry, in other words, science. If somehow it now is bereft of its true nature, we need to consider what happened and why, and what effect this loss is having on our academic enterprise and on society as a whole.

Some readers may be startled at the assertion that philosophy and science are essentially the same. How can I have the audacity to say that philosophy, which, as everybody knows, is vague, imprecise, abstract, and "metaphysical," is the same thing as hard-nosed, rigorous, factual, experimental science? I answer that when we take a full, panoramic view of our intellectual history and academic life, that broad perspective enables us to put aside many of the stereotypes we have inherited, including our stereotypical views of philosophy and science. When we look in this manner at the long tradition of writers in "philosophy," we see that it is a great deal more like science than we have been led to believe, and "science," for its part, turns out to be much more speculative and "philosophical" than most people realize. History reveals these things to us, if we will but study it with breadth and imagination. If one takes each rational, factual step, and watches as each individual strand is woven into the tapestry of the argument, gradually a whole new tableau emerges, one so rational and sensible that we wonder why it was not apparent long before. The answer is that it is a synthesis of many diverse elements, components that we are accustomed to consider only in isolation from each other.

But back to Randall. Perhaps you noticed that in the passage quoted above, he started referring to philosophy with the pronoun "she." That is the beginning of an allusion, which he then develops, to the famous work of Boethius, *The Consolation of Philosophy*. Anicius Manlius Severinus Boethius (c. 480–524 A.D.) was a Roman statesman and intellectual who fell out of favor with the emperor Theodoric and was condemned to death. In this work, which he wrote in prison while awaiting execution, he imagines philosophy appearing to him in the form of a woman, Dame Philosophia or Lady Philosophy:

> While I silently pondered these things and decided to write down my wretched complaint, there appeared standing above me a woman of majestic countenance whose flashing eyes seemed wise beyond the ordinary wisdom of men. Her color was bright, suggesting boundless vigor, and yet she seemed so old that she could not be thought of as belonging to our age. Her height seemed to vary: sometimes she seemed of ordinary human stature, then again her head seemed to touch the top of the heavens. And when she raised herself to her full height she penetrated heaven itself, beyond the vision of human eyes. Her clothing was made of the most delicate threads, and by the most exquisite workmanship; it had – as she afterwards told me – been woven by her hands into an everlasting fabric. Her clothes had been darkened in color somewhat by neglect and the passage of time, as happens to pictures exposed to smoke. At the lower edge of her robe was woven a Greek [pi], at the top the letter [theta], and between them were seen clearly marked stages, like stairs, ascending from the lowest level to the highest. This robe had been torn, however, by the hands of violent men, who had ripped away what they could. In her right hand, the woman held certain books; in her left hand, a scepter.[2]

Then in a series of dramatic and poetic conversations, Dame Philosophy consoles Boethius and helps him rise above his earthly travail to contemplate the supreme good toward which he is going.

That was Boethius' vision of Lady Philosophy. Here is Randall's:

> And so, in ignorance of her deeds, it is idle to analyze philosophy's character. It is far wiser to tell the story of her life. She belongs to the oldest profession in the world: she exists to give men pleasure, and to satisfy their imperious needs. When young and blooming, she was a favorite of the rich but cultivated and discriminating Greeks, who kept

her in idleness for the sheer delight of her conversation. She had not even to lift a finger; and it was rumored that the gods loved her and her alone. But as she grew older, her charms faded, she waxed more austere, and took to giving sound advice on every occasion. And when the Romans burst into her garden, with their American moralism and fear of idleness, they led her off and set her to work as the handmaiden of Morality. She has been a working-girl ever since. Most of her life she has spent in serving Theology; but she had quite an easy time of it, especially toward the end, when her mistress was too decrepit to watch her goings-on. From this servitude she was rescued by a handsome young admirer who loved to hear tales of her ancient glory; but she was soon enslaved again by Science, who set her to work clearing fields and putting up fences. Science found her invaluable in private, but was apt to cut her dead in public. She has just put in a century working for the faith of our grandmothers; but the old lady died at last, bequeathing her effects to the brazen young Neo-Orthodoxy, who will have nothing to do with her. At present, she is entertaining proposals from the rich but ailing old Capitalism, and from the up-and-coming heirs of Marx and Lenin, earning her board and keep in the meantime by doing some cleaning up for the physicists, and angling hopefully for an invitation to set up housekeeping in UNESCO. For all the hard work she has done, she is scarcely an honest woman; and notoriously she can bake no bread. For centuries she has been a campfollower: you will find her always where the fighting has been fiercest, wherever men have been torn loose from their familiar domestic ties, when their wives have been left behind, or have run away, or are just grown too wrinkled and old. She consorts with men, comforts men, tells them what they want to hear; and with the wisdom of her incredible experience she teaches them how to win. No wonder countless soldiers in the strife of ideas have thought her the one woman in the world, *das Ewig-Weibliche*, and have sworn to her undying allegiance. But *mutabilis semper femina*; she turns up in some other camp with a new set of finery. She is indispensable, but quite without conscience.[3]

That is clever, and as a one-page summary of the history of philosophy, it is not bad, but what a comedown from Boethius it is! Dame Philosophia isn't a lady. She's a whore. Randall always did have a nasty sense of humor. More than once, I felt the sting of his caustic tongue. Yet he combined wit and insult so skillfully that one was uncertain whether to be offended or amused, especially since his mockery had a way of boomeranging. Consider the foregoing passage: if Dame Philosophy is a whore, what does that make Randall – her procurer?

Moreover, Randall begs the question just as he did in the passage quoted earlier: The wise old philosopher has seen it all. He loves it, but he doesn't believe any of it. But how does he know that philosophy is just a succession of contending and ultimately meaningless ideas?

However, Randall was far from alone in this view of things. Waves of skepticism and cynicism not only pervade contemporary philosophy, but ripple through many other disciplines at the end of the twentieth century. It is hard to be sure whether our lack of a unified vision of human knowledge and human life is a symptom or a cause of our *fin-de-siècle* malaise. Probably it is both. Whatever the precise cause-effect relationship, clearly the writers whom we call the "great philosophers" have been at the center of Western intellectual life since ancient times. Since they also form the heart of the discipline called "philosophy," looking at that discipline from a broad perspective may not only reveal what ails it, but shed light on other important questions as well.

The reader will notice that I write the words "philosopher" and "philosophy" in quotation marks. So many of these marks will occur in the following pages that it may seem as if I am playing fast and loose with punctuation. My purpose, however, is to avoid the verbal confusion into which discussions of the nature of philosophy so easily fall.

Indeed, many people seem to be in doubt about what the word "philosophy" means, and not just professional philosophers, as those who work in the field call themselves. "Oh, philosophy! That's something like psychology," I remember a man saying after striking up a conversation with me in a restaurant. Or as a lady commented to me across a restaurant table, "There'll always be a need for philosophy. People want to know about the meaning of life." I remember also the casual remark of a student, "Oh, I like philosophy! I always liked bull sessions." Or that of a woman who had taken a course in the subject some time before: "Ah yes, philosophy! [Pointing to a chair] Is that a chair?"

Not only does this vagueness and uncertainty exist in the popular mind, but it is noteworthy that even the professors in the discipline feel the need to call themselves "professional philosophers." Normally, we do not speak of professional physicists, professional mathematicians, professional chemists, professional astronomers, geologists, biologists, *et al.* If someone says he or she is a physicist or chemist or biologist or mathematician, we assume the speaker is a professional, unless told otherwise. Even with less high-powered areas of research like psychology, sociology, anthropology, history, etc., we do the same. The case is similar with doctors, dentists, lawyers, engineers, architects, and virtually all other professions and occupations. The name alone connotes professionalism. However, the word "philosopher" suggests an inherent absence of professionalism, and not necessarily in a bad sense. To some extent, the popular conception of a philosopher resembles that of a mathematician, that is, an absent-minded professor. Einstein, who embodied this stereotype and breathed new life into it, combined the images of the scientist and the philosopher. Still, everybody has at least some concrete idea of what a mathematician or a physicist does, whereas people are much less certain about what a philosopher does and tend to regard someone identifying himself by that name as an eccentric. Randall wrote of getting into casual conversations with seatmates on airplanes and telling them not that he was a philosopher, but a historian. That was the truth and nothing but the truth, but not quite the whole truth.

A similar encounter on an airplane is reported by the contemporary philosopher David Hall, who tells of a five-week trip to several Asian countries, where his hosts "were not only reputable philosophers but influential government advisors,"* and even Japanese businessmen wanted him to explain to them the philosophy of Nietzsche. His trip concluded, there he sat, on a jet plane homeward bound for the U.S.A., reflecting on the pleasant, but discomfiting contrast between the high regard Asians had for philosophy and its uncertain status back in the West:

> Certainly the most striking impression drawn from my visit was that, beyond the many courtesies extended to me simply by virtue of my status as a foreign visitor, I had been treated with extra kindness because I was a philosopher. Such treatment contrasted readily with that which members of the philosophic clan are accustomed to receive within Western societies. For at least since Socrates' fatal toast to the health of the Athenian establishment, the Western philosopher has enjoyed a rather modest social and political status.[4]

He did not have to wait long for the charm of his visit to wear off:

> My seatmate on the flight from Tokyo to New York was a Manhattan investment banker. We had talked for a few minutes about

---

* *I.e.*, the same group of people were both philosophy professors and government advisors.

current crises in international finance – the flight of capital from Hong Kong, and so on. Finally, it came.

"And what do *you* do?"

"I'm a philosopher." (To her credit, the silence was brief, the shuffling almost unnoticeable.)

"Ahhh . . . *ha*! An intellectual!" she jibed. Laughing, she added, "But what do you *do*?"

Though we were less than a hundred air miles from the Japanese coast, I suddenly felt I was at home.[5]

I guess it all depends on whom you are talking to. For example, when I was a graduate student and was skiing one day at Winter Park, Colorado, I got into a conversation with my seatmate on the chair lift, who turned out to be an airline pilot. "And what do *you* do?" he asked. I said rather apologetically that I was a graduate student in philosophy, and maybe that was not a very practical line of work. "Oh, no!" he exclaimed, interrupting me. "That's one of the most important things you can do."

Had Hall been sitting in the cockpit rather than the cabin, he might have got an entirely different response. At 40,000 feet with, as one of them put it, hours of boredom punctuated by moments of sheer panic, pilots spend lots of time looking at the sky, the stars, and the ground or the ocean beneath them. In that lofty environment, they do not have to be Antoine de Saint-Exupéry to think eternal thoughts, at least occasionally. High above the clouds, at the controls of those marvelous machines, surely they feel the sublimity expressed by Sophocles:

> Wonders there are many
> None more wonderful than man

as well as the humility of the Psalmist:

> When I consider the heavens, the work of thy fingers . . .
> What is man, that thou art mindful of him?

It may be that we Westerners are not quite the Philistines Hall thinks we are. Let us consider his comment that "since Socrates' fatal toast to the health of the Athenian establishment, the Western philosopher has enjoyed a rather modest social and political status."

Certainly it is true that the professional philosopher today has a dubious status in our society. But was it always thus? Beginning right after Socrates, we note that Plato doesn't quite fit Professor Hall's observation. He was, after all, invited by Dionysius, the ruler of Syracuse, to reform the Syracusan state on the model of the ideal state in his dialogue *The Republic*. Then there was Aristotle, who, starting off as tutor to a crown prince named Alexander, maintained his association with this fellow Alexander when the latter became King of Macedon and Greece and led his armies over much of the civilized world. Aristotle was the intellectual spearhead of the drive to make Greek civilization dominant in the world. Both Alexander and Aristotle died prematurely, but in large measure their efforts succeeded, as they made Greek culture available ultimately to the whole world.

Well, Plato and Aristotle may have been exceptions to the modest status of philosophers, and it's a long way from their time to the present. But wait – there seem to be more exceptions. By 146 B.C., the ascendancy had passed from the Greeks to the Romans. In that year, the latter completed their conquest of Carthage and also assumed control of Greece. Now that they had a polyglot empire stretching across much of the Mediterranean, a group of intellectuals led by the victorious general Scipio Africanus were looking for a body of ideas to provide a rationale for the newly established Roman Empire. They chose the Stoic philosophy of universal brotherhood and universal reason as the official philosophy of the Empire. Still later, in the first century B.C., Marcus Tullius Cicero (106–43 B.C.), a leading attorney and politician and the foremost orator of his day, translated Greek philosophic works into Latin and wrote numerous dialogues of his own, which have been studied for many centuries. Cicero wasn't just a philosopher who advised statesmen; he *was* both a philosopher and a statesman. Nor was he alone. In the second century A.D. the emperor Marcus Aurelius also was a Stoic philosopher.

Amazing, isn't it, how the list just seems to go on. After the rise of Christianity, St. Augustine (353–430 A.D.) developed a philosophy and theology of Christian Platonism that not only was the intellectual heart of medieval Christianity, but influenced both Luther and Calvin. Luther and Calvin in turn were philosopher/theologians who revolutionized Christianity and society with their Protestant theology and institutions. Augustinian Platonism also influenced Galileo and Descartes and the other founders of modern mathematical science.

In the thirteenth century, St. Thomas Aquinas showed that Aristotle's ideas could be Christianized, and gave a whole new direction to medieval intellectual life. Even after medieval scholasticism died out, Thomas's ideas have remained a bulwark of the Roman Catholic Church. They underwent a revival in the nineteenth and twentieth centuries, as they enabled the Church to fit Darwinian evolution into its framework of belief.

In the seventeenth century, Descartes caused a revolution in intellectual life with his mind-body dualism and his advances in mathematics. His fame was so great that Queen Cristina of Sweden all but kidnapped him. She sent a ship commanded by an admiral to where Descartes was living in the Netherlands to fetch him to Sweden to be her private tutor. Also in the seventeenth century, Spinoza corresponded with the leading scientists of his day and may have been acquainted with the DeWitts, the chief executives of the Netherlands. Leibniz too was a leading figure in the intellectual life of his day, for a time was the dominant influence in German thought, and was famous all over Europe. Locke is known as "the father of modern psychology" and was the chief theoretician of England's Glorious Revolution of 1688 and of American independence a century later. In addition to writing treatises in philosophy, Berkeley was a scientific researcher and a bishop. Hume was hardly a philosopher laboring in obscurity but a famous writer whose ideas provoked continuing controversy. Kant, though very much an academic, still was the major influence in the succeeding 200 years of philosophy, and his work had repercussions in many other disciplines. Hegel had a profound effect on the study of history and on the social sciences. His work stimulated Marx, whose effect on intellectual life and on society was even more sweeping. Later on, in America, Dewey caused a revolution in education.

The foregoing list is not complete but is more than enough to make the point. For more than 2,000 years the influence of the people whom we call philosophers has been enormous. The assertion that their status has been modest is a monumental misstatement. The problem is not the public's mistaken view of philosophy, but rather the mess the so-called philosophers have made of their discipline. Befuddled by their own internal problems, they have been helpless to prevent Academe from becoming excessively specialized or to overcome the modern dualism between the sciences and the humanities. Far from helping others eliminate these ills, far from providing the unity and coherence that would bring other disciplines back together, the "philosophers" offer some of the worst examples of incoherence and disunity to be found in Academe. That is why "philosophy" is held in such low esteem.

Perhaps the reader has not stopped to reflect on the fact that the array of specialized departments and disciplines that constitute the university at the end of the twentieth century is only about a century old. While the university as an institution goes back to medieval Europe, and many disciplines trace their ancestry back to the ancient Greeks or even earlier, many of the academic fields we know today did not become organized into professions until the latter part of the nineteenth century. At that time, when all the other fields were becoming professional disciplines, "philosophy" had to be one too. But the twentieth-century professional philosophers never quite figured out exactly what they were doing, what precisely made "philosophy" different from the sciences as well as from the humanistic disciplines, of which it might seem to be one. "Philosophy" was not systematic or empirical enough to be science, yet it was more literal and rigorous than the arts. So what was it then? Many attempts were made to answer this question. Indeed, as another of my teachers, Justus Buchler, said, there has been more "metaphysical self-consciousness," as he called it, in the twentieth century than in the 2,000 years preceding. Small wonder, because "philosophy" never before had conceived of itself as a discipline with its own method and content separate from all the rest.

Typical of the answers given was that of William James, who defined philosophy as "the residuum of questions left unanswered." In other words, as soon as a solution to a problem or set of problems was found, it ceased to be philosophy and became science. Thus, philosophy by definition was distinct from science.

This view may have been influenced by Immanuel Kant (1724–1804) and certainly accords with the view stemming from him, known as "foundationalism." That is to say, philosophy seeks to explore the foundations, the *Grund* or *Gründe* as Kant would say, of all particular disciplines. Thus, we have philosophy of science, philosophy of art, political philosophy, etc. Kant's work has been the most influential in the field for the past 200 years. His theories have had a great deal to do with the way the discipline has defined itself.

Both of these views accord with the popular understanding of the *word* "philosophy," which is used by many people. Although most of them have never studied the *subject* formally, they use the word in a clear and coherent way. Thus, when a salesman speaks of his "sales philosophy" or an athletic coach of his "coaching philosophy" or a businessman of his "business philosophy," and so on, the meaning is clear: the principles by which the individual guides his or her activity.

These three definitions are consistent with one another. After all, where do the principles of any field or activity come from? How can we justify them? Discovering, comparing, and justifying principles is very much like studying fundamental unanswered questions, if not the same thing. These are questions about which reasonable people can disagree. In other words, they are philosophical questions.

According to Kant, the human reason is doomed to ask itself questions it never can answer, pose problems to itself it never can solve. Chief among these are what he called "the antinomies of reason," which are contradictions that, in his view, follow from the nature of reason itself. For example, it is perfectly plain to anyone who has ever stopped to think about it that the world must have a beginning and an end; yet it seems equally apparent that time and space are infinite and that the world cannot, strictly speaking, have any beginning or end. Then common sense tells us that everything consists of simple elements, that there must be some ultimate elements – atoms, or subatomic particles, or whatever – out of which everything is made; yet at the same time, how can there be any ultimate components of being? You can just keep on dividing forever. Thirdly, we presume that free will exists; are we not the causes of our own actions? Yet science tells us that everything has a cause, everything is determined. Finally, it must be the case that there is some necessary being underlying all the changes and movements we see around us – if absolutely everything were contingent and subject to chance, how could the universe exist? But what then is this absolute being? Everything in our experience seems temporary and contingent.

Every human being at some time in his or her life has thought about these parodoxes or contradictions, however briefly. It is a natural tendency of the human mind. Kant stated them more abstractly than the average person would do and made them one of the cornerstones of his system. He likened the natural tendency of the reason to reflect on such questions to the foam produced by the ocean as it beats against the shore. No matter how much you scoop off, more will arise. He might just as easily have drawn a comparison with Sisyphus, the mythical Greek king condemned in Hades eternally to roll uphill a heavy stone that always rolled back down.

Without for the moment pronouncing on the correctness or incorrectness of Kant's views, we recognize that they influenced the formation of the contemporary discipline that goes by the name of "philosophy" and that organized itself as a discipline in the latter part of the nineteenth century. Perhaps the reader will think I am overdoing things – the quotation marks, the cautious, diffident way of talking about "philosophy" – as if I were doubting its very existence. On the other hand, systematic doubting is precisely what René Descartes, "the father of modern philosophy," made the hallmark of his method, even to the point of trying to doubt his own existence. Beginning with Descartes and on through the next century, eight major writers as well as some lesser ones wrestled with the same set of problems. The other seven were Hobbes, Spinoza, Locke, Leibniz, Berkeley, Hume, and Kant. Kant's monumental writings put the capstone on the ideas of his predecessors. Their combined efforts form the core of what has come to be known as "modern philosophy." Since the discipline of "philosophy" focuses its attention principally on "modern philosophy," it reflects the concerns of the writers from Descartes through Kant, whose uncertainty about human knowledge was intensified by their latter-day successors and imitators. The field has emerged in the twentieth century with a very skeptical cast, a problematic turn of mind that is evident not only in its perennial identity crisis, but in all aspects of its activity. As Richard Rorty, a major contemporary "philosopher," succinctly puts it:

> Cartesian . . . skepticism seems to us so much a part of what it means to "think philosophically" that we are amazed that Plato and Aristotle never confronted it directly.[6]

In truth, the lady I quoted earlier had the right idea when she pointed to a chair and said, "Ah, philosophy! Is that a chair?"

I have no quarrel with the ordinary English meaning of the *word* "philosophy." The general public uses it in a clear, consistent, and acceptable way. The question is, does that word properly name an academic discipline? Is there really a discipline called "philosophy" whose function it is to deal with fundamental questions and raise doubts about the reality of our perceptions? Is there actually an academic field whose subject-matter *by definition* is "the residuum of questions left unanswered"? Do the professors who call themselves "professional philosophers" really devote their time to asking questions that never can be answered? Perhaps if we take a quick look at the tradition of writers who preceded the philosophy professors of today, we will be able to see how narrow and artificial the current discipline is.

Notes

1. J.H. Randall Jr., *The Career of Philosophy, Vol. I, from the Middle Ages to*

the Enlightenment (New York and London: Columbia University Press, 1962), pp. 3–4.

2. *The Consolation of Philosophy*, tr. Richard H. Green (Indianapolis: Bobbs-Merrill, 1962), pp. 3–4.

3. Randall, *op. cit.*, pp. 4-5.

4. David Hall, "On Putting Philosophy in its Place: And what do *you* do?" *Nova* (alumni magazine of the University of Texas at El Paso), 20, No. 2 (Dec. 1984), pp. 3–4.

5. *Ibid.*, p. 5.

6. Richard Rorty, *Philosophy and the Mirror of Nature* (Princeton, N.J.: Princeton University Press, 1979), p. 46.

2
A Brief History of "Philosophy"

When we look at "the history of philosophy," that is to say, the whole tradition stretching from the ancient Greeks onward for more than 2,000 years, we see that the interests of the writers in it were very broad. The texts are highly interdisciplinary. They range over many different fields. Indeed, even the "modern philosophers" turn out, on closer inspection, to be less skeptical than our contemporaries would have us believe.* To a man, the writers from Descartes through Kant were closely allied with science, or even were scientists in their own right. Descartes was a co-inventor of analytic geometry and tried to extend mathematical analysis to all fields of inquiry. Locke was trained as a physician; he contributed so much to the development of psychology that he earned the soubriquet "the father of modern psychology"; he was the political theorist whose ideas justified the Glorious Revolution of 1688 in England and later inspired the American war of independence. Far from representing himself as a skeptic, he described himself as "a willing underlabourer for Mr. Newton." Spinoza for his part corresponded with the leading scientists of the day and stated his ideas in the form of a mathematical system. Leibniz was a co-inventor of the calculus. Berkeley did research in optics. Kant was a physics and astronomy professor before writing the *Critique of Pure Reason* and other "philosophical" works. Hume and Hobbes, who had literary inclinations, were very

---

* As a matter of convenience, I shall often speak of the eight major writers from Descartes through Kant as a group and call them the "modern philosophers." Strictly speaking, every modern writer in "the history of philosophy" should be so designated. Although it would be more precise to call those eight the "early modern philosophers" or the "classical modern philosophers," it soon becomes awkward. Since it is they who define the current discipline, I give them terminological pride of place. The nineteenth- and twentieth-century writers are then referred to by their respective centuries.

much interested in what we now call the "social sciences," and used the natural sciences as a model for their theories.

Not only were the above-named thinkers involved with science, but they were concerned to extend its benefits to human life, while preserving human values in one form or another. They never let the difficulties they encountered in explaining the foundations of knowledge impede them from pursuing their central concerns. The problems were something to be worked past so that people could get on with the business of science. Thus, the "modern philosophers" were playing the unifying role that their successors today are *not* playing.

However, in the twentieth century we have lost the certainty of the Newtonian world-view that made it easier for the earlier writers to play that role. In addition, with the enormous growth of specialized knowledge, the study of non-Western cultures, and the disruption caused by two World Wars, the task of intellectual and moral unification has become more formidable. Looking back toward the seventeenth and eighteenth centuries in light of all that has happened since, the twentieth-century professors of "philosophy" think they see something in the problems of their predecessors that the latter themselves did not see.

While many of the "philosophers" of the twentieth century, like Whitehead, Dewey, and Wittgenstein, also have had connections with the sciences, the picture is more cloudy than it was two centuries ago. For one thing, the Newtonian universe has been superseded by Einsteinian relativity, the esoteric world of subatomic physics, the indeterminacy of quantum mechanics, and a more uncertain cosmology. At the same time, the pursuit of knowledge has expanded beyond all previous bounds. More researchers are active now than in all the centuries preceding. There is not even a remote possibility of any one person knowing it all. Indeed, that ideal was abandoned more than three centuries ago, although a few diehards like Pascal, Goethe, Mill, and Peirce made valiant attempts to fulfill it. It is difficult even to have a unified picture of the whole or maintain necessary cooperation among disciplines. The extreme specialization in the pursuit of knowledge, together with the already existing gap between the sciences and the humanities, not only causes intellectual confusion but undermines and weakens the coherence of society.

These developments were just starting to occur or were in the offing toward the end of the last century when "philosophy" was defining itself as a discipline. Originally, the term "philosophy" had a much wider meaning than it does today, and for most of the past 2,500 years, it preserved that broader sense. The Greek word *philosophía* means literally "the love of wisdom" – in other words, the *pursuit* of wisdom or of knowledge. This meant its systematic pursuit, or what we nowadays call "science." Anyone familiar with the achievements of Greek science, comprising the work of Archimedes, Eratosthenes, Euclid, Aristarchus, Apollonius of Perga, Ptolemy, and others, knows that it deserves that name in the fullest sense of the word. Thus, for more than two millennia, the term *philosophía* or "philosophy" included what we now call "science." It is only recently that people have tried to make a hard and fast, ironclad, watertight or airtight distinction between the two, and despite a lot of palaver, they have not succeeded.

Kant's "critical philosophy," embodied in *The Critique of Pure Reason*, *The Critique of Practical Reason*, and *The Critique of Judgment*, as well as lesser writings, marked a turning point in the attempt to distinguish philosophy from science. In his view, there exists a long metaphysical tradition dealing with ultimate questions that cannot be answered. Kant's ideas foreshadowed the twentieth-century discipline of "philosophy."

While histories of the lives and thought of Western "philosophers" had first been written in ancient times, their authors did not systematically interpret and classify the individual thinkers. Early in the nineteenth century, Georg Wilhelm Friedrich Hegel (1770–1831) attempted to treat "the history of philosophy" systematically. This was one aspect of his effort to fit human ideas and human history into one all-encompassing theory. In his *Einleitung in die Geschichte der Philosophie* (*Introduction to the History of Philosophy*) he distinguishes the British use of the word "philosophy," which, like the Greek term, included all the sciences, from his own narrower use of the word.

Like Kant, Hegel thought philosophy was distinct from science, but his conception of it was more grandiose. He had in mind a set of principles and concepts from which all specialized areas of human knowledge and endeavor flowed. These, according to him, constituted a superscience. In calling the attempt to discover these principles "philosophy," Hegel was using the word in its traditional sense, but confining it to the most abstract level of human thought. In the Western intellectual tradition, a small number of thinkers have made similar claims for their theories. These include Plato (427–347 B.C.), Plotinos (205–270 A.D.), and Karl Marx (1818–1883). Plato did not work out enough of the details of his theory of ideas to turn it into a scientific system, nor did Plotinos with his theory of the One and the emanations. Hegel did work out some of the details, while Marx and his followers really tried to turn their ideas into a science, with consequences familiar to us all. For more than a hundred years the influence of the Marxists was very great, but it has waned. In the twentieth century came the Freudians, who also tried to apply their ideas to a wide range of disciplines, but they too are far less important than they used to be. More closely identified with the discipline of "philosophy" have been the various schools of thought that have operated within it in this century – the logical positivists, the analytic philosophers, the pragmatists, the Whiteheadians, the phenomenologists, and the existentialists – but all of these latter-day groups have had only a shadow of the authority and influence that previous writers in the tradition have had.

Hegel called his lectures on intellectual history *Introduction to the History of Philosophy*, but you would not recognize standard history of philosophy in them, *i.e.*, the version we have become accustomed to in this century. Nevertheless, when scholars in the late nineteenth century began to write the kind of history of philosophy we would recognize as such, they were influenced by Hegel's notion that there was such a subject-area and that it could be treated systematically. The pioneers of this type of history were German writers, primarily Windelband, Ueberweg, and Erdmann. Others in England, France, and the United States followed in their footsteps, among them John Herman Randall Jr. and the Jesuit father Frederick Copleston.

Given the traditionally broad interpretation of the word "philosophy," the question was what was to be included or excluded under that heading. It was easy enough to exclude the Greek mathematicians and astronomers. Whatever "the history of philosophy" meant, it was safe to assume it was narrower than that. But a great deal of what did get included was scientific in any reasonable interpretation of the term, like the writings of the pre-Socratic nature philosophers, at least some of the dialogues of Plato, such as the *Timaeus* and the *Theaetetus*, the scientific treatises of Aristotle, and the atomistic theories of the Hellenistic thinkers, as well as all the psychological and "epistemological" writings to be found throughout the tradition.

The point is that no hard-and-fast criterion existed for inclusion or exclusion. What emerged was a tradition of writers who clearly had built on each other's work. Any historian worth his salt could spot connections all over the place and describe them, even if their precise nature and extent remained a matter of individual interpretation.

Thus, a working consensus was arrived at – for example, the division into ancient, medieval, and modern periods, and the division of "modern philosophy" into the "British empiricists" and the "Continental rationalists." Those of us who majored in "philosophy" were all trained to make these and other bread-and-butter distinctions in terms of which the discipline was defined. On closer inspection, it was apparent that such distinctions as that between the British empiricists and the Continental rationalists were less than solid, indeed, very rickety in places. But we never questioned them enough to undermine the framework or paradigm that constituted "philosophy" as a discipline. A great deal of coherence obviously existed within individual clusters of writers: the pre-Socratics, Plato and Aristotle, the Hellenistic thinkers, the medieval thinkers, and above all, the group beginning with Descartes and ending in Kant. The post-Kantian writers, a diverse group of thinkers and schools, still had many threads connecting them with their predecessors.

This intellectual tradition was called "the history of philosophy" without there being any resolution of the ambiguous use of the word "philosophy" and of the overlap between it and "science." It remained unclear precisely what made "philosophy" a distinct discipline in the new academic scheme of things. This is particularly apparent from its relationship to "psychology," another field newly organized as a discipline during this period. The movement that came to dominate "psychology" was behaviorism, founded by John Watson early in the twentieth century and led later by B. F. Skinner. Both in their experimentalism and their anti-mentalism, the behaviorists were distinct from the "philosophers." However, consider the following from William James, who, resisting the separatist trend, ranged freely over both fields:

> No conventional restrictions *can* keep metaphysical and so-called epistemological inquiries out of the psychology books.[1]

James was one of the dominant figures in psychology at Harvard in the late nineteenth and early twentieth centuries. At Columbia, philosophy and psychology were in the same department until 1920. Thus, although "experimental psychology" had begun to identify itself as a distinct field fifty years earlier, it continued to be associated with "philosophy" well into this century. Indeed, when we consider the phenomenologists and the psychiatrists right up to the present, it is clear that the two fields have never fully parted. The phenomen- ologists are a group of "philosophers" who are very much interested in experimental psychology. The psychiatrists, and not just the Freudians and Jungians, have frequently had recourse to "philosophic ideas." The relationship between the two disciplines can be compared to that between theoretical and experimental physics, which stayed within the same discipline, whereas "philosophy" and "psychology" split apart. The separation may have had as much to do with differences in temperament and narrow dogmatism as with inherent differences in subject-matter.

Consider "epistemology" or "theory of knowledge," which the "philosophers" understand to be the heart of their discipline. The chief writers in "epistemology" are the "modern philosophers" of the seventeenth and eighteenth centuries. However, the term apparently was not coined until the mid-nineteenth century, the first period in which the *Oxford English Dictionary* records its use.[2] While no one would deny that "epistemology" is different from "behaviorism," we can well ask what distinguishes it from "cognitive psychology." Note that "history of psychology" courses include many of the same writers to be found in "the history of philosophy," particularly the ones in "modern philosophy"! Of how many disciplines claiming to be distinct from one another could such a statement be made? While we can assume that "the history of psychology" considers Descartes-through-Kant with a somewhat different emphasis, it is hard to believe that the difference is greater than that between, say, theoretical and experimental physics.

The fact that "philosophers" and "psychologists" should have separated in the first place serves to remind us that internecine conflict often is fiercer than battles with external enemies. History records the bitterness of many such schisms, such as those between Socialists and Communists, Protestants and Catholics, Shiite and Sunni Moslems, and so on.

The term "epistemology," a coinage of the mid-nineteenth century, was taken up in the twentieth to help justify the skeptical cast of twentieth-century "philosophy." The emphasis on "the problem of knowledge" came to pervade the discipline, despite its constant protestation that it was overcoming or working past or outgrowing this set of issues. In fact, it was constantly recasting its skeptical epistemology into one or another form. The discipline wandered around in a post-Kantian morass, as if the "philosophy professors" were trapped in one of the circles of Dante's *Inferno*. The main body of this skeptical, nominalistic movement was constituted by Ludwig Wittgenstein and the other Oxford-Cambridge ("Oxbridge") linguistic and "analytic" "philosophers," together with the "logical positivists" of Austria and the American adherents of these two groups. The prevailing unsystematic approach was, taken all in all, veddy British. Or rather, veddy English – or at least veddy English of a certain caste and period, the England of the '20's and '30's. One doesn't write *about* anything. One just writes. One doesn't philosophize about anything in particular. One just philosophizes. One eschews systems. One simply makes points. That is how one does philosophy. Anything else simply isn't *doing* philosophy. I say, regarding that object over there in the corner – is that a chair?

The style of this "philosophizing" varies with the cultures in which it occurs. As Bertrand Russell observed, in psychological experiments with rats, American rats scurry all over the place before they find their way out of a maze, whereas German rats sit down and calmly figure a way out. Extending this example to humans, American "analytic philosophers" adopted a more intense and frenetic mien as they made their points, but they went round and round in the same skeptical circles as their more measured and leisurely British colleagues.

So far, I have sketched two of the key elements in the make-up of contemporary "philosophy." The third nuclear element is logic, together with what can be called "dialectics," *i.e.*, training in the analysis of concepts, terms, and arguments that presupposes formal logic, but goes beyond it in content. Certainly, argument and debate are an essential part of "philosophy," but logic, particularly given the great advances in it made since the middle of the nineteenth century, is closely tied to mathematics. Except for the fact that it was invented by Aristotle, whose works are included in "the history of philosophy," one wonders what logic is doing in "philosophy" at all. Not only does mathematical logic resemble mathematics, but its applications are in mathematics, the physical sciences, computer science, and the compilation of actuarial data. Logic also is related to rhetoric, but rhetoric is the province of two other newly defined fields of the last hundred years, namely "English" and "communications." Again, there is no inherent reason for locating it in "philosophy."

In short, the three central components of "philosophy" are a) "the history of philosophy," whatever precise area of intellectual history that term might encompass, b) "epistemology," whatever its exact relationship to cognitive psychology might turn out to be, and c) logic, which is closely connected with mathematics on the one hand and rhetoric on the other. If the three nuclear components of "philosophy" really belong to other disciplines, then it is clear that the existence of "philosophy" as an independent field is more apparent than real.

Now it might seem that in attacking the integrity of "philosophy" I am questioning the validity of my own doctorate, which is in the field going by that name. But not so. Instead of having a degree in one field, I have a degree in three – in my case, four, because mine would include linguistics as well as the other three. One could make an analogy with business and finance and compare this to a stock split. The splitting of a corporation's shares is a sign that it is prospering and providing an increasing return to its shareholders. The typical case is two shares for one, but here we have a three- or four-way split! If the "professional philosophers" understood the nature of their own field better, they would understand what a good deal this is.

In addition to the three nuclear components of "philosophy," some further ones exist, which I will discuss shortly. Meanwhile, if the three aforenamed specialties do not in reality constitute a discipline, does this mean they are unworthy of being studied? Of course not. Logic/dialectics already is partly located in the two other fields with which it is naturally connected. As for "the history of philosophy," that is a branch of intellectual history and could just as easily be taught in history departments.

As soon as I put these words to paper, I hear in my imagination a chorus of objections. What about the "metaphysical" systems and theories that form the heart of "the history of philosophy"? What would they be doing in *history*? Philosophy isn't history. You couldn't teach it in history departments!

First of all, I reply, if "philosophy" isn't closely related to history, why do the writers in "the history of philosophy" comprise the bulk of its subject-matter? No other discipline except history itself is so preoccupied with the study of history, let alone its own history. Why is this so? The answer is that while the various metaphysical, epistemological, and ethical theories and systems have their respective adherents, nothing even close to a method exists within "philosophy" for evaluating their truth-claims. If a decision procedure could be found, then "philosophy" would become a branch of science. Since the different writers in "the history of philosophy" are obviously connected with each other, the twentieth-century "philosophers" can do little else but study them within a historical framework. But what they are doing is primarily history, not science.

It should be clearly understood that all history involves analysis and criticism. It is far more than gathering facts and making a chronicle, whether it be political history, military history, social and economic history, art history, the history of ideas, or any historical study whatsoever. For example, much of this essay is historical criticism, not "philosophy," except in the superficial sense that it deals with a discipline that calls itself by that name. It also could fall under the heading of what Karl Mannheim called "the sociology of knowledge."

Making "the history of philosophy" part of intellectual history allows its students ample room to "philosophize" about it, *i.e.*, to analyze, criticize, and develop the theories within it. If in any instance that development reaches the point where we have a theory with truth-claims that can systematically be tested, well and good. The notion that "philosophy" *by definition* is a field that deals only with untestable ideas comes, as stated earlier, from Kant, and is belied by numerous examples from "the history of philosophy" itself. All theories are judged by their explanatory power, *i.e.*, by their consequences, whether the consequences are logical and abstract or whether they explain and predict physical phenomena. There is no such thing as a "philosophical" theory as distinct from a "scientific" one. As Gertrude Stein might have put it, a theory is a theory is a theory.

This truth is not apparent from the way the "professional philosophers" study and teach "the history of philosophy." They study this or that problem in this or that writer and almost always are diffident about pronouncing on the truth-claims of the people they are considering. This is akin to literary criticism and art criticism or literary history and art history. It is not a unique form of cognition called "philosophizing."

The diffidence about truth-claims among professional philosophers reflects the Cartesian skepticism that Rorty speaks about, that "seems to us so much a part of what it means to 'think philosophically.'" Indeed, we do not even have to call the skepticism "Cartesian." It might just as easily be Wittgensteinian, Humean, Kantian, or whomever you like. The bottom line is that "philosophy" today boils down to skeptical "epistemology," where the skeptics even are dubious about the problems constituting "epistemology" itself. In short, "philosophy," *qua* discipline, is a parody of itself.

To see this more clearly, let us consider "epistemology" or "theory of knowledge" a bit further. The heart of it is the set of problems regarding human knowledge raised by the eight writers from Descartes through Kant. In the twentieth century, without the certainty of the world-picture of Newtonian science, these difficulties bulked much larger than they had before – so large, in fact, that they gave the whole discipline a skeptical cast. Thus, in the parlance of the 20th-century "philosophers," the expressions "theory of knowledge" and "the problem of knowledge" became almost synonymous.

All of "philosophy" came to be viewed from this skeptical perspective. Instead of making a serious effort to keep the various disciplines from going their separate ways, the "philosophers" engaged in prolix or pedantic criticism of the writers in "the history of philosophy" or in some cases abstruse system-building. All the seemingly diverse movements of twentieth-century "philosophy": Anglo-American analytic philosophy, pragmatism, existentialism, phenomenology, and process philosophy exhibit some or all of these traits.

Subordinate or derivative areas within "philosophy" were affected as well. Thus, ethics, typically a part of the systems of thought of the various thinkers in the tradition, was turned into "meta-ethics."

Readers unfamiliar with the jargon of "philosophy" may wonder what the difference is between "meta-ethics" and plain old ethics. To clarify the distinction, let us first consider the Greek prefix *metá*. It means 'with,' 'among,' or 'after,' and it also can mean *change*, whether of place, condition, plan, etc. When used to form compounds in English, it often has a connotation of mysterious change, as in *metamorphosis*, 'transformation.' The words "metaphysics" and "metaphysical" *sound*, as it were, metaphysical. In twentieth-century "philosophy," "meta" has been employed to rename certain traditional areas that still have a role in the newly organized discipline. The term lends a certain cachet to areas or modes of study that might seem impossibly dull, sterile, or difficult were they not given an impressive-sounding name. The change in terminology reflects the Kantian view that philosophy deals with the foundation or ground of other fields. "Meta-ethics," for example, deals with the foundation or ground of ethics. In fact, it is a thinly disguised form of epistemology, as it tries to explain or explain away the existence of ethical terms and concepts in a framework in which human knowledge itself remains in question. Thus, meta-ethics has gotten stuck in the same skeptical quagmire as the rest of "philosophy."

All of the foregoing comments add up to a double criticism: a) "philosophy" as a discipline doesn't know what it is doing, and b) it doesn't do it well. The two are related. If it knew what it was doing, it would do it better, and if it did it better, it probably would understand what it is doing.

In this precarious condition, "philosophy" is in no position to perform the function specified by Rorty, namely "to underwrite or debunk claims to knowledge made by science, morality, art or religion" based on its "special understanding of the nature of knowledge and of mind."[3] During the seventeenth and eighteenth centuries, the "modern philosophers" might legitimately have claimed to be doing this. Yet even then, they tended to think of themselves in more modest terms than Rorty uses, as when Locke called himself "a willing underlabourer for Mr. Newton." Given the current state of "philosophy," Rorty's assertion reads like a bad joke. With its skeptical attack on its own foundations, "philosophy" hardly can have much to say about the foundations of other disciplines.

As noted earlier, "philosophy" is neither unifying disciplines, nor coordinating them, nor adjudicating disputes or boundaries among them. In recent years, the person to make the most significant contribution to bringing disciplines back together has been Noam Chomsky, a professor of linguistics who is truly interdisciplinary and who sets an example the "philosophers" would do well to follow.

Indeed, "philosophy" is so ill-conceived and ill-defined that it does not know what to do with its own material. It doesn't give a very coherent overview of its own history, as I shall show in Part Two of this essay. It does not use that history to make connections with and among other disciplines. It cannot even be certain whether it is primarily an historical discipline or an analytic one. Since it defines itself in terms of the writers in "the history of philosophy," yet has no decision procedure for sorting out their truth-claims, it must be essentially history of ideas.

In my mind I can hear a chorus of protests rising to greet this conclusion: No, no, philosophy is an analytic discipline with its own unique problems and its own approach to them. Yet one readily can see how uncertain the "philosophers" are about this key issue. No clear distinction exists between "the history of philosophy" and the subdivisions of the discipline that draw most of their content from it: metaphysics, epistemology, philosophy of mind, ethics, aesthetics, etc. It is mainly a matter of emphasis – or just personal taste – whether one calls oneself a specialist in the history of philosophy or in one of the subdivisions.

If we ask what are the unique problems that constitute "philosophy," what is the core around which it is organized, the answer clearly is "the problem of knowledge," that is to say, skeptical epistemology. Yet from the ancient Greeks to the twentieth century the writers in "the history of philosophy" have ranged over many disciplines. There is a great deal more in it than just epistemology, let alone the skeptical form of epistemology that now prevails. Moreover, contemporary "philosophers" question the validity of skeptical epistemology itself. They incessantly claim to have worked past the difficulties of the seventeenth- and eighteenth-century writers, but that development always turns out not to have occurred just yet – understandably, because not knowing what to substitute for the problem of knowledge, they dare not eliminate it. So round and round they go.

A partial exception to these criticisms are Catholic and other religious institutions, which start from a realist perspective, not a skeptical one, thanks to their acceptance of revealed truth as part of their religious faith. "Philosophy" remains the handmaiden of theology, much as it was in the middle ages. The unifying framework is Platonistic and/or dualistic, and the discoveries of science in one way or another are fitted into it. This is what has been done since the time of St. Augustine, who synthesized Platonism and Christian faith. Even St. Thomas Aquinas fit his Aristotelianism into a Platonic framework. From this perspective, it is possible to view "the history of philosophy" in a very different light from the skepticism that prevails elsewhere in the discipline. Much of what I have to say might seem less radical to a Catholic professor of philosophy than to a secular one. I got used to the Thomist professor Paul Miller, under whom I studied after Randall, writing on my term papers: "This may be news to my colleagues, but not to me." Be that as it may, it still is highly unlikely that everything I am telling you in this essay is known to any Thomist worth his salt, and indeed, was already known back in the thirteenth, greatest of centuries. If that should turn out to be true, how wonderful! But if so, why are more people not aware of it – the rest of the philosophy professors, the scientists, the general public? It really would be news.

From the perspective of a Catholic philosopher, and particularly a Thomist, it is easy enough to see how closely philosophy is connected with all the other disciplines, to gainsay skeptical epistemology, and, at least in principle, to deny the mind-body dualism. Nevertheless, I know how long it took me to see in Aristotle solutions to the dilemmas of "modern philosophy." Maybe the claims I make for Aristotle *are* implicit in the writings of St. Thomas. If so, that suggests they already exist in Aristotle. Furthermore, the journey from the implicit to the explicit can be long and arduous. Thus, while students and teachers at Catholic colleges and universities may be more readily disposed than others to believe what I say, I strongly suspect that the connections of which I speak have heretofore not been made explicit by anyone.

One further qualification needs to be made in regard to philosophy in its current incarnation. Look at any philosophy department or program in the Western world and compare it with any other. You are likely to find the same subdivisions of the discipline, similar reading lists, and the people within the discipline working together to maintain it as an entity.

I do not deny that a unity exists, but it is superficial. Even the underlying unity of "the history of philosophy" is poorly understood. Thus, students frequently emerge from courses in "philosophy" unsure of what they have learned, unable to state philosophy's relationship to other disciplines, unable even to talk about it coherently. That has been my own observation, which is supported by reports of colleagues and even more cogently by declining enrollments.

The fact that a discipline in this condition still can have a superficial unity is nothing new. The same could be said of Ptolemaic astronomy in the time of Copernicus, scholastic philosophy in the late medieval and early modern periods, the Sophists during the time of Socrates, the skeptics in the Hellenistic period, and doubtless about astrologers, phrenologists, faith healers, *et al.* A body of thought or opinion may well be unified, but it may also be mistaken.

Still, what about logic? Surely the philosophers do a good job in that area! But logic is a specialized field on its own, with axioms, theorems, and well-defined procedures, and with numerous applications. Indeed, after a century and a half in which much useful and interesting development has occurred, logic already is semi-independent from "philosophy." College and university catalogues usually cross-list logic courses in mathematics and computer science along with philosophy. This is understandable because its chief uses are in doing proofs in mathematics and the sciences, setting up computer programs, developing actuarial tables, and of course training people to be logicians.

Moreover, when it comes to presenting logic to non-specialists, the "philosophers" do a mediocre job. The history of the subject usually is presented in a casual and haphazard way, so the student has a hard time understanding terms, conventions, and procedures – when they were developed and why they are used. To make matters worse, little communication occurs between the people in "philosophy" and those in "English," so the relationship between formal logic and rhetoric remains unclear. Finally, the dialectical skills that the philosophy professors hone are largely brought to bear on the pseudo-problems of skeptical epistemology – with not especially brilliant results, as we can see by the state "philosophy" is in.

The "philosophers" continually remind us of how logical and keenly analytic they are. We would expect, therefore, that by this time they would have figured out a clear and consistent definition of the word "philosophy" and stuck to it. On the contrary, one of the prime examples of their confusion is their ambiguous use of that very word. If they profess to know anything at all, it is how to use words precisely. Yet they cannot even be clear about the word that names what they are doing.

Perhaps this seems harsh. Maybe their skepticism has a positive side and their uncertainty is a virtue, another sign of their endlessly inquiring minds. They might seem to be imitating Socrates, the icon of philosophy, who professed to know nothing. However, Socrates' profession of ignorance was filled with irony. Behind it lay the theory of ideas, a doctrine as opposite from skepticism as any body of ideas could possibly be.

Unlike Socrates, when the skeptical "philosophers" of today claim to know nothing, they really mean it. Moreover, Socrates was a gadfly, a pain in the neck to the Athenian state and to many individuals in Athens. Can you name any "philosophy" professors who are behaving like that today? They aren't even doing it in Academe. In addition to the intellectual problems already mentioned, think of all the current ills of academic life: the stifling bureaucracy, the business mentality encroaching on intellectual decisions at all levels, the excessive pressure to publish, the steady decline in standards, the exploitation of adjunct faculty, the excesses of political correctness, the phony job searches, the corruption in the athletic departments, and so on. It is hard to imagine the present-day "philosophers" stirring things up in an effort to correct these ills, and drinking the hemlock of negative tenure decisions and lost positions. No, they cannot be called "Socratists," disciples of Socrates. "Pseudo-Socratists" would be a better name for them.

Other terms might be just as descriptive. Consider Kant's comment that metaphysical questions are like the foam produced by waves beating against the shore. No matter how much of it you scoop away, more constantly appears. If Kant is right that human reason is burdened with questions that never can be answered, and if "philosophy" is the discipline that studies such questions, then a good name for it would be "metaphysical foam-scooping," and the "philosophers" could rightly be called "metaphysical foam-scoopers."

Or comparing what they are doing to Sisyphus, who was condemned for all eternity to roll uphill a stone that never made it to the top, but always rolled back down again, we could just as easily call them Sisypheans. Given their conception of "philosophy," this too would be a good name.

Nor is it the only possibility classical antiquity offers us. There was also Procrustes, a legendary bandit who would tie his victims to an iron bed. If they were too small, he would stretch them, and if they were too large, he would chop their legs off. Hence in modern English the adjective "procrustean" means producing conformity in a ruthless or arbitrary way.[4] Since twentieth-century "philosophy" tries to squeeze the highly interdisciplinary tradition it arbitrarily calls "the history of philosophy" onto the procrustean bed of epistemology, on which it manifestly does not fit, we might as well call "philosophy" Neo-Procrusteanism.

Or thinking of the lady who summed up "philosophy" with the question, "Is that a chair?", we could make up something from the Greek, such as "," that is, people who ask, "Is that a chair?" Or else one could simply invent a term containing all three major functions I have described, such as "epistemologicoideologicologists" or "logicoepiste- moideohistorians," concoctions worthy of Aristophanes and suited to the Cloud-Cuckoo-Land of skeptical epistemology. Maybe all these terms do not sound as edifying and as dignified as "philosopher," but they also avoid the vagueness and ambiguity with which that term is currently used. Whichever term we use, it should be clear that the existence of "philosophy" as a discipline is more apparent than real. It is in reality a collection of intellectual pursuits brought together by circumstance in the form of a discipline, ill-conceived and ill-defined. If it already is in a moribund state and most of it already has parallels and connections with other disciplines, why not help nature take its course and break up "philosophy"? Let us now examine whether that would be feasible and what would result if we did it.

Notes

1. William James, *Coll. Ess. & Rev.*(1920) 399, cited in the *Oxford English Dictionary*, Supplement (Compact Edition, Vol. III).

2. See entries under "epistemology" and "epistemological" in the original

edition of the *Oxford English Dictionary*, and those under "epistemol-ogical," "epistemologically," and "epistemologist" in the Supplement.

3. Rorty, *op. cit.*, p. 3.

4. *The American Heritage Dictionary*, 2nd College Edition.

3
The Break-Up of "Philosophy"

It should be understood that "philosophy" would be broken up rationally. It would not be sold at auction to the highest bidder or shipped to the junkyard to be scrapped and sold for parts. What I am proposing is to take its component activities and locate them in the appropriate disciplines. To some extent, as noted earlier, this has happened. Connections already exist between "philosophy" and a range of other disciplines. Even where components of "philosophy" have not already migrated to other fields, we at least can see the affinities and the potential for fruitful contact. Indeed, if we cast the departmental blinders from our eyes and examine what is truly contained in the writings that constitute "philosophy," we very quickly see that most of it is a mixture of psychology, anthropology, sociology, political science, linguistics, history, and literature. There also are connections with mathematics and the natural sciences.

Let us proceed then. To begin with, mathematical logic already is partly located in mathematics and computer science. If philosophy departments ceased to exist, it still would have a home. The informal and traditional part of logic could be associated with English composition and rhetoric. A weak connection exists now, and it could be made stronger. About a hundred years ago, when "English" was evolving into the discipline we know today, it took over composition and rhetoric, which could just as easily have been shared with "philosophy." In any event, logic would be the easiest of the major components of "philosophy" to relocate in other disciplines.

The subordinate components – philosophy of art, philosophy of science, philosophy of religion, political philosophy, etc. – are in a similar position and would also be easy to assign to their respective subject-areas.

Ethics would be more complicated to deal with, even though here too the move already has gotten under way. Medical and business ethics, often called "applied ethics," have detached themselves from "philosophy" and are taught in medical and business schools. They are associated with their respective professions more than with "philosophy." The contents of the textbooks in these two areas strongly reflect everyday ethical issues in business and medicine. Not much comes from the writers in "the history of philosophy."

At certain times in the past, ethical systems actually have been employed to guide people's lives. The Hellenistic/Roman period springs to mind. During that time, Stoic and Epicurean ideas were used for this purpose in a manner comparable to modern psychotherapy. Hellenistic ethics also has had adherents in the modern period. For example, in the nineteenth century, Cicero's *De Officiis* (*Of Duties*) was used in the English public schools to train young members of the English upper class and poorer boys who would emulate them. Moreover, both in past centuries and at present, ethical concepts have played a part in religious education. Platonism has long served Christianity in this role.

Aside from the foregoing examples, if we but glance at the potpourri of self-help and personal improvement books and advisors available to the public, it is obvious what little connection these have with academic ethics, which is primarily "meta-ethics." Meta-ethics studies the foundations and the principles of ethics, which are based on the "metaphysical" theories and principles of the great thinkers of the past. Hence, it is really a part of metaphysics. But since there is no consensus about the truth or falsity of "metaphysics," the study of it is primarily historical. Thus, "meta-ethics" could be taught as part of "the history of philosophy" and would end up wherever the latter does. At the same time, as noted earlier, it too is a disguised form of "epistemology," so it could wind up wherever epistemology does. The reader unfamiliar with the ins and outs of "philosophy" may find this all a bit confusing. Suffice it to say that the "philosophers" never have drawn any clear boundaries between ethics and metaphysics, epistemology, and the history of philosophy.

Finally, ethics is associated with psychology, anthropology, sociology, political science, and literature. Some of the connections between "philosophy" and these other disciplines already exist. They could be strengthened, particularly in the interdisciplinary atmosphere the break-up of "philosophy" would create.

The objection may be raised that ethics is an area of theory very different from the empirical sciences of anthropology, psychology, etc. Immanuel Kant, to be sure, stated that opinion. Nevertheless, it is exactly that view I am questioning. Having some sort of ethical beliefs and standards is a universal human trait, yet there is widespread disagreement and uncertainty about the details of ethics and about its foundations. Thus, the study of ethics is a part *both* of the history of ideas *and* of the various social sciences to which it obviously is related. Coordinating the interdisciplinary study of ethics is a job made to order for a group of professors calling themselves "philosophers," and it is one they most certainly are not doing. If they were, the current disarray would not exist. We would have a much more coherent idea of the nature of ethical concepts and their role in human life. There is no guarantee that merely redistributing the study of ethics in the manner described would cause this desirable development to occur, but it would be a start.

Having come thus far in the break-up of "philosophy," we have yet to decide what to do with the history of philosophy and epistemology. Given all that was said in Chapter 2 about the history of "the history of philosophy," it is easy to figure out where it should go, namely, into history departments. I can imagine the dismay, the horror, and the anger with which philosophy professors will greet this proposal. Nevertheless, the change would prove to be a positive one. Almost immediately, the confusion, the ambiguity, and the obscurity now beclouding that subject-matter would begin to lift.

I am speaking from observation of students and colleagues and from my own long struggle to master "the history of philosophy." The confusion about evaluating the ideas in this tradition, their relation to each other, and their relationship to other disciplines is very great. Thinking of them as the core of a nebulous discipline called "philosophy" only obscures them and makes them much harder to comprehend. While it might look as if we were downgrading "the history of philosophy" by putting it into history departments, the result would be just the opposite. Just as, in Clemenceau's words, war is too serious a matter to be left to the generals, "the history of philosophy" is far too important to be left to the "philosophers." Not only do they ignore or misunderstand the genius of their own best writers, but they obscure it in a fog of pseudo-problems.

As soon as "the history of philosophy" migrates to history departments, the fog will begin to lift. Picture, if you will, a group of former philosophy professors finding themselves in this new environment. Of course they will ask themselves, "What are we doing here?" and their new colleagues in history will put that same question to them. In attempting to reply, they will have to confront the fact that much of "the history of philosophy" is already studied in other fields, *e.g.*, psychology, political science, literature. What have the "philosophers" been doing that is so special, and why have they been so isolated from these other fields? In their new situation, it will be very hard for them to duck these issues. If they utter a lot of mumbo-jumbo about "the problem of knowledge" and try to pretend they are adjudicating differences among disciplines, they will make themselves laughingstocks.

However, I strongly suspect that a healthy self-criticism will dominate the discussion. Imaginative proposals will be made, new ideas will emerge, and we will have the beginnings of real cooperation among disciplines that for too long have been isolated from one another.

Our task is almost complete, and the last part should be easy. All we need find is a place for epistemology, and it seems obvious that its place is in psychology and/or cognitive science. Once again, the change has already begun to occur. Some of the people in epistemology and philosophy of mind, a related area of "philosophy," have expertise in artificial intelligence, neural networks, etc. Conversely, there are people in the latter fields who are familiar with epistemology and philosophy of mind.

While a portion of the boundary with these other disciplines has already been eroded, epistemology remains the heart of "philosophy," and combining it with psychology may not be as easy as it first appears. Indeed, "philosophy" and "psychology" split apart in the first place because of profound differences of method and of emphasis on the part of individuals who otherwise had many ideas and interests in common. This state of affairs still obtains, and it is a bad omen for bringing them back together. Internecine conflicts often are more bitter than any other kind. Anyone who has observed the rancor and suspicion that many psychologists, particularly behaviorists, and philosophers display toward each other knows what I mean. Thus, despite all that the two disciplines have in common, it would be harder to relocate epistemology in psychology than to bring any other part of "philosophy" together with its corresponding field. The epistemologists, for all their professed skepticism about their own problems and their denial of the realism of Plato and Aristotle, still cling to their own form of mentalism, *i.e.*, phenomenalism and subjectivism, like sailors in a battered and leaky boat that is slowly sinking. Their mentalist vessel is not very seaworthy, yet they hang on to it for dear life. Meanwhile, Plato and Aristotle, who are not far away in a sleek and fast ship, could pick them up and bring them to shore, but, weak from fatigue and exposure, blinded by the glare of the sun, and distracted by the turbulence of wind and wave, they cannot see their would-be rescuers. The psychologists on a nearby passing freighter could also rescue them, but fearing the ship is in the hands of behaviorist pirates who would rob them of their minds, they refuse to be taken aboard.

But let us imagine that one way or another, the hapless epistemologists are rescued, either by the psychologists or by the cognitive scientists, who also are close by. This scenario makes sense, for if the other members of "philosophy" already have joined other disciplines, the epistemologists can hardly go it alone. Furthermore, it is not out of the question to imagine that they and the cognitive scientists and/or psychologists might do each other some good. Some of the interest in theory that was lost when "psychology" went gung-ho for behaviorism might be regained. This development has partly occurred with the resurgence in recent years of cognitive psychology and the rise of "cognitive science." The latter includes cognitive psychology and overlaps with computer science and neurology. Since it still is defining itself, epistemology might find a real place for itself there.

Moreover, having to function in an observational, experimental environment would do the epistemologists a great deal of good. They would be forced to look more closely at their own dogmas than is possible in the narcissistic fog of skeptical discourse within which they have been stumbling for so long. The introduction of a scientific spirit might clear the air.

The question is, how much of epistemology would survive in this environment? Like the "historians of philosophy" finding themselves in history departments, they could hardly escape asking themselves, what are we really doing? Is it science? Or is it metaphysical foam-scooping, *i.e.*, asking ourselves questions to which we know there is no answer, partly because of the way the questions have been framed. If the latter turned out to be correct, then "epistemology" would simply disappear – and maybe that would be the best way to deal with it. In any case, because of the close connection between "epistemology" and "the history of philosophy," at least some of the epistemologists could join their colleagues in departments of history.

On the other hand, the epistemologists might succeed in getting the cognitivists and the behaviorists to question some of *their* own dogmas: materialism, anti-mentalism, etc. Thus, while epistemology might not survive in its present form, portions of it would live on in a new synthesis with psychology, a Hegelian *Aufhebung*, as it were.* This would seem to be the most desirable outcome.

---

* *Aufheben*, the verb from which the noun *Aufhebung* is derived, means (among other things) to cancel and yet to preserve, as in a new synthesis.

All of these changes do not mean that the word "philosophy" would disappear from the language. True, it no longer would name an ill-conceived academic discipline, since that discipline would cease to exist. But the general public would still employ the word as it does now to mean the guiding principles in any field of activity whatsoever. Furthermore, the word would retain its traditional meaning of *philosophía*, the pursuit of wisdom or knowledge, including what we mean nowadays by "science." We would still use the expression "Doctor of Philosophy," in which the word has its traditional sense.

At this point, I can imagine myself being accosted by skeptics, either philosophy professors or faculty from other fields or members of the public, who might say, "Come on now. You've had your little joke, but do you really expect us to believe that we can no longer speak of the philosophy of Nietzsche or Kant or Hegel? And what about Plato? Are you actually trying to tell us that we shouldn't call Plato a *philosopher*? You can't be serious!"

I would answer that the problem is not in the words themselves, but in the fact that they are used in a very confusing way, and that the ambiguity helps conceal the dubious status of the discipline. Once the latter is revealed, it is easy to see how optional the terminology is. Thus, when we speak of "the philosophy of Nietzsche" or Kant or whomever, all we mean is the *thought*, the ideas of that individual. It then remains to decide what field or fields those ideas encompass. In the case of Nietzsche, they include psychology, anthropology, intellectual history, literary criticism, art criticism, musicology, literature, linguistics, and perhaps more. Just because a man writes essays that range widely over many fields does not make him *ipso facto* a "philosopher." We can also speak of "the philosophy of Nietzsche" in the more restricted sense in which a businessman might speak of his "business philosophy" or an athletic coach of his "coaching philosophy" – in other words, the set of principles by which the individual guides his or her activity. In regard to Nietzsche, this would mean his central or controlling ideas.

Let us take another example, Kant. How can I maintain that Kant's writings are *not* works of philosophy?** Above all, think of that weighty tome, *The Critique of Pure Reason*. It seems to be the quintessence of what any intelligent person would mean by the word! But not so. On the contrary,

---

** Except, of course, as Kant himself defines it. But that is exactly the point of
   view I am opposing, the view of philosophy as metaphysical foam-scooping.

more than any other work in the whole tradition, that book is the very essence of what philosophy-with-quotation-marks really is: a mixture of intellectual history, psychology, and logic. (I reiterate that intellectual history, like any other form of history, includes criticism.)

Okay, what about Hegel, the man who "stood philosophy on its head," the one who said all history is the working out of an idea? Wasn't he the philosopher *par excellence*? It is true that, like Plato and Plotinos, Hegel thought he had discovered a superscience, an abstract system that transcended all other forms of science and in terms of which everything in the universe could be understood. One might argue that this is by definition a *philosophical*, rather than a scientific system. But first of all, Hegel did not succeed in establishing the truth of his metaphysical superscience, and there are no prospects that any latter-day Hegelian will do so either. That is why the study of Hegel *qua* metaphysician is part of the history of ideas. At the same time, Hegel tried to apply his principles to all specific sciences. To the extent that he established the truth of his ideas or influenced other scholars, it was in specific disciplines like history, economics, political science, etc. This too would suggest that his ideas were essentially scientific in character, and not "philosophical" in some mysterious and ineluctable sense of the word and certainly not in the skeptical sense of twentieth-century "philosophy."

The case is similar in regard to Plato. In the first place, many of his dialogues – the so-called "dramatic dialogues" – are literary works. Probably no other writer combined literature and ideas so perfectly. But are the dialogues inherently *philosophical*? Here too a wide range of subjects is discussed: politics, psychology, rhetoric, linguistics, literary criticism, aesthetics, ethics, anthropology, sociology, history, education, cosmology, mathematics. The dialogues also are a biographical portrait of Socrates, a figure comparable to Jesus. To be sure, they contain the theory of ideas, a "metaphysical" theory par excellence. But once again, it remains unproven, and we don't have schools of Platonists trying to prove it and develop it. While over the centuries many scientists have been influenced by Plato's thought, as have many artists and writers, this argues for the connection of philosophy with other disciplines, not its separateness.

Granted that we might want to cling to the habit of calling the great writers of the tradition "philosophers" precisely because in being so interdisciplinary they embody the traditional sense of the word. However, if we do so, we should recognize that the usage is entirely optional and that we are not making thereby a hard and fast distinction between "philosophy" and "science." We should keep in mind that "science" rests on "metaphysical," *i.e.*, unproven, assumptions and concepts. What is "matter"? What is "force"? What is "energy"? What are space and time? What is the nature of living organisms? The scientists themselves used to be called "philosophers."

In any case, the break-up of "philosophy," once it occurs, will have repercussions in other disciplines and will begin immediately to benefit Academe as a whole and society at large. But I am getting ahead of myself here, and will deal with these issues in later chapters.

I am making it all sound so easy, but maybe some would resist these changes. The skeptical epistemologists – the Rortys, the Quines, the Sellarses, *et al.* – despite all their questioning of the foundations of their own discipline, would, I suspect, be less willing to join other disciplines than anybody else in "philosophy." This is apparent from Rorty's own summing up of the situation at the conclusion of *Philosophy and the Mirror of Nature*. First he acknowledges the discipline's uncertain prospects:

> The conversational interest of philosophy as a subject, or of some individual philosopher of genius, has varied and will continue to vary in unpredictable ways depending upon contingencies. These contingencies will range from what happens in physics to what happens in politics. The lines between disciplines will blur and shift, and new disciplines will arise, in the ways illustrated by Galileo's successful attempt to create "purely scientific questions" in the seventeenth century. The notions of "philosophical significance" and of "purely philosophical question," as they are currently used, gained sense only around the time of Kant. Our post-Kantian sense that epistemology or some successor subject is at the center of philosophy (and that moral philosophy, aesthetics, and social philosophy, for example, are somehow derivative) is a reflection of the fact that the professional philosopher's self-image depends upon his professional preoccupation with the image of the Mirror of Nature. Without the Kantian assumption that the philosopher can decide *quaestiones juris* concerning the claims of the rest of culture, this self-image collapses. That assumption depends on the notion that there is such a thing as understanding the essence of knowledge – doing what Sellars tells us we cannot do.[1]

This sounds almost plaintive. "Philosophy" in its brief career has never resolved the conflicts about its own nature and problems, let alone deciding conflicting claims among other disciplines. Rorty hems and haws as he seems to recognize the weakness of his position:

> To drop the notion of the philosopher as knowing something about knowing which nobody else knows so well would be to drop the notion that his voice always has an overriding claim on the attention of the other participants in the conversation. It would also be to drop the notion that there is something called "philosophical method" or "philosophical technique" or "the philosophical point of view" which enables the professional philosopher, *ex officio,* to have interesting views about, say, the respectability of psychoanalysis, the legitimacy of certain dubious laws, the resolution of moral dilemmas, the "soundness" of schools of historiography or literary criticism, and the like. Philosophers often do have interesting views upon such questions, and their professional training as philosophers is often a necessary condition for their having the views they do. But this is not to say that philosophers have a special kind of knowledge about knowledge (or anything else) from which they can draw relevant corollaries. The useful kibitzing they can provide on the various topics I just mentioned is made possible by their familiarity with the historical background of arguments on similar topics, and, most importantly, by the fact that arguments on such topics are punctuated by stale philosophical clichés which the other participants have stumbled across in their reading, but about which professional philosophers know the pros and cons by heart.[2]

In the same paragraph he has gone from "an overriding claim on the attention" of other disciplines to "useful kibitzing"! When was the last time "professional philosophers" had an overriding claim on the attention of other disciplines? I mean of course something on the level of importance of Descartes, Locke, Leibniz, Berkeley, Hume, Kant, *et al.* If they do not have "a special kind of knowledge about knowledge (or anything else)," how can they even do useful kibitzing – whatever that might be? But the comment that takes the cake is the one about "stale philosophical clichés." Just who is spouting stale philosophical clichés these days? Who is going round and round in narrow circles, if not the "philosophers"? While other academic disciplines that have been conceived too narrowly and are artificially separated from each other may also be guilty of this failing, "philosophy" surpasses them all. It is the one *least suited* to play the role of gadfly today. Rorty had a fling at that role with the publication of this book, and we can see from its conclusion that he goes nowhere with it. In the same breath in which he admits the moribund state of "philosophy," he tries to deny its consequences:

> The neo-Kantian image of philosophy as a profession, then, is in-

volved with the image of the "mind" or "language" as mirroring nature. So it might seem that epistemological behaviorism and the consequent rejection of mirror-imagery entail the claim that there can and should be no such profession. But this does not follow. *Professions can survive the paradigms that gave them birth.* [Emphasis added.][3]

I wonder what professions Rorty is thinking of. The ones that come to mind are the Ptolemaic astronomers, the medieval scholastics, the Sophists – that is, if they survived the destructive criticism of Socrates – and the skeptics of the Hellenistic period. Rorty has had kind words for the Sophists, so presumably he at least has them in mind.

The answer, I suspect, is that deep in their hearts, Rorty and the others are not really convinced that the problems of modern philosophy are pseudo-problems. In this respect, they *are* very much like the Ptolemaics and the Scholastics, *et al.* They are not ready even to consider, let alone to embrace the alternatives. In the words of Hamlet, they would rather bear those ills they have than fly to others that they know not of. And so Rorty, like Hamlet, continues dispassionately to contemplate suicide for the profession while trying to decide what it is that will really die:

> In any case, the need for teachers who have read the great dead philosophers is quite enough to insure that there will be philosophy departments as long as there are universities. The actual result of a widespread loss of faith in mirror-imagery would be merely an "encapsulation" of the problems created by this imagery within a historical period. I do not know whether we are in fact at the end of an era. This will depend, I suspect, on whether Dewey, Wittgenstein, and Heidegger are taken to heart. It may be that mirror-imagery and "mainstream," systematic philosophy will be revitalized once again by some revolutionary of genius. Or it may be that the image of the philosopher which Kant offered is about to go the way of the medieval image of the priest. If that happens, even the philosophers themselves will no longer take seriously the notion of philosophy as providing "foundations" or "justifications" for the rest of culture, or as adjudicating *quaestiones juris* about the proper domains of other disciplines.
>
> Whichever happens, however, there is no danger of philosophy's "coming to an end." Religion did not come to an end in the Enlightenment, nor painting in Impressionism. Even if the period from Plato to Nietzsche is encapsulated and "distanced" in the way Heidegger suggests, and even if twentieth-century philosophy comes to seem a stage of awkward transitional backing and filling (as sixteenth-century philosophy now seems to us), there will be something called "philosophy"

> on the other side of the transition. For even if problems about representation look as obsolete to our descendants as problems about hylomorphism look to us, people will still read Plato, Aristotle, Descartes, Kant, Hegel, Wittgenstein, and Heidegger. What roles these men will play in our descendants' conversation, no one knows. . . . The only point on which I would insist is that philosophers' moral concern should be with continuing the conversation of the West, rather than with insisting upon a place for the traditional problems of modern philosophy within that conversation.[4]

But Rorty has just told us that "[t]he lines between disciplines will blur and shift, and new disciplines will arise." Yes, and "the great dead philosophers" will still be read, but not necessarily in "philosophy departments." "Philosophy" as a discipline will come to an end because it was a fiction to begin with. Rorty comes close to admitting this when he speaks of an "encapsulation" of its problems within a historical period. Given his skepticism both about hylomorphism (Aristotelianism) and about "the traditional problems of modern philosophy," *i.e.*, skeptical epistemology, what is there left for "the philosopher" to kibitz about? The concluding line about "the conversation of the West" (a vague concept he adumbrated earlier) sounds high-minded, but with the ground cut out from under "philosophy," it is hard to imagine what the "philosophers" might contribute to it.

Reading these comments, we are led even more strongly to ask why "philosophy" should continue to exist as an independent discipline. There is nothing left to justify that status, yet it is striking how blithely Rorty embraces contradictory views or simply begs the question – it is hard to say which. When in the face of all the negative admissions, he still maintains that "there will be philosophy departments as long as there are universities," he is saying, in effect, that a university without philosophy is inconceivable. But he has just been at pains to tell us that it *is* conceivable. Similarly, after 400 pages of knocking the great dead philosophers off their pedestals, he asserts that they will always be read, yet admits that he does not know to what end or why.

No matter. The "philosophers" will persist, in some form or other. As we have seen, the problem is partly verbal confusion and partly the ill-conceived nature of "philosophy," of which the verbal confusion is a symptom. The virtue of Rorty's book is that he rushes in where the other "philosophers" fear to tread and trumpets their ambiguities, ambivalences, and self-contradictions. They are intelligent people who grasp that they have been backed into a corner, but their cleverness is exercised in trying to rationalize an ever-more-indefensible position rather than in looking for a way out of it. "Professions can survive the paradigms that give them birth." Philosophers are "useful kibitzers." There is not much difference between Rorty's way of putting it and Randall's or any of the others'. "A philosophic idea . . . soon seems but a chain of meaningless sounds." Dame Philosophia is a whore. Ah, you Westerners are Philistines. You don't appreciate the finer things.

In telling seatmates on airplanes that he was a historian, Professor Randall was staying on *terra firma* to describe himself. The term "philosopher" might be dubious, but a historian he certainly was. He apparently made the leap to the conclusion that I have come to after much reflection. In any event, he could hardly have said, "I'm a pimp for Lady Philosophy."

One wonders, what does Rorty tell fellow passengers on airplanes when they ask him how he earns his living? Does he say, "I'm a kibitzer at the University of Virginia"? Or "I'm a Sophist at the University of Virginia"? No, I suspect that first he admits to being a philosophy professor, and then when they ask him what philosophy professors do, he tells them about all the participants in the great conversation of mankind, and so on.

"Useful kibitzing" indeed – there are more picturesque and vigorous terms for it. I am reminded of the student who said to me when I told him what my field was, "Oh, philosophy! I love bull sessions!" One can imagine David Hall answering his seatmate when she asked him what he does, "I'm an academic gadfly, a sort of conscience of the university and all-faculty b.s. artist." She might have scratched her head for a few seconds and then exclaimed, "Aah . . . ha! You're a philosophy professor!"

Unfortunately, that is what "philosophy" as an academic pursuit conjures up in the public mind, and while the public perception may be somewhat rough about the edges, it is essentially sound. Picture to yourself, dear reader, the state of affairs of the discipline when eminent professors of it publicly make the admissions I have cited. It is barely a step or two farther to think of them as bullshit artists. It seems hardly cruder than what they say about themselves.

Be it so that most of the instructors and professors of "philosophy" go along day by day, teaching their classes, grading their exams, serving on committees, publishing an article now and then, getting their promotions and their tenure, just carrying on and doing their job, part of the silent majority of Academe, leading their little lives of quiet desperation. Do I really mean to call all of these good people bullshit artists? Probably not all of them or even most of them. More likely it is a case of most of the people some of the time, and some of the people most of the time. In any event, the fact remains that "philosophy" is an ill-conceived pseudo-discipline, based on a set of confusingly stated pseudo-problems whose questionable status its professors recognize, but which they reiterate and revise and repeat *ad infinitum*. Using more refined language, one can compare them to the Sophists, the Scholastics, the Ptolemaics, but it amounts to the same thing. They are the self-appointed custodians of a most wonderful intellectual tradition, yet they have at best an inkling of its true greatness. In their skeptical palaver, they are like cockerels on a dungheap. Underneath that dungheap is a gold mine, but they don't know it, and don't know that they don't know it, and don't want to know that they don't know that they don't know it, let alone that they don't know it. Now there's a problem of knowledge for you, and it is not a pseudo-problem, but a genuine epistemological problem, the ignorance of the "philosophers."

Meanwhile, a host of ills beset higher education that cry for the attention of those who would be the true heirs of Socrates, Plato, and Aristotle. Where are the gadflies of yesteryear? Someone needs to be calling to account the arch-community songsters of Academe, the bureaucrats, the academic careerists, the self-serving administrators, the pandering presidents ready to ride every wave of politically correct opportunism, the operators of academic sweatshops, the promoters of their cronies, the writers of superficial articles to gain tenure and promotions, the composers of fake grant proposals, the conductors of phony job searches, the compilers of meaningless statistics, the attackers of the First Amendment, the devious deans, pedantic professors, corrupt coaches, venal alumni, and intellectually lazy students who populate our far-flung campuses. In the words of François Rabelais, that Renaissance reformer, they beshit themselves most foully. In the cockpit of academic bull-throwing, and in the arena of public bull-throwing, they ladle it out in derrick-size shovelfuls. Truly their fecality is Gargantuan and needs the invective of a Rabelais to do it justice. Call them

> brattling gabblers, licorous gluttons, freckled bittors, mangy rascals, shite-a-bed scoundrels, drunken roysters, sly knaves, drowsy loiterers, slapsauce fellows, slabberdegullion druggels, lubbardly louts, cozening foxes, ruffian rogues, paultry customers, sycophant-varlets, drawlatch hoydons, flouting milksops, jeering companions, staring clowns, forlorn snakes, ninny lobcocks, scurvy sneaksbies, fondling

fops, base loons, saucy coxcombs, idle lusks, scoffing braggards, noddy mea-cocks, blockish grutnols, doddipol joltheads, jobbernol goosecaps, foolish loggerheads, flutch calf-lollies, grouthead gnat-snappers, lob-dotterels, gaping changelings, codshead loobies, woodcock slangams, ninnie-hammer fly-catchers, noddie-peak simpletons, turdy-gut, shitten shepherds, and other such like defamatory epithets.[5]

While the "philosophers" can hardly be blamed for all the ills of higher education, they could be pointing them out and leading the way to their solution. Instead they are part of the problem. Along with many others in Academe, they are prisoners in Plato's cave. Perhaps the dungheap I left them on a few paragraphs back is really located there. You recall the myth of the cave in Plato's *Republic*, where the people are chained from childhood and can see only shadows of puppets on the wall in front of them.

Yes, the "philosophers" are there in Plato's cave, groping about in the dim light. And what is that I see? A trapdoor marking the entrance to a long passageway. Even in the darkness, they follow the leaders of the profession, who lift the door open and make their way along the passage. It leads to a dark forest, which turns out to be the one described by Dante at the beginning of the *Inferno*:

> Nel mezzo del cammin di nostra vita
> mi ritrovi per una selva oscura
> ché la diritta via era smarrita.

> Midway in the journey of our life
> I found myself in a dark forest
> Because I had strayed from the straight path.
>   (Canto I, 1–3)***

The "philosophers" have strayed from Plato's cave to Dante's Inferno! Drawn onward as if by a fatal attraction, they rush ahead, and we lose sight of them. Uncertain about what to do next, we linger while hours pass. Indeed, we completely lose track of time and have no idea how much of it has elapsed when suddenly the two famous guides appear before us. Led on

---

*** Unless otherwise stated, all translations are by the author.

through the forest by Dante and Virgil, we reach the Gate of Hell, inscribed with the fateful words:

> ... PER ME SI VA TRA LA PERDUTA GENTE ...
> LASCIATE OGNE SPERANZA, VOI CH'INTRATE.

> Through me the way runs among the lost people ...
> Abandon all hope, you who enter here.
> (Canto III, 3, 9)

And we hear Virgil saying to Dante:

> "Noi siam venuti al loco ov' i' t'ho detto
> che tu vedrai le genti dolorose
> c'hanno perduto il ben de l'intelletto."

> "We have come to the place where I have told you
> Where you will see the sorrowful people
> Those who have lost the benefit of the intellect."
> (Canto III, 16–18)

Finally, Virgil conducts us along with Dante to the eighth circle of Hell, where we encounter the committers of ordinary fraud. Among them are found the crowd of academics I just was castigating, the university presidents and deans, the bureaucrats, the coaches, the professors, even some students. Then we reach an evil-smelling lake bubbling with foul vapors where we espy a group of people flailing with their arms, struggling to keep their heads above the noxious ooze. "Who are those people?" Dante asks Virgil. *"Quale gente sono quelli?"*

> Mi rispose il fedele guida, "quelli
> professori sono di filosofia,
> condannati fin ai menti a nuotare
> In eterno in la propria cacca."

> My faithful guide answered me, "Those
> Are professors of philosophy,
> Condemned to swim up to their chins
> For eternity in their own *cacca.*"

Let us leave the desecrators and destroyers of philosophy swimming in their own excrement and, returning to the upper world of daylight, resume our narrative. We have put "philosophy" out of its misery, cutting out its diseased heart, skeptical epistemology, and redistributing the healthier parts to the appropriate areas of the academic corpus in a series of organ transplants. But will those transplanted parts be recognizable in their new environment? Will we truly be able to say, "'Philosophy' is dead; long live philosophy"?

My answer is yes. In the next section, I will show how this can come about. Taking my cue from various comments of Rorty and Randall, I will explain how philosophy can come back to life and be restored to its proper place in the new interdisciplinary scheme of things that I envision.

I will be far from carrying the burden of demonstrating all this on my own shoulders alone. I will have helpers, both ancient and modern. In one of the passages quoted above, Rorty observes, "It may be that . . . 'mainstream,' systematic philosophy will be revitalized once again by some revolutionary of genius." Unbeknownst to Rorty because of his narrowminded view of "philosophy," such a person already has come upon the scene, namely, Noam Chomsky. Rorty certainly has heard of Chomsky, but despite his prattling about the great conversation of mankind, he overlooks the fact that nearly forty years ago, Chomsky began the revival of traditional, interdisciplinary philosophy, what philosophy used to be. I will show that it is possible to go much farther than Chomsky has done by combining "modern philosophy" and modern science with the ideas of an even greater genius, Aristotle.

Notes

1. Rorty, *op. cit.*, p. 392.

2. *Ibid.*, pp. 392–93.

3. *Ibid.*, p. 393.

4. *Ibid.*, pp. 393–94

5. François Rabelais, *Gargantua*, tr. Sir Thomas Urquhart, ch. XXV.

Part 2
The Life of Philosophy

4

The Unity of the Tradition and the Attempt to Deny It

In the preceding pages I outlined the problems faced by the contemporary discipline of "philosophy." In the chapters that follow I will propose a solution to them. The project upon which I am embarking is something like what Kant did in his *Prolegomena to Any Future Metaphysics*, which he published in 1783 as an introduction to *The Critique of Pure Reason*, that had appeared in 1781. Kant divided up the *Prolegomena* so as to answer the following four questions:

1. How is pure mathematics possible?
2. How is pure natural science possible?
3. How is metaphysics in general possible?
4. How is metaphysics as a science possible?[1]

In similar fashion, I will attempt to answer the question, how is breaking out of the problematic situation of contemporary philosophy possible? Since Kant helped create that situation, it may be poetic justice to use his method as an antidote. However, I am doing so because it is a logical approach. Having attempted in the preceding chapter to connect "philosophy" with other disciplines, I will simply pick up where I left off, beginning with the connections between different parts of "the history of philosophy" that have been minimized, misunderstood, or overlooked by the "philosophers."

It turns out that "the history of philosophy" is a more coherent tradition than the "professional philosophers" themselves seem to realize. They seem concerned to emphasize the *differences* among the various thinkers in the tradition rather than their common themes. The following passage from Richard Rorty's *Philosophy and the Mirror of Nature* states this mind-set very plainly and contains some further relevant comments:

> Almost as soon as I began to study philosophy, I was impressed by

the way philosophical problems appeared, disappeared, or changed shape, as a result of new assumptions or vocabularies. From Richard McKeon and Robert Brumbaugh *I learned to view the history of philosophy as a series, not of alternative solutions to the same problems, but of quite different sets of problems.* [Emphasis added.] From Rudolph Carnap and Carl Hempel I learned how pseudo-problems could be revealed as such by restating them in the formal mode of speech. From Charles Hartshorne and Paul Weiss I learned how they could be so revealed by being translated into Whiteheadian or Hegelian terms. I was very fortunate in having these men as my teachers, but, for better or worse, I treated them all as saying the same thing: that a "philosophical problem" was a product of the unconscious adoption of assumptions built into the vocabulary in which the problem was stated – assumptions which were to be questioned before the problem itself was taken seriously.

Somewhat later on, I began to read the work of Wilfrid Sellars. Sellars's attack on the Myth of the Given seemed to me to render doubtful the assumptions behind most of modern philosophy. Still later, I began to take Quine's skeptical approach to the language-fact distinction seriously, and to try to combine Quine's point of view with Sellars's. Since then, I have been trying to isolate more of the assumptions behind the problematic of modern philosophy, in the hope of generalizing and extending Sellars's and Quine's criticisms of traditional empiricism. Getting back to these assumptions, and making clear that they are optional, I believed, would be "therapeutic" in the way in which Carnap's dissolution of standard textbook problems was "therapeutic." This book is the result of that attempt.[2]

Certainly the *method* Rorty recommends has merit: discovering unsound assumptions and dissolving pseudo-problems. The assumptions need not be unconscious, as he suggests they are, but merely arbitrary, like the hard-and-fast distinction made by Locke and Descartes between the primary and secondary qualities of perception. However, one can apply Rorty's method to his own ideas. He states that the history of philosophy is not very coherent, "a series, not of alternative solutions to the same problems, but of quite different sets of problems." Then in the next paragraph, when he speaks of "the assumptions behind most of modern philosophy," he seems to be vitiating, if not contradicting his earlier statement. If part of the history of philosophy is very coherent, why would the rest of it not be so? Did the modern philosophers have nothing in common with their predecessors? Did they invent a whole new set of problems? Consider what he has to say in comparing the ancient and the modern philosophers:

> To see the difference between [Aristotle's] argument and the various Cartesian and contemporary arguments for dualism, we need to see how very different these two epistemologies are. Both lend themselves to the imagery of the Mirror of Nature. But in Aristotle's conception intellect is not a mirror inspected by an inner eye. It is both mirror and eye in one. The retinal image is *itself* the model for the "intellect which becomes all things," whereas in the Cartesian model, the intellect *inspects* entities modeled on retinal images. The substantial forms of frogness and starness get right into the Aristotelian intellect, and are there in just the same way they are in the frogs and the stars – *not* in the way in which frogs and stars are reflected in mirrors. In Descartes' conception – the one which became the basis for "modern" epistemology – it is *representations* which are in the "mind." The Inner Eye surveys these representations hoping to find some mark which will testify to their fidelity. Whereas skepticism in the ancient world had been a matter of a moral attitude, a style of life, a reaction to the pretensions of the intellectual fashions of the day, skepticism in the manner of Descartes' *First Meditations* [sic] was a perfectly definite, precise, "professional" question: How do we know that anything which is mental represents anything which is not mental? How do we know whether what the Eye of the Mind sees is a mirror (even a distorted mirror – an enchanted glass) or a veil? The notion of knowledge as inner representation is so natural to us that Aristotle's model may seem merely quaint, and Cartesian (as opposed to Pyrrhonian "practical") skepticism seems to us so much a part of what it means to "think philosophically" that we are amazed that Plato and Aristotle never confronted it directly. But if we see that the two models – the hylomorphic and the representative – are equally optional, perhaps we can see the inferences to mind-body dualism which stem from each as just as optional.[3]

First Rorty tells us how very different the two epistemologies are and later says they are equally optional. Well, which is it? If they are so very different from each other, how does he know they are equally optional? Conversely, if they are equally optional, how different from each other can they be? Furthermore, if they both "lend themselves to the imagery of the Mirror of Nature" (*i.e.*, a realist epistemology in which the mind mirrors the natural world), it sounds as if they are indeed alternative solutions to the same problem!

Rorty appears to be contradicting himself at every turn. However, the virtue of his book is that he comes right out in the open and does what nearly everybody else in "philosophy" is doing in a less obvious and more prolix, convoluted manner. He flaunts the arbitrariness and the self-contradiction of contemporary "philosophy." In so doing, he makes it easier for us to point out its questionable assumptions. Despite all their protestations to the contrary, the philosophy professors have become so locked into these assumptions that they seem unable to break out from them, although they have been talking about doing so for the past hundred years. Even if Rorty really succeeds in doing so, what is he offering us in their place?

At least a consensus seems to exist that there is a set of assumptions underlying most of "modern philosophy." That is a start. Indeed, if any movement in "the history of philosophy" can lay claim to unity and coherence, it is the small band of theorists from Descartes through Kant, who were active from about 1620 to about 1800. They read each other's works; some of them actually corresponded with each other; and they were all connected or concerned with science.

It turns out that the modern writers are closely connected not only with each other, but with the ancients as well. Alfred North Whitehead observed that "the history of philosophy is a series of more or less extended footnotes to Plato and Aristotle." That observation is truer than perhaps Whitehead himself realized.

Like many students in the twentieth century, I wrestled for years with the problems of the seventeenth- and eighteenth-century writers. When in the early '70's, I saw in Aristotle a solution to their problems, it was obvious that a closer connection existed between them and the ancients than I had realized. But I did not grasp how close the connection was.

In the fall of 1979 I had the opportunity to teach the history of ancient philosophy, and then in the spring of 1980, the history of modern philosophy. In the latter course, I recognized something I previously had been completely unaware of, namely that Hobbes' *De Corpore* contains a point-by-point rebuttal of key positions in Aristotle's *De Anima*. Indeed, the title of the former treatise means "Of Body" or "On Body," while the latter means "On the Soul." Given the close criticism of Aristotle in Hobbes' treatise, the opposition of the titles can hardly be an accident.

One can disagree when Hobbes tries to reduce Aristotle's concepts of the substantial unity of the organism (the *psyché* or "soul") and the unity of the mind to mechanical forces. But at least *he is speaking literally to Aristotle's key arguments.* Hobbes was a literal-minded man, and in *De Corpore* he displays this trait to perfection.

In order to see this, I had to be thoroughly familiar with *De Anima*, especially Book III, which deals with the mind, as well as with other psychological texts and passages in Aristotle. Since I had written my Ph.D. dissertation several years before on these very texts, you could say I was primed to make the discovery. Nevertheless, when it occurred, I was amazed that so close a connection existed between Aristotle and one of the modern writers. As I continued to teach the course, I found something similar in Locke, and it was equally unmistakable. I came to see that all eight major writers of "modern philosophy" were dealing with the same set of problems; they were using an Aristotelian vocabulary; and to a large extent, they were reacting, directly or indirectly, to Aristotle's formulation of the issues. In Berkeley and Hume this occurs at one or two removes: both are responding to Locke, who is reacting to Aristotle. In Leibniz and Spinoza, two of the "Continental rationalists," there also is obvious borrowing and reshaping of Aristotelian terms and concepts. As for Descartes and Kant, who formulated the paradigm of "modern philosophy," each provides a view of mind and body parallel to that of Aristotle, but in contrast with his theory, theirs are dualistic. The connection between the human mind and human values on the one hand and the physical world of science on the other becomes difficult, if not impossible, to explain. Moreover, the former have to be defended against the perceived threat from the latter.

In short, "the history of philosophy" is just the opposite of what Rorty says it is: Rather than being "a series . . . of quite different sets of problems," it is very much *a series of alternative solutions to the same set of problems* – or if not totally the same set of problems, something close to that.

In light of this way of viewing the tradition, distinctions like that between the "British empiricists" and the "Continental rationalists" bulk much smaller than in the conventional view. This turns out to be a big improvement. The "modern philosophers," no longer part of a nebulous discipline, become not less, but more important in the intellectual scheme of things.

The reader may wonder, is there no sense of the close relationship between Aristotle and the modern writers in the standard histories such as those of Randall and of Copleston? While references to Aristotle occur from time to time in their respective discussions of the modern writers, not even a hint is dropped of the connection of which I am speaking. Still, the reader might object: If famous scholars like these have not written of this relationship, maybe it does not exist. Who are you to challenge them? If the relationship really exists and they have overlooked something so basic, their very competence is in question – and not only theirs, but that of Rorty, Quine, Sellars, McKeon, Brumbaugh, Hartshorne, and all the rest.

I answer that yes, I *am* challenging virtually the entire field of "philosophy," but not by presenting arguments or texts dreamed up *ex nihilo*. I am appealing to the modern writers, not just individually, but *as a group*, and not to them alone, but *in conjunction with* Aristotle. A commonality exists among them that transcends their differences. Once perceived, it gives us a view very different from the customary one we get by looking at them in the isolated manner employed by the twentieth-century skeptical "philosophers." While there is a long tradition, beginning in the first century B.C., of commentators on Aristotle, the "modern philosophers," without being recognized as such, comprise the best group of commentators on Aristotle in the whole tradition.

A few facts and observations about the Aristotelian texts will help make this point clearer. Nobody knows what happened to Aristotle's writings for 250 years from the time of his death in 322 B.C. to when they resurfaced in the first century B.C. They are treatises in the form of lecture notes, and they tend to be very concise. This makes them more difficult to understand than if all the key ideas were fully explained, but we are lucky to have them at all. Their conciseness compels us to explicate and develop them more than we have to do for the "modern philosophers," whose ideas are stated at greater length. However, in explicating Aristotle, the "modern philosophers" prove to be invaluable.

Take the question of the unity of mind. This is a key issue for both ancient and modern writers. However, in the Aristotelian corpus only one passage deals with it directly, although it is either mentioned or implied in many places and is central to any reconstruction of Aristotle's psychology.[4] I did not recognize the importance of this question from reading Aristotle, but rather from reading the *modern* writers. It appears in all eight of them, starting from Descartes and leading up to Kant. They all either affirm or deny it. Kant above all affirms it strongly, and it plays a more obvious role in his thought than in that of anybody else in the tradition. Thus, when I was getting to know the Aristotelian texts well, had I not come to them with the mind-set of the modern writers, I might have overlooked not only this, but many other important features of Aristotle's psychology.

Thus, around 1970, when I was still a graduate student and the brilliance of Aristotle was dawning on me, I first spotted his argument for the unity of mind and wrote a term paper on it. Then I worked out many of the details of his psychology in my Ph.D. dissertation, completed in 1974. Later, as noted above, I saw in detail the closeness of the connection between the modern writers and Aristotle. However, the former were not keen to acknowledge their debt to him, so even when they rebut him, it is mostly by allusion. Someone unfamiliar with Aristotle will not realize what is going on, but to the reader who is familiar with the Aristotelian texts, the allusions are unmistakable. For example, when Hobbes denies the unity of mind, he says not a word about *De Anima*, III, ii, 426b8–30, but the reader who knows that passage recognizes the allusion. The argument is cast in almost identical terms, and Hobbes simply denies what Aristotle asserts.[5] He takes the same piece of evidence, the same set of observed facts that Aristotle does, and draws a diametrically opposite conclusion. Thus, he gives one the opportunity to think very carefully about the issue that is at stake – that is, if one realizes with whom Hobbes is arguing. It is an excellent test, and in my judgment, Aristotle withstands it.

This is one dramatic example of the interaction of the "modern philosophers" and Aristotle, an interaction that is manifold and ongoing. There is nothing cut and dried about it. The modern writers help one see Aristotle's genius, and he in turn highlights the best in them. The brilliance of his solutions serves to show how well the moderns grasped and stated the problems. They may have been mistaken, but at least they were dealing with the most important issues. Even if one is convinced that Aristotle's views prevail, one still must explain *why*: why, for example, his argument for the unity of mind is correct, and why Hobbes fails to rebut it; why Aristotle's "realistic" theory of perception and knowledge is correct, rather than the subjectivism that many of the "modern philosophers" embrace; why Locke's absolute, unbridgeable gap between "primary" and "secondary" qualities of experience is unfounded; and why Aristotle is correct in asserting that "substance" (*i.e.*, substantial being) is actuality or form, rather than potentiality or matter, as Locke asserts. One must show that Aristotle had an adequate, scientific explanation of free will as opposed to the determinism of Hobbes and Spinoza. One must also show that Aristotle adequately explained how the mind moves the body, in contrast with Descartes' Rube Goldberg explanation. Finally, one must explain why Kant's convoluted conceptual framework for preserving both human values and scientific laws is unnecessary. The things Kant placed *outside* of nature in order to preserve them can be found safe at home within nature.

All this can be done, and to many it probably sounds too good to be true. We are so accustomed to dualism, reductionism, and skepticism that we can hardly believe a genuine alternative to them exists. Indeed, my primary aim in this essay is to provide enough evidence to satisfy the reader that it does. The first step is to recognize that the intellectual tradition conventionally known as "the history of philosophy" is far more unified and coherent than Rorty, Randall, and other contemporary "philosophers" would have us believe. It is cooperative and cumulative in a manner and to a degree that seems almost completely to have escaped them, and thereby it truly is a part of science.

Moreover, the interaction between Aristotle and modern writers need not be confined within the artificial boundaries of "philosophy." A similar relationship exists with a contemporary writer of genius, Noam Chomsky, Professor of Linguistics at MIT. Like the "modern philosophers," and without intending to be so, Chomsky proves to be as great a commentator on Aristotle as anybody else in our intellectual tradition.

Nearly forty years ago, Chomsky caused a revolution in linguistics by reviving the idea of a universal grammar underlying the particular grammars of all human languages. This is an old idea that goes back at least as far as Aristotle and is implied in Plato. Chomsky used it together with related ideas to re-establish connections among three twentieth-century disciplines that had been defined too narrowly and had drifted apart from one another, namely "philosophy," "psychology," and "linguistics."

Chomsky's enduring contribution, I suspect, will be the brilliant way in which he removed the boundaries separating these disciplines and explained what questions a theory of language and mind should answer. At the same time, he provided his own specific answers to those questions, including the view that the universal grammar is innate and that semantics is not part of linguistics.

In other words, Chomsky provided *both* prolegomena to a theory of language and mind *and* a specific theory. The latter much more than the former caused the bitter controversies his work has aroused. Unfortunately, the two are mixed together so closely in his writings that the less controversial part tends to be overshadowed. People tend to take an "all-or-nothing" view of him.

I was introduced to Chomsky's ideas during the early 1970s, around the time I was getting to know the texts of Aristotle very well. By stipulating what a theory of language and mind should contain, Chomsky helped me to see that such a theory was implicit in the writings of Aristotle. Thus, Chomsky is in the same complementary relationship with Aristotle as are the modern philosophers, a parallel that brings home all the more strongly how artificial are the boundaries between disciplines.

I am not alone then, a solitary figure pitted against the pseudo-discipline of "philosophy." The tradition itself, together with new allies such as Chomsky, bears witness against the narrowness of small-minded scholars. On the one hand, we have a group of professors styling themselves "philosophers" who take a skeptical and critical view of the very subject they profess. On the other hand, the giants of the tradition, by the brilliance of their common themes even when they disagree, overshadow the pygmies of today, with their skeptical "epistemology" and confused claims to separate identity for their illusory discipline.

But how do we know that the giants really are giants and the pygmies pygmies? The obvious way is by checking out the things I have stated, that is, by comparing my account of the traditional writers with the conventional one, and far more important, by looking at the primary sources. Thus, readers can decide for themselves. However, that can be a lengthy and difficult process. I will try to make a satisfactory general argument, a *prima facie* case, without going into a mass of details.

First of all, as Rorty himself says, and Randall and the others would agree, "the great dead philosophers" will continue to be read. In the sciences, by contrast, textbook versions have long since replaced the original treatises of Archimedes, Euclid, Galileo, Newton, Darwin, *et al.* It may indeed be better, as the students do at St. John's College in Annapolis and Santa Fe, to study science by reading its great books, but it is not necessary. However, in "philosophy," it is necessary to study the primary sources.

Nevertheless, we are asked to accept the diminished view of the primary sources offered by Randall, Rorty, Quine, Sellars, & Co. Dame Philosophy is a whore; to be a philosopher is to be a professional skeptic – however they state it, it amounts to the same thing. Rorty thinks that by rebutting Descartes, Locke, *et al.* he is *a fortiori* doing the same to Plato and Aristotle. It is taken for granted that the "modern philosophers" rebutted the ancients, so if we refute the moderns, we have refuted the whole tradition. As for the medieval writers, Rorty and most of the others don't even bother with them: they only offer *outré* theological versions of Plato and Aristotle.

This treatment of its own sources is unique to "philosophy." The physicists do not do it to Galileo, Newton, Faraday, Maxwell, Planck, and Einstein. The mathematicians do not do it to Euclid, Archimedes, Leibniz, Fourier, Euler, Riemann, and Gauss. The English professors certainly don't do it to Shakespeare and Milton. The musicologists don't do it to Bach, Mozart, and Beethoven. Only the "philosophers" are busily engaged in cutting their own leading lights down to size.

While not everybody in "philosophy" accepts the primacy of the modern writers over the ancients, the skeptical epistemologists or professional skeptics are in the majority by far. A minority who would oppose them simply do not have the means to do so effectively. Nor do I mean to paint them all with a broad brush. For example, Randall, who unlike Rorty does not lump together the epistemologies of Aristotle and the moderns, gives intermittent signs of trying to break away from relativism and skepticism, but is unable to do so.

Ancient or modern, in times to come "the great dead philosophers" will still be read. Despite their mistakes, they will endure, and they will outlast Rorty and Randall and the other contemporary "philosophers." Without going into the question exhaustively, I will use Randall to pinpoint why this is so, because I know his writings well enough to find some specific answers.

In his book on Aristotle Randall comments that the latter has little to say about the nature of language and mind:

> For Aristotle . . . [t]here can be no "imageless thought." It is surprising that, for a man so wedded to *logos,* to language, as Aristotle, he seems to have been, psychologically, as much of a visualist as the major British empiricists. . . . This suggests what is undoubtedly the chief lack in the text of the *De Anima* as it stands. There is to be found in it no treatment of *logos*, of language and communication, in connection with knowing – there is no treatment of *logos* in functional terms. In treating *logos* Aristotle is always the formalist, the *logikos*, never the functionalist, the *physikos*.[6]

It is surprising to *me* that someone so wedded to *logos*, to language, as *Randall* should have failed to see the theory of language and mind so strongly implied in so many passages in Aristotle. It was the subject of my Ph.D. dissertation, and I discovered it not through Randall, but through Chomsky. In the dissertation, I cite a series of passages from different Aristotelian texts, explicate them, compare them, and synthesize them in order to show how powerful it is. Randall cites just one of them in denying that Aristotle had such a theory. His denial would have much more force had he considered the rest of the passages. Furthermore, except for the comments just quoted, he posits no criteria for making the negative judgment. He would have had to a) speak to the criteria for a theory of language and mind laid down by Chomsky (or comparable ones), and b) show that Aristotle does not meet those requirements. Randall doesn't do either of these things. Indeed, let us look for a moment at the one passage he cites:

> It is impossible even to think without an image. The same process oc-
> curs in thinking as in drawing a diagram; for in this case although we
> make no use of the fact that the magnitude of a triangle is a finite quan-
> tity, yet we draw it as having a finite magnitude. In the same way the
> man who is thinking, though he may not be thinking of a finite magni-
> tude, still puts a finite magnitude before his eyes, though he does not
> think of it as such. And even if its nature is that of a magnitude, but an
> unlimited one, he still puts before him a finite magnitude, but thinks of
> it as a magnitude without limit.[7]

Aristotle is telling us that the mental images by means of which we think are *symbols*; our thinking is inherently linguistic. The words we create express and develop the natural symbolism of our thought. The foregoing passage is strong evidence that Aristotle did have a theory of language and mind, but somehow Randall draws the opposite conclusion. However, if something that should be there isn't immediately apparent, try looking for it. Scholarly texts can be compared to archeological sites: you have to do some digging. If Aristotle made such a promising start, and Randall *finds it surprising* that he didn't continue, the implication is that perhaps he did. If it is surprising that Aristotle didn't continue, it *wouldn't* be surprising if he did. So maybe he did! But Randall does not draw these inferences, made plausible by his own comments. In the last paragraph of the book, he observes, "[Aris-totle's] view of the relation of *logos* to things is far too simple."[8] On the con-trary, Randall's view of Aristotle's view of *logos* is far too simple!

In other words, it is not I alone against Randall, or even Chomsky and I, but Chomsky and I and Randall himself against his own interpretation. I am not trying to psychoanalyze Randall, but only to show that the seeds of a more positive view of Aristotle can be found in Randall's work, but he does not develop them.

Aristotle's theory of language is brilliant, but Randall doesn't even know it exists. Similarly, his chapters on Aristotle's psychology provide lit-tle or no sense of Aristotle's genius. The same is true of Randall's discussion of Aristotle's theory of ethics, politics, art, and the nature of living organisms. Each of these areas of Aristotle's thought deserves a much longer treatment than Randall gives them – a chapter or two here, a portion of a chapter there do not suffice.

By contrast, the claim made earlier in this essay about Aristotle and the modern writers is stronger than any Randall makes for him. Equally strong and more far-reaching are the claims I make for Aristotle's views on psychology, linguistics, the social sciences, and the nature and origin of life: that Aristotle was ahead of modern science in these areas, and that science must understand and develop his ideas. These matters will be discussed at length in Chapter 8.

Sometimes Randall does present a more exalted vision of Aristotle. Then Lady Philosophy stops being a whore and becomes Boethius' Dame Philosophia, her head touching the clouds. But the moments do not last. I do not mean to sound overly critical of my teacher, whose memory I revere. It is just that I am trying to get a precise idea of why the great thinkers of the tradition will survive their modern commentators and critics.

Unfortunately, the prevailing view of the tradition among contemporary "philosophers" is the narrower view. They are "micro-scholars." Even when their research is solid, it tends to be too narrow. Some cases are much worse than others, and one can learn to recognize the symptoms. For example, to a true micro-scholar the texts are filled with difficulties and badly need the help of the commentators. When one of them tells us that "X gets into difficulty here," and "we have to restate his position for him," or says plaintively, "If we can just help X out here," it is likely we are reading a work of small-minded scholarship. Yet despite the microscopic examination of texts and problems, the Lilliputian scholars fail to shed much light on them. One of the surest signs of their microscholarship is the inordinate amount of time they spend discussing the opinions of their colleagues. They clearly are much more concerned about the latter than about the texts themselves and finding solutions to the real problems the texts raise.

It would be interesting and amusing to ferret out more characteristics of small-minded scholarship. However, the criteria and the examples given suffice for now. To conclude with an example that I already have touched on, consider the relation between Hobbes and Aristotle on the question of the unity of mind. Hobbes takes a firm position on this issue. He rebuts Aristotle, a very solid thinker, from the standpoint of modern science, a body of knowledge that also is very solid. In other words, he squarely faces a key problem. He brings the strongest and clearest arguments of modern materialist science to bear on the strongest anti-materialist arguments in the tradition, those of Aristotle. It is true that Hobbes is vulnerable to some severe criticisms, and the commentators do not stint in pointing them out. Nevertheless, Hobbes striking out still looks better than Randall and Rorty and all the others hitting home runs, and we can see why. The latter are minor leaguers, and he is playing in the majors.

George Santayana pictured the great philosophers conducting dialogues in limbo, and, extending this idea, we can imagine them interrupting their discourses to play a game of baseball. There is Aristotle on the mound for the Ancient All-Stars and Hobbes, playing for the Modern Marvels, stepping up to the plate in the late innings with bases loaded and two out. Hobbes works the count to three and two, and then on the next pitch, he hits a long fly ball down the left field line. We hear the voice of the announcer, "What a screaming line drive! It looks like it's outta here! Bye-bye, baby! It's going, going, going, and it goes – foul!" Then on the next pitch, Hobbes strikes out. How 'bout that! Yes, he strikes out, but it's off Aristotle's pitching, and off that same pitching he almost hits a home run.

As noted earlier, the great writers of the tradition are dealing with the larger issues and they are talking to each other and helping each other much more than is commonly realized. The commentators and the critics are, generally speaking, working within a much narrower compass. Thus, we can see why the giants are giants and the pygmies are pygmies. In light of these insights, in the next chapter I will show how we can rethink the conventional view of "modern philosophy."

Notes

1. Immanuel Kant, *Prolegomena to Any Future Metaphysics*, tr. Lewis White Beck (Indianapolis: Bobbs-Merrill, 1950), Preamble [279–80], p. 27.

2. Rorty, *op. cit.*, Preface, xiii–xiv.

3. Rorty, *op. cit.*, ch. 1, "The Invention of the Mind," pp. 45–46.

4. Plato clearly influenced Aristotle on this question. The argument for the unity of mind in *De Anima* III, ii, 426b8–30 strongly resembles the one in Plato's dialogue *Theaetetus 184b–185e*. The passage in the *De Anima* is the only explicit statement of this key concept in Aristotle. However, it is

alluded to, presupposed, or implied in subsequent chapters of Book III. (See the Appendix of this essay.)

5. See Thomas Hobbes, *Elements of Philosophy concerning Body*, Ch. XXV, "Of Sense and Animal Motion," Sect. 8.

6. John Herman Randall, Jr., *Aristotle* (New York: Columbia University Press, 1960), pp. 95–96.

7. Aristotle, *Parva Naturalia: De Memoria* 1: 449b32–450a6, quoted in Randall, *op. cit.*, p. 96.

8. Randall, *op. cit.*, p. 300.

5
Rethinking "Modern Philosophy"

The view of the tradition I am proposing is very different from all the micro- and pseudo-scholarship. While the standard history of philosophy is not swept away, it is modified and put into a wider context. Consider the conventional distinction in "modern philosophy" between "British empiricism" and "Continental rationalism." That distinction is dwarfed by the fact that all the writers from Descartes through Kant were trying to comprehend science and to find a proper place in the world depicted by science for the human mind and human values. If we look at the writers who comprise "modern philosophy" in light of this new paradigm, we will see how much more comprehensible they become, how much more unified and coherent than Rorty and the other skeptics would have us believe. In this chapter I will sketch the modern writers as they would appear in the new paradigm. While outlining the key points in the rethinking of "modern philosophy," I will try to show a) that the essential ideas in "the history of philosophy" can be explained simply, clearly, and precisely, and b) how sharply focused the problems of "philosophy" really are.

A. Descartes and Augustine

Let us begin at the beginning with Descartes and his famous saying *Cogito, ergo sum* (I think; therefore, I am), which occurs in his *Discourse on Method*. That work, together with his *Meditations on First Philosophy*, is generally considered to mark the founding of "modern philosophy." This saying is part of an argument in which Descartes purports to make all doubts about the reality of the physical world come to rest against the rock-hard certainty of his self-awareness: He can doubt everything in the world around him, but he cannot doubt that he is doubting. Indeed, the more he doubts, the surer he is of his own existence, the surer he is that he is the one doing all the doubting. My essential criticism of this argument is that Descartes tries to stretch an undeniable truth of logic to cover a dubious hypothesis in psychology (or, if you prefer, "epistemology"). In the end, he appears to recognize the inadequacy of his position, and he falls back on a form of Platonism. Both the *Discourse* and the *Meditations* follow this basic plan.[1]

"I think; therefore, I am" is an informal statement of what appears to be a simple logical argument, which we can restate more precisely in order to examine it carefully. As just stated it is an *enthymeme,* that is, a syllogism with one of the premises understood, in this instance, the major premise. The latter would read as follows: "All things that think are things that exist." Thus, the argument would run: "All things that think are things that exist; I am a thing that thinks; therefore, I am a thing that exists." (For the purposes of this discussion, we can disregard possible differences in meaning between "am" and "exist," as Descartes is not distinguishing between them.)

The foregoing is known as a categorical syllogism, and it can be restated in hypothetical form. For simplicity and clarity, let us do that:

If I think, I am. (By hypothesis.)
I think._____
Therefore, I am.

This argument has the following logical form:

If p, then q.
p_____
q

The logical form of Descartes' argument is simple enough because the text makes abundantly clear that the major premise is presupposed. The difficulty in the argument is not logical, but psychological.

At this point, it is crucial to note that a very similar argument occurs in the writings of St. Augustine, and is surely the ultimate source of Descartes' argument, although the latter does not acknowledge it. He may well have learned it from his teachers at the Jesuit college of La Flèche. Here is St. Augustine's argument:

> 73. If you do not grasp what I say and doubt whether it is true, at least make up your mind whether you have any doubt about your doubts. If it is certain that you do indeed have doubts, inquire whence comes that certainty. It will never occur to you to imagine that it comes from the light of the sun, but rather from that "true light which lighteth every man that cometh into the world." It cannot be seen with these eyes, nor with the eyes which seem to see the phantasms of the brain, but with

those that can say to phantasms: You are not the thing I am seeking. Nor are you the standard by which I put you in your rightful place, disapproving of all that is base in you, and approving of all that is beautiful. The standard according to which I approve and disapprove is still more beautiful, so I approve more highly of it and prefer it not only to you but to all those bodily shapes from which you spring. Now think of the rule in this way. Everyone who knows that he has doubts knows with certainty something that is true, namely, that he doubts. He is certain, therefore, about *a* truth. Therefore everyone who doubts whether there is such a thing as *the* truth has at least *a* truth to set a limit to his doubt; and nothing can be true except truth be in it. Accordingly, no one ought to have doubts about the existence of *the* truth, even if doubts arise for him from every possible quarter. Wherever this is seen, there is light that transcends space and time and all phantasms that spring from spatial and temporal things. Could this be in the least destroyed even if every reasoner should perish or grow old among inferior carnal things? Reasoning does not create truth but discovers it. Before it is discovered it abides in itself; and when it is discovered it renews us.[2]

It is very worthwhile to compare Augustine's version of the argument with Descartes'. We note that Augustine clears up the doubting state of mind almost immediately, whereas Descartes lingers over it for page after page. We must keep in mind, of course, that Augustine had gone through years of doubt and self-questioning, eloquently described in his autobiography, *The Confessions*. Once he had resolved his uncertainties with a mixture of Platonic theory and Christian faith, he did not need to linger over them in developing and expounding his ideas.

By contrast, Descartes was trying to clear away the Aristotelian scholasticism that still dominated the thought of his time and to build a proper foundation for the mathematical method that he wanted to extend to all fields of knowledge. This method was based on analytic geometry, of which Descartes was the co-inventor. He was trying to be rigorous, to subject his ideas to the strongest possible test. He tried to doubt as many things as he could as hard as he could, in order to arrive at the greatest possible certainty. Thus, as he proceeds in the *Meditations*, he finds that he can doubt the existence of every conceivable physical object. In particular, his eye lights upon a piece of wax, which looks solid and permanent. Yet when he holds it to the fire, it melts, and he recognizes the uncertainty to which all physical objects are subject. Yet the more he doubts, the more certain he is that he is doubting. Doubting is a form of thinking, and "if I think, I am."

Just as his compatriot Louis XIV said, *"L'état, c'est moi"* ("The state, that's me" – customarily, but less accurately translated "I am the state"), we can picture Descartes saying, *"Le douteur – c'est moi."* The doubter – that's me. *I* am the doubter.

"*I* am the doubter, and the more I doubt, the surer I am that it is I who am doubting." But that is exactly the problem, and with a little imagination, we can see why. Take that piece of wax, for example. Instead of it sitting there quietly and calmly letting Descartes doubt its existence, imagine it suddenly vanishing. We can picture Descartes' reaction. *"Que diable! Où s'est-il évanoui ce maudit morceau de cire? Est-ce que je me trompe?"* (What the devil! Where did it go to, that damn piece of wax? Am I deceiving myself?) And then we can imagine it suddenly reappearing in another part of the room, then disappearing and reappearing again and again. How many times would this have to happen before Descartes would doubt whether or not he was doubting, or would wonder whether or not he was dreaming, or would start to doubt his own existence? We can carry this yet farther and think of it as a scene from a horror movie, a Cartesian creature feature, in which the wax pops in and out of walls, floors, and ceilings, assumes grotesque shapes, and so on. We can imagine Descartes so despondent and distraught from all of his metaphysical doubting that he takes to drink, starts hallucinating, and in his delirium experiences even more nightmarish doubt.

What is truly doubtful in all of this is the privileged position of the "I" that supposedly is doing all the doubting. How can it sit there as calm as the eye of a hurricane while all its perceptions other than its perception of itself are whirling about it in utter chaos? Moreover, when I say "all its perceptions," I do not just mean the inanimate objects lying about the room. What about Descartes' own body? After all, that's part of "extended substance," *i.e.*, the physical world. What might Descartes think if he suddenly found himself missing an arm, a leg, an ear, an eye, or other body parts?

In short, you cannot get the certainty of the mind or the self or the "I" using a solipsistic argument. You cannot derive the certainty of the self from the uncertainty of the perceptions. The *Cogito* is essentially a psychological argument, and if you follow out its psychological implications, *i.e.*, if the perceptions really are uncertain, you see that the minor premise cannot be established. You really do doubt whether or not you are doubting. Thus, the argument fails.

So where does that leave Descartes? Is his whole philosophy a shambles? Let us backtrack a little and compare Descartes' version of the argument with that of St. Augustine.

The first thing we notice is that Augustine doesn't push the doubting very far. He immediately appeals to a higher authority. As his further comments make clear, all that the doubt serves to do is remind him of the certainty that already is there in his own mind, a combination of Christian faith and Platonic ideas.

Lo and behold, Descartes ultimately follows the same path, but with so many twists and turns that we might not realize what is happening if we did not look closely. Immediately after the *Cogito*, he presents several proofs of the existence of God, the guarantor of all truth, including that of mathematics. This, together with the *Cogito*, should be enough to lay all his doubts to rest, but no, he keeps on raising doubts right on to the last page of the *Meditations*. He questions not only the physical world and his perception of it, but even the things he finds in his own mind. Could the truths of mathematics be false? Could God be a deceiver? While God has the power to deceive us or to allow us to be deceived, He would never do that because He is good.

In the end, God is the source of all truth, just as He is in Augustine. God, together with all the truths that come from Him, prominent among which are the truths of mathematics, stands as a bulwark against all the uncertainties of the physical world. It is the faith of a scientist, but faith nonetheless, and one that is constantly tested, as he concludes, ". . . we must in the end acknowledge the infirmity of our nature."

One can hardly resist drawing a comparison with St. Augustine because the parallel is so striking. Like Descartes a man of great intelligence, Augustine arrived at his faith after a long spiritual journey. Born in 354 A.D. in what is now Algeria, he became a Christian in 387. In 397 he was appointed bishop of the North African city of Hippo, an office he retained until his death in 430. During this time the Roman Empire was collapsing, people were blaming its ruin on the Christians, and the last four months of Augustine's life were spent with Hippo besieged by the Vandals.

Augustine's rich experience included a wide range of ideas and beliefs, which continually were tested. Surrounded by many sources of doubt, did he maintain the serenity of his faith? His voluminous writings suggest that he did. There is no sense of the anguish and soul-searching of his earlier life that is so eloquently described in the *Confessions*. But there is no sense either that his mind ever came to rest in a dogmatic certainty. He is always questioning. His is a living faith.

In this respect, Descartes and Augustine are similar, and the style of several of their key works reflects the similarity. The *Confessions* is an autobiographical meditation in which Augustine is speaking to God. The *Discourse on Method* and *Meditations on First Philosophy* are autobiographical soliloquies whose personal style parallels that of the *Confessions*.

We must not, however, overlook the critical differences between them. Augustine is uninterested in acquiring scientific knowledge of the physical world. For him, as for Plato and Plotinos before him, the material world is only an imperfect copy of the ideal world. It is the latter they are trying to reach, and they are interested in science only insofar as it serves that purpose.

Descartes, on the other hand, is a mathematician and scientist who is very much interested in the physical world. Ancient atomism, the very atomism Augustine rejected in the *Confessions*, is revived in the 1620s by the intellectual circle to which Descartes belongs. Despite his doubts, Descartes accepts the reality of the world of atoms and molecules. He wants to acquire scientific knowledge of it and subdue it to human purposes. The mathematics he develops is a new and wonderful tool for doing so, and he goes ahead and applies it full tilt. But except for the fact that the mathematical concepts do apply to the physical world – and it is a major exception – Descartes has a hard time explaining how mind and matter are related. His clumsy attempt to show how the mind acts on the body through the pineal gland only serves to highlight the inadequacy of his explanation. And so we have dualism.

In fact, the dilemma is of his own making. He sets it up with his hard-and-fast distinction between thinking substance (mind) and extended substance (body). Once Descartes has locked himself up inside his head and thrown away the key, it is no wonder he can't figure out how to escape. Just as when I imagined the piece of wax flying about the room, it is tempting to compare "the founder of modern philosophy" to Frankenstein, and "modern philosophy" to a horror movie. Nor is the comparison frivolous. By Descartes & Co.'s account of things, the brain could just as easily be immersed in liquid in a glass case, with wires sticking out of it connecting it to the rest of its body located elsewhere in the room. The point is that dualism is a forced and constrained non-solution to the question of the relationship between mind and body or mind and matter. Descartes' attempt to make the connection via the pineal gland was not taken seriously even in his own time, and more sophisticated attempts like Leibniz's "pre-established harmony" were no more satisfactory.

Once again, we can see the dilemmas of the modern thinkers more clearly by making a comparison with St. Augustine. At a critical juncture in his life, just before his conversion to Christianity, Augustine went through an episode of emotional agony in the garden of the house where he lived with a friend. Speaking to God in the *Confessions*, he recalls this incident vividly, and it prompts him to reflect on the relationship of body and mind:

> There was a little garden belonging to our lodging, of which we had the use just as we did of the whole house, for the host, the owner of the house, did not live there. There the tumult in my breast had carried me, where no one might impede the fiery lawsuit that I had entered into against myself, until it came to an outcome that you knew, but I did not. . . .
>
> At length in those seethings of delay I did so many things with my body that sometimes men will to do and cannot, if either they do not have the very limbs to do them or if those limbs are bound with chains or weakened by feebleness, or however they may be hindered. If I tore my hair, if I struck my forehead, if with my fingers locked together I hugged my knees, what I willed to do, I did. But I could have willed it and not done it, if the mobility of my limbs had not yielded to me. So many things, therefore, I did, where the will was not the same as the power; and I did not do what both with incomparable emotion pleased me more fully, and what, as soon as I willed it, I then could do, because as soon as I willed it, I then certainly willed it. For there the power is the same as the will, and to will it was already to do it; yet it was not done, and my body was submitting more easily to the slightest wish of my mind, so that at a nod my limbs would be moved, than my mind was to itself in carrying out its own great act of will in the will alone.
>
> 9. Whence this wonder? And for what reason? . . . The mind commands the body and is immediately obeyed; the mind commands itself, and is resisted. The mind commands that the hand be moved and it happens so easily that the command can hardly be distinguished from the execution; yet the mind is mind and the hand is body. The mind commands the mind to will, and it is not something else, yet it does not do it. Whence this wonder? And for what reason? It commands, I say, that it will, and would not command unless it willed, and does not do what it commands. But it does not fully will; therefore it does not fully command. For it only commands insofar as it wills, and insofar as it does not do what it commands, thus far it does not will, since the will [itself]

commands that there be a will – not something else, but itself! And so the full will does not command; hence, there does not come to be what it commands. For if it *were* full, it would not command that it be, because it would already be. Therefore, it is not a wonder partly to will and partly not to will, but a sickness of the mind, that not whole, it rises, borne upward by the truth, [yet] weighed down by habit. Hence there are two wills, because one of them is not whole, and to this one is present what is lacking in the other.[3]

Notice that Augustine does not try to explain the *mechanism* of the relationship between mind and body. Unlike Descartes, he doesn't confine the mind to the brain and then try to figure out how it is connected to the rest of the body. Whatever the physical process is, it is obvious that mind and body are connected. The paradox is that it is easier for the mind to control the body than to control itself. The latter is far more important to Augustine than learning the details of the mind-body relationship or developing a science of the body.

By contrast, Descartes wants to use the Platonic certainty he finds within his own mind to get back into the world of his body, the physical world. But having put that world so completely in doubt, he has a hard time doing it. He is one of the founders of a mathematical science of the physical world, a crusader for science who fervently believes in the physical world, yet on the other hand, he doesn't believe in it. This is not just dualism, but schizophrenia. It is something like the state of mind of St. Augustine in the passage just quoted. That passage is a prescient commentary on the schizophrenia of modern Western society.

The objection has been made that Descartes was one of the most cocksure individuals who ever lived and that his doubts were really only "metaphysical," just an intellectual exercise. To be sure, he was no solipsist, a person who believes only in his own existence. One can hardly imagine him, say, in bed with his girlfriend, suddenly experiencing an acute attack of doubt. "I am absolutely certain of my own existence, my dear, but I am unsure if you really exist. Perhaps you're just a figment of my imagination." However, we ought not to overlook the contradictory nature of his ideas and of modern thought as a whole. Descartes was a mathematician with a high standard of certainty, and he discovered that the metaphysical foundations of his thought were in doubt, that he needed a higher power to remove their uncertainty, that he couldn't give a rigorous answer to the skeptics, the followers of Montaigne. In short, I am suggesting that the cocksureness was real enough, but that the doubts were equally real. Why else would he have bothered to write the *Discourse on Method* and *The Meditations*? Even after he completed these treatises, the worm of doubt remained to gnaw at him. He may have been an amateur at metaphysics, but he was not a superficial mind.[4]

I remember that for years I struggled with Descartes' writings before I began to understand all of this. Descartes gets bogged down and he drags the reader into the muck with him. However, with the help of St. Augustine, we can see what he really is up to and avoid this quagmire or be pulled out of it if we get caught in it. Or to switch metaphors, without the light that Augustine shines on him, we all too easily fall into the trap of trying to figure out a connection that cannot be figured out, of trying to solve a problem that has been formulated in such a way that it cannot be solved. Seen in light of Augustinian Platonism, the Cartesian dualism can rightly be called Frankensteinian Platonism.

In Augustine, the argument from doubt serves as a check, to remind you of the truths you already have in your mind in goodly supply. Augustine wisely does not push the argument too far, else he would get into the same kind of trouble Descartes does. Like Augustine, Descartes sees the escape route from the uncertainties of the physical world, but unlike him, he wants to go only part way on it. He uses the truth he finds within his own mind as a buttress against the uncertainty of the world outside his mind. In the end, God has to be the guarantor of the physical world as well, and someone certain only about the contents of his mind might choose to doubt the very existence of the latter. If, on the other hand, one should be skeptical that God is out there performing this function, then there *is* no guarantor, no ground of our perceptions. We have only to read Descartes carefully to see Berkeley and Hume lurking in the wings.

Descartes is the exemplar of modern dualism not only because he formulates it so dramatically but because he tries so valiantly to embrace both sides of it. The crux of the problem, however, is not Descartes' *statement* of it, but that modern science accepts the world of atoms and molecules as the primary reality, and then has difficulty understanding mind and human values or finding a place in nature for them. All the "modern philosophers" begin with this scientific paradigm and its built-in dilemma. Contrary to what Rorty says, they are all proposing *alternative solutions to the same problem.* Moreover, the solutions they propose have much more in common than the twentieth-century "philosophers" would have us believe.

The *Cogito* is rightly regarded as the entry point to "modern philosophy," and studying its original Augustinian form gives us a whole new perspective on it. But in order to gain this perspective, it is necessary to compare closely the two versions. As noted in the previous chapter, the members of the tradition illuminate each other better than anyone else seems able to do. The texts themselves remain far richer, more fertile, and more original than anything the historians and commentators have to say about them. While Randall, for example, in his history of philosophy mentions the influence of Augustinian ideas on Descartes, he merely alludes to Augustine's version of the *Cogito* without actually quoting it or discussing it. This omission significantly weakens Randall's commentary on Descartes, which otherwise is interesting and informative.[5]

That is to say, it weakens the commentary for those who actually have studied and compared the texts. For those who have not, it has a far different effect. In addition to making the texts harder to understand, the failure to let them shine their light upon each other diminishes not only the individual texts but also their combined effect. It allows minor leaguers like Randall and Rorty to look good at the expense of the all-stars. It makes the pygmies bulk larger than the giants.

The pygmies look bigger than the giants and the tradition turns to jumble and confusion. False problems arise and multiply, and a pseudo-discipline comes into being. That is what happens when the history of ideas is presented according to the lights of the relativists and skeptics. Maximize the differences. Minimize the common themes. Accentuate complexity. Decentuate unity. Do your best to keep the texts from speaking for themselves.

The way to test what I say is to compare the texts with each other and then see what the commentators have to say about them. Perhaps it sounds easy, but I remember how long it took to attain the vantage point from which I now survey the tradition. In Randall's course in the history of philosophy, which I took as an undergraduate, the Augustinian version of the *Cogito* was not assigned, so I never knew it existed until I studied Plotinos and Augustine with Paul Miller. Discovering it was an eye-opener, but even then I did not see the relationship between Descartes and Augustine clearly enough. So deeply engrained are the conventional ways of reading "the history of philosophy" that one can fail to think through and beyond them until the right stimulus occurs. An essay, which is a form of self-examination, can provide that stimulus. It was so for St. Augustine, for Montaigne, for Descartes, and for countless others, including myself.

B. Locke

If we compare dualism in the *rationalism* of Descartes with the form it takes in the *empiricism* of Locke, we will see that it is just as arbitrary in the one as it is in the other.

The clearest and most fundamental expression of dualism in Locke is the distinction he makes between what he calls "primary qualities" and "secondary qualities." By the former he means the inherent characteristics of bodies (*i.e.*, of physical objects): number, size, figure, solidity, motion and rest. The latter are the subjective perceptions caused by the former: sensations of touch, including hardness and softness, sharpness and dullness, heat and cold, etc; perceptions of taste, smell, color, and sound:

> 11. The ideas that our complex ones of substances are made up of, and about which our knowledge concerning substances is most employed, are those of their secondary qualities; which depending all (as has been shown) upon the primary qualities of their minute and insensible parts; or, if not upon them, upon something yet more remote from our comprehension; it is impossible we should know which have a *necessary* union with one another . . .
>
> 12. Besides this ignorance of the primary qualities of the insensible parts of bodies, on which depend all their secondary qualities, there is yet another and more incurable part of ignorance, which sets us more remote from a certain knowledge of the co-existence or *inco-existence* (if I may so say) of different ideas in the same subject; and that is, that *there is no discoverable connection between any secondary quality and those primary qualities which it depends on.* [Emphasis added.]
>
> 13. That the size, figure, and motion of one body should cause a change in the size, figure, and motion of another body, is not beyond our conception; the separation of the parts of one body upon the intrusion of another; and the change from rest to motion upon impulse; these and the like seem to have *some connexion* one with another. And if we knew the primary qualities of bodies, we might have reason to hope we might be able to know a great deal more of these operations of them one upon another: but our minds not being able to discover any connexion betwixt these primary qualities of bodies and the sensations that are produced in us by them, we can never be able to establish certain and undoubted rules of the *consequence* or *co-existence* of any

secondary qualities, though we could discover the size, figure, or motion of those invisible parts which immediately produce them. We are
so far from knowing *what* figure, size, or motion of parts produce a yel-
low colour, a sweet taste, or a sharp sound, that we can by no means
conceive how *any* size, figure, or motion of any particles, can possibly
produce in us the idea of any colour, taste, or sound whatsoever: *there
is no conceivable connexion between the one and the other.* [Emphasis
added.][6]

The foregoing is one of the central passages in Locke's writings. It states a
position that has been presented to countless numbers of students, including
myself, as gospel, with the primary qualities updated in light of scientific
discoveries made since Locke's time. On the one hand, science tells us that
light is electromagnetic vibrations; on the other hand, we have sensations of
color. On the one hand, wave-like vibrations occur in the air; on the other
hand, we hear sounds. On the one hand, atoms and molecules are constantly
in motion; on the other hand, we have sensations of heat and cold. The case
is similar for our perceptions of taste and smell. On the one hand, there are
chemical reactions, and on the other our subjective perceptions.

I recall in the spring of 1980 describing this position to my students in
the history of modern philosophy. Several of them objected, "But this theory defies common sense. Why are we studying it?" By that time, I too had
seen through it, and I shared their discomfort. I remember struggling to explain to them its historical importance. Although I succeeded in mollifying
their discontent, I was uncertain of my own rationalization. But then I came
upon the foregoing passage, and its arbitrariness hit me with full force: according to Locke, not only is there no *discoverable* connection or resemblance or identity between these two sets of phenomena; no such
connection, resemblance, or identity is even *conceivable*! Now I truly could
justify studying this viewpoint because we need to grasp how arbitrary it is
and to see its consequences for Western thought and Western culture.

In Locke's time, chemistry was in its infancy and little was known
about electricity. The existence of atoms was presupposed, as it had been in
ancient times, but was not experimentally confirmed. Although Galileo,
Newton, *et al.* had already appeared on the scene, modern science still was
young. Thus, there was some justification for Locke to be cautious about the
extent and the limits of human knowledge because so much less was known
in his time than in ours. Nevertheless, he goes beyond mere caution. If we
know so *little* about the atoms, how can he know so *much* about what we can

and cannot know about them? How does he *know* that a connection between primary and secondary qualities is neither discoverable nor conceivable?

Actually, the same distinction exists in Descartes, although he does not give it those names. He brings it up briefly in the Sixth Meditation and quickly goes on to other things. The reason it plays a smaller role in his thought is that, being a "rationalist," he believes that certain ideas or concepts, like those of mathematics, are innate, and he is more concerned with these.

To say that certain ideas are innate does not mean that we are conscious of them from the moment of birth, but that we may discover them in our minds at different times in our lives. This is an old idea. In Plato's dialogue *Meno*, Socrates calls the process of rediscovering the ideas already existing in our minds "recollection."

At the beginning of his *Essay*, Locke vigorously attacks the doctrine of innate ideas. This is the fundamental difference between him and Descartes. However, despite this difference, they find themselves in the same quandary. Descartes' dualistic version of Platonism is, as I said, Frankensteinian. He has us pent up inside of our skulls with our innate ideas and mental images derived from the senses; we are connected with our bodies and with the world outside our bodies in a most peculiar way, via the pineal gland.

According to Locke, we don't have innate ideas, just mental images, the secondary qualities, which supposedly are derived from the world of the senses, the primary qualities; but given the extreme position he takes, it is unclear how we get from the secondary qualities back to the primary qualities, or how we got from the primary qualities to the secondary qualities in the first place. While the primary qualities *cause* the secondary qualities, we know of their existence only *by means of* the secondary qualities. Furthermore, as we just saw, no connection between the two is either discoverable or conceivable. If you don't believe Locke could be saying all these self-contradictory things, just read the *Essay*. Whereas Descartes' version of the dualism is schizophrenic, Locke's is simply muddled. He is the archetypical, quintessentially muddleheaded Englishman.

At least that is the Locke of the *Essay*, where he describes himself as "a poor underlabourer for Mr. Newton." In his political writings, where he is busy fomenting revolution or justifying it, he is much more rationalistic, constantly making eloquent appeals to universal reason. So maybe he is schizophrenic too!

I can remember how slowly and how gradually I worked my way out of the dilemma of dualism to a *critical realism* or *neo-Aristotelian realism*. Late in the 1960s and early in the 1970s, when I still was a graduate student, I was starting to see resemblances between the primary and the secondary qualities. It occurred to me first that with sounds, particularly low-pitched ones, you can *hear* vibrations. That certainly is a resemblance, and it made me question the whole distinction. Also at that time I was reading Aristotle's *De Anima* more carefully than I had ever done before. One of the things I grasped from his account of perception was the similarities between the sensations of touch and the qualities of the objects that cause them: hard and soft, sharp and dull.

In these examples, the resemblance between the secondary and the primary qualities is fairly clear. But what about our other sense-perceptions? It is not so obvious how differences in the motion of molecules can be perceived as sensations of heat and cold. The case is similar for color, taste, and smell, and their respective causes. However, if a resemblance can be found for sound and touch, does it make sense to argue that an unbridgeable gulf exists for our other percepts? How could the connection be *undiscoverable* and *inconceivable* for some types of perception and not for all? That would be another dualism. Amazing, isn't it? Just as you rid yourself of one dualism, another springs up to take its place!

Maybe we can get a clue to the relationship by imagining how, over evolutionary time, living creatures developed sense-organs for these other types of perception. Biologists theorize that the flesh of organisms became sensitive to a variety of physical phenomena, and the respective sense-organs gradually developed. For example, certain areas of skin became more and more sensitive to the impinging electromagnetic radiation. It must have taken many millions of years for eyes to evolve. From mere reverberations of air waves upon skin, eventually the various components of the ear developed: the eardrum, vibrating bones, etc. There must have been many gradations before the sense-organs reached the level of development with which we are familiar. Between the mere impingement of electromagnetic radiation and the perception of color, a transitional stage most likely occurred early on. It is very hard to believe that the dualism existed right in the process of evolution, as if by Darwinian magic: now you see the primary qualities; now you don't. Or rather, at one moment only primary qualities exist in the sense organ, and at the next moment, only secondary ones, as the Lockean/Cartesian dualism springs into existence *ex nihilo*. On the contrary, the transitional stage must have been something like the resemblances between sound and touch and their respective physical motions that I was describing above. That is, the perception of color was so crude and limited that the transition or the resemblance was perceived by the creature with the primeval organ. As the visual organ became more sophisticated, the transition between light as photons or waves and light as colors was no longer apparent.

The structure of certain currently existing eyes lends support to this explanation. For example, many (if not all) insects have eyes with thousands of facets. They have thousands of images of the same object instead of one overall visual field. Thus, we can imagine a much earlier stage of evolution in which crude eyes picked up relatively small individual batches of photons, and what they "saw" was a much more primitive version of color than what eyes can see today.

A similar evolution can be envisioned for all the other "secondary" qualities. Needless to say, the Darwinian theory of evolution was one more major scientific theory that did not exist in Locke's day. Furthermore, even though Darwin worked out his theory in the historical context of a mechanistic science of matter, he has more in common with Aristotle than with dualists like Descartes and Kant. The latter regard living bodies, *i.e.*, all non-human living creatures, as mere machines obeying the mechanical laws of physics. In order to preserve the integrity of the human mind, which after all exists in an animal body, they somehow have to locate it outside of nature.

Aristotle, the pioneer biological researcher, was wrong on many specific points. Still, he had a view of the *scala naturae*, the ladder of living beings, that is comparable to Darwin's. Aristotle is thought not to have believed in biological *evolution*: a concept of the *eternality* of the different species is usually inferred from other aspects of his thought. However, he understood the concept of biological species and was fully aware of the interbreeding of different species. From there, it is only a few steps to the notion of evolution. It is far easier to revise Aristotle's biology in light of Darwin than his physics in light of Newton. In any event, the evolutionary view of perception strongly supports a neo-Aristotelian, biologically based *realism* in preference to a Cartesian/Lockean/Kantian materialist, mechanist, and dualist *phenomenalism.*

C. Realism and Phenomenalism; Hume and Kant

For readers unfamiliar with the jargon of epistemology, "realism" is the hypothesis that our experience is of the reality that truly exists. In other words, there's really a world out there beyond our sense-organs. We are part of it, and our perceptions of it, corrected where necessary by science, are accurate. "Phenomenalism" or "representationalism" is the view that our experience is of our own perceptions, *i.e.*, what comes in through our five senses. But our perceptions are subjective. We have no way of knowing what is behind them causing them. If what we perceive is only something subjective, then even our scientific knowledge is only of the order of our own perceptions. Additional problems arise, such as how we know other minds. How does each of us *know* that anybody besides him- or herself exists? Descartes confronts this problem and puts his faith in God that all those folks out there aren't dummies or monsters put there by an evil God or by the Devil just to fool him.

Descartes' position is a mixture of realism and phenomenalism. He believes that the mathematical ideas and other abstract concepts he finds in his mind are real. Like Plato, he thinks these ideas are innate. Descartes also believes in the reality of the world of atoms and molecules. His problem is getting from one to the other via the uncertain medium of the senses.

Locke also is both a realist and a phenomenalist, although he denies that any of our ideas are innate. He believes in the reality of the physical world that our perceptions reveal to us, but the perceptions themselves are subjective phenomena, and he cannot explain the connection between them and the physical world. Berkeley has a lot of fun exposing Locke's self-contradictions, and he decides the issue in favor of phenomenalism, saying that "to be is to be perceived" (*esse est percipi*). However, he asserts that God is standing behind our perceptions guaranteeing their order and stability and thereby qualifies his phenomenalism decidedly. Hume then dispenses with God or anything whatsoever standing behind the perceptions and appears to be a total phenomenalist and a skeptic. Nevertheless, Hume turns out to be a realist, but in a cagey and ironic way, as we shall see.

Hobbes and Spinoza both are realists, but Hobbes is a reductionist who tries to explain all mental processes in terms of the motion of atoms and molecules. Hobbes' materialism is about as extreme as materialism can possibly be. He not only contradicts Aristotle, but is the polar opposite of Plato. For the latter, the physical world is only a pale reflection of the world of ideas, whereas for Hobbes ideas are a sort of efflorescence or by-product of the motion of matter. Hobbes' anti-mentalism is so strong that, reading him, it is hard for us to understand where the mathematical laws governing the motions of the atoms could come from.

Like Hobbes, Spinoza believes in the scientific world of atoms and molecules. Those atoms and molecules do indeed constitute what we call "matter," but they also have a mathematical structure or form that can be grasped by the human mind. Thus, Spinoza is not a reductionist like Hobbes. He does not try to reduce everything to matter. Like Aristotle, he conceives of the universe as a combination of matter and form. However, he rethinks the Aristotelian concepts of matter and form in terms of the mechanistic, mathematical world of modern science. Spinozism is Aristotelianism with the biology removed, as if the universe were one vast machine. The question remains, who is right, Spinoza or Aristotle? I shall have more to say in this chapter and in Chapter 8 on the ability of Aristotle's ideas to solve the problems of "modern philosophy" and on their applicability to modern science.

Like Spinoza, Leibniz also is a realist and a rationalist, but he is less mechanistic than Spinoza. With his concept of *monads*, which he substitutes for the traditional Aristotelian concept of *substance* (substantial being), he tries to explain both the motions of atoms and the processes of living organisms while avoiding reductionism. To some extent, Leibniz anticipates twentieth-century physics. His ideas are brilliant and suggestive, but his writings, although voluminous, are fragmentary. The concept of monads does not seem to be an improvement on the Aristotelian substances. Leibniz's exposition of it is less detailed and less precise than Aristotle's explanation of substance, and the pre-established harmony is an implausible solution to the mind-body dualism. Leibniz did not solve any of the problems of "modern philosophy," but at least he tried to bring Aristotelian realism into modern science and to avoid materialist reduction.

Thus, when we look at the seven major representatives of "modern philosophy" who preceded Kant, we see that the conventional view of them is very misleading. Phenomenalism or representationalism did *not* predominate to the extent that we have been taught. Hobbes, Spinoza, and Leibniz were realists. As we shall see later , Hume, the alleged arch- phenomenalist, turns out to have been a realist too, or at least to have escaped the dogmatic consequences of his position. The phenomenalism in Descartes and Locke is mixed with realism. Even Berkeley, a purer representative of this view than the others, has God standing behind the phenomena.

The true phenomenalist was Kant, the man who digested and synthesized the work of his predecessors and gave us the nearest thing we have to a definitive version of "modern philosophy." Because he was so influential, we tend to look at the others from his perspective. Kant takes as a given the subjectivism and phenomenalism that he finds in Locke, Berkeley, and Hume. He accepts Locke's distinction between primary and secondary qualities as well as another key idea of Locke, namely that our perceptions are discrete and individual, like atoms. According to this view, any object that comes to us through our five senses is really a collection of atomic percepts: color, shape, temperature, hardness or softness, sharpness or dullness, sound, taste, smell. Because they happen to be conjoined in space and time, we think of them as constituting one single object. But strictly speaking, all that is present to our senses is a conglomeration of individual perceptions. The origin of this theory is no mystery. It was inspired by the atomic theory of matter, which goes back to the ancient Greeks (*átomos* in Greek means uncut, uncuttable, indivisible) and has a long history in classical thought. It was revived in the 1620s and soon was accepted as gospel by nearly all modern thinkers. The physical world was understood to contain a vast collection of little billiard balls, continually colliding and forming and destroying objects. The motion of these atoms upon our sense organs, also composed of atoms, produces individual percepts which themselves are like atoms: a patch of color, a sensation of warmth, a touch, a taste, a smell, and so on.

In sum, Kant's phenomenalism comes from the mind-body dualism, the distinction between primary and secondary qualities, and the atomic view of perception. Think of Descartes: I can doubt everything in the physical world, but I cannot doubt that I am doubting. At least I am certain of my own consciousness. Then Locke: what I am conscious of is secondary qualities, and there is no discoverable connection between them and the primary qualities they depend on. What I perceive is not what is really out there, but my own perceptions. Furthermore, the latter are discrete, like atoms.

The foregoing concepts or hypotheses, taken individually, are serious obstacles to knowledge. Together they make a formidable combination of phenomenalism, subjectivism, and skepticism. Each one of us is locked up inside his or her brain, conscious of his or her own existence, but uncertain about the reality of the physical world "out there." We can't figure out how the mind is connected to the body, or how the mind moves the body. We don't understand the relationship between our perceptions and the atoms that we believe cause them; we're uncertain what is really holding together the objects formed by the perceptions supposedly caused by the atoms, and what is more, we're not even sure the atoms are really there. This is what happens when people try to explain the physical world completely in terms of matter, yet want to preserve traditional views of mind while at the same time making questionable assumptions about it. It is a dubious theory of knowledge that cannot escape its own self-contradictions. Different "modern philosophers" tried out different combinations and variations of ideas in an attempt to avoid the quandary their incompatible views forced them into.

No one was more conscious of the self-contradictions in Locke's position than George Berkeley, who had great fun exposing them in his *Three Dialogues Between Hylas and Philonous*. In this work, Philonous ("Lover of Mind," *i.e.*, Berkeley) repeatedly pins down Hylas ("Mr. Matter," *i.e.*, Locke) and forces him to admit his inconsistencies. In the *Dialogues* and in the *Principles of Human Knowledge*, mind wins out, matter disappears, and God takes its place as the ground of our perceptions. This is perfectly consistent given Locke's assumption about the relation of primary and secondary qualities. All that remains is for Hume to take Berkeley one step farther and deny the need for any ground. Then all we have is sense impressions and mental images formed from them. This is not to say that the impressions we get through the senses don't appear to be solid and hard and hot and cold and in motion and in contact with each other, etc. We can still speak of them in the normal, commonsense way. It is just that we have no idea that there is anything real behind them, that there is any ground behind them. They are just phenomena or appearances (which is what the word *phainómena* means in Greek.)

In addition to removing the ground of our perceptions, Hume also carried the implications of the atomic theory of perception to their limit. If all of our perceptions are atoms, how can there be any necessary connection between them? Hume denied that any such connection exists. Thus, no one physical event necessarily causes any other, and scientific laws become merely contingent descriptions of phenomena. Of course these phenomena are orderly, and we can have scientific formulas and rules like Galileo's and Newton's to describe and predict them. But it is misleading to call the former "laws" because there is nothing fixed or absolute about them. The sun might not rise tomorrow morning. Gravity might cease to exist. Pigs might fly. The probability of these events occurring is low, but still, there is no necessity in the "laws" that supposedly preclude them.

All this looks like pure phenomenalism and skepticism, and most people understood it that way. Indeed, Kant takes the key ideas of Descartes, Locke, and Hume as a given. Starting from these assumptions and conclusions, Kant builds his system. According to him, the necessary connection missing in Hume comes not from the outside world, but from within the mind; it is the way the mind is constituted. We can discover scientific laws in nature because the mind is set up to impose causal laws on the phenomena that come into it through the senses. That is how it is "programmed," as we would say today. The mind contains built-in categories to do this, and our sense organs are naturally constituted so that we perceive space and time in the form of Euclidean geometry. Thus, modern science, based on Newton's laws and the work of Galileo and Kepler and many others, is possible.

Kant saves science, or at any rate our belief in the foundations of science, from Hume's skeptical attack, but what a price he pays! While he gives us genuine scientific laws, he defines nature as "the content of appearances" (*der Inhalt der Erscheinungen*), so that what the laws tell us about is appearances, not what things are in themselves. We do not know what is really out there in the world, just what comes in through the senses together with the form the mind imposes on these raw phenomena. In other words, the subjectivism and phenomenalism Kant finds in Locke, Berkeley, and Hume is still there. We have scientific knowledge, *but only of the phenomena*! As if that weren't bad enough, not only are we precluded from ever gaining knowledge of the physical world in itself, but we can't even know ourselves, either as pure rational beings (whom he calls *noumena*), nor as physical beings, *i.e., phaenomena*.[7] Last but not least, Kant has no way of explaining or removing the dualism. Wisely, he does not follow up on the vain attempts of his predecessors to do this – he leaves the pineal gland to Descartes – and simply asserts that it is perfectly consistent to talk about nature as deterministic and human beings as possessing freedom. That is because we are talking about two different realms, the sensible and the intelligible. Fine, but how are they connected? Kant has no answer. In place of one he has an elaborate set of conditions, possibilities, and presuppositions.[8]

The edifice that Kant builds also contains the presuppositions of Newtonian science about cause and effect, space, time, and motion. These lead him to further skeptical conclusions, namely the antinomies of reason described earlier in this essay (in Chapter 2).

What Kant achieves is significant, but it also is frustratingly, tantalizingly limited. The categories of the understanding and the Euclidean form of our perceptions only combine with the raw data of the senses to produce *our experience* – nothing more. He constantly uses the word "transcendental" to describe this process and its components. *The Critique of Pure Reason*, Kant's chief work, is divided up (after the Introduction) into The Transcendental Doctrine of Elements and The Transcendental Doctrine of Method. The former, which makes up the bulk of the essay, consists of the Transcendental Aesthetic, the Transcendental Analytic, and the Transcendental Dialectic. The question is, what is actually being transcended?

To be sure, positing innate ideas puts Kant, broadly speaking, within the Platonic tradition. But in Plato's dialogues, notably in the myth of the cave, Socrates claims that the prisoners in the cave actually can escape and attain a higher reality. Socrates, as Plato depicts him, makes a serious case, in his ideas and by his example, that such a higher realm is attainable. If so, this truly would be transcendence. Kant, however, repeatedly and emphatically denies that such transcendence is possible.

Kant does not even escape from phenomenalism. The irony is that, roused (as he said) from his dogmatic slumbers by Hume, he arrives at a more rigid skepticism, subjectivism, and phenomenalism than Hume ever had. Still, he "transcends" the radical consequences of a pure phenomenalism, and that is no small thing.

However, Hume transcends those consequences too, although it is less obvious that he does so. Consider the following passage:

> But though this be the only reasonable account we can give of necessity [that there is no necessary connection], the contrary notion is so riveted in the mind . . . that I doubt not but my sentiments will be treated by many as extravagant and ridiculous. What! The efficacy of causes lie in the determination of the mind! As if causes did not operate entirely independent of the mind, and would not continue their operation, even though there was no mind existent to contemplate them, or reason concerning them. Thought may well depend on causes for its operation, but not causes on thought. This is to reverse the order of nature, and make that secondary, which is really primary. To every operation there is a power proportioned; and this power must be placed on the body that operates. If we remove the power from one cause, we must ascribe it to another; but to remove it from all causes, and bestow it on a being that is noways related to the cause and effect, but by perceiving them, is a gross absurdity, and contrary to the most certain principles of human reason.

I can only reply to all these arguments, that the case is here much the same, as if a blind man should pretend to find a great many absurdities in the supposition, that the colour of scarlet is not the same with the sound of a trumpet, nor light the same with solidity. If we have really no idea of a power or efficacy in any object, or of any real connection betwixt causes and effects, it will be of little purpose to prove that an efficacy is necessary in all operations. We do not understand our own meaning in talking so, but ignorantly confound ideas which are entirely distinct from each other. I am, indeed, ready to allow, that there may be several qualities, both in material and immaterial objects, with which we are utterly unacquainted; and if we please to call these *power* or *efficacy*, it will be of little consequence to the world. But when, instead of meaning these unknown qualities, we make the terms of power and efficacy signify something, of which we have a clear idea, and which is incompatible with those objects to which we apply it, obscurity and error begin then to take place, and we are led astray by a false philosophy. This is the case when we transfer the determination of the thought to external objects, and suppose any real intelligible connection betwixt them; *that being a quality which can only belong to the mind that considers them.*[9] [Emphasis added.]

We have been led to believe how different from each other the empiricists and the rationalists are. This distinction is the bread and butter of the conventional version of "modern philosophy." Yet in the foregoing quotation, one of the key passages in Hume, we have the essence of *Kant's* thought! Indeed, Hume could hardly have put it more succinctly. One is reminded of the comment made by the noted orator Edward Everett to Abraham Lincoln, after the latter's speech at Gettysburg. It will be remembered that there were two Gettysburg addresses, the first by Everett and the second by the President. After Lincoln had finished, Everett came over to him and commented, "Congratulations, Mr. President. You said in two minutes what it took me more than two hours to say." In the same vein, we can imagine Kant meeting Hume in Limbo and telling him, "Congratulations, Herr Hume. You said in two paragraphs what it took me over 700 pages to say!"

I am not maintaining that the positions of Hume and Kant actually are identical. Nevertheless, the ways in which they conceive the basic issues are so similar that we should be very careful not to prejudge how different from each other they turn out to be. For example, nothing seems more different from Hume than Kant's formidable framework of "transcendental" ideas, but the problem is that it doesn't really transcend anything. Kant for his part was well aware of all the trouble he was going to, as is clear from the following passage, cited first in German and then in translation:

> Wenn wir also durch diese kritische Untersuchung nichts Mehreres lernen, als was wir im bloss empirischen Gebrauche des Verstandes, auch ohne so subtile Nachforschung, von selbst wohl würden ausgeübt haben, so scheint es, sei der Vorteil, den man aus ihr zieht, den Aufwand und die Zurüstung nicht wert.

> If, therefore, we do not learn anything more through this critical inquiry than what we would have achieved as a matter of course, even without such subtle investigation, in the merely empirical use of the understanding, it appears that the advantage one draws from it is not worth the expense and the preparation.[10]

He immediately responds to his own criticism that it *is* worth the trouble. We shall get to his explanation shortly.

Meanwhile, and by the same token, if we can fault Kant for having said too much, we can just as easily ask why Hume said so little, why he did not spell out more of the details of the abstractions the mind imposes on the phenomena. To understand Hume's minimalist approach, consider the following passage, one of the most famous in his writings:

> When we run over libraries, persuaded [that all our knowledge comes from experience], what havoc must we make? If we take in hand any volume; of divinity or school metaphysics, for instance; let us ask, *Does it contain any abstract reasoning concerning quantity or number?* No. *Does it contain any experimental reasoning concerning matters of fact or existence?* No. Commit it then to the flames, for it can contain nothing but sophistry and illusion.[11]

Hume enjoyed shocking people, but in the foregoing he is not merely indulging his sense of humor. Dogmatic speculation and meaningless abstraction not only have impeded the advance of knowledge, but have led to sectarian conflict and fed political and religious fanaticism. Hume can manage perfectly well without them, thank you, and by so doing, he sets an example for others. If in the process, he can shock a great many stuffy, narrow-minded people, why, what fun!

It may well be that we are naturally inclined to think in terms of necessary connection and similar metaphysical concepts, but Hume regards such notions as "fictions," a word which in the eighteenth century meant "hypotheses." We can see from the following how he sets his priorities:

> As to those *impressions*, which arise from the *senses*, their ultimate
> cause is, in my opinion, perfectly inexplicable by human reason, and
> 'twill always be impossible to decide with certainty, whether they arise
> immediately from the object [Newton and Locke], or are produced by
> the creative power of the mind [the Cambridge Platonists], or are de-
> rived from the author of our being [Berkeley]. Nor is such a question
> any way material to our purpose. We may draw inferences from the co-
> herence of our perceptions, whether they be true or false; whether they
> represent nature justly, or be mere illusions of the senses.[12]

The interpolations are Randall's. Hume only alludes to these other writers
in passing rather than mentioning them by name and considering their theories in detail. This makes it all the more plain that to him creating metaphysical "fictions" or hypotheses is a natural tendency or function of our minds.
It matters less what the specific hypotheses are than the fact that we cannot
help creating them. He wants us to recognize them for what they are so that
we will see their limitations.

Now let us return to Kant's answer to the question he asks himself in
the passage cited above. Why is he going to all this trouble?

> Nun kann man zwar hierauf antworten: dass kein Vorwitz der
> Erweiterung unserer Erkenntnis nachteiliger sei, als der, so den Nutzen
> jederzeit zum voraus wissen will, ehe man sich auf Nachforschungen
> einlässt, und ehe man noch sich den mindesten Begriff von diesem
> Nutzen machen könnte, wenn derselbe auch vor Augen gestellt würde.
> Allein es gibt doch einen Vorteil, der auch dem schwierigsten und
> unlustigsten Lehrlinge solcher transzendentalen Nachforschung
> begreiflich, und zugleich angelegen gemacht werden kann, nämlich
> dieser: dass der bloss mit seinem empirischen Gebrauche beschäftigte
> Verstand, der über die Quellen seiner eigenen Erkenntnis nicht
> nachsinnt, zwar sehr gut fortkommen, eines aber gar nicht leisten
> könne, nämlich, sich selbst die Grenzen seines Gebrauchs zu
> bestimmen, und zu wissen, was innerhalb oder ausserhalb seiner
> ganzen Sphäre liegen mag; denn dazu werden eben die tiefen
> Untersuchungen erfordert, die wir angestellt haben. Kann er aber nicht
> unterscheiden, ob gewisse Fragen in seinem Horizonte liegen, oder
> nicht, so ist er niemals seiner Ansprüche und seines Besitzes sicher,
> sondern darf sich nur auf vielfältige beschämende Zurechtweisungen
> Rechnung machen, wenn er die Grenzen seines Gebiets (wie es
> unvermeidlich ist) unaufhörlich überschreitet, und sich in Wahn und
> Blendwerke verirrt.

> Now to be sure we can answer to this that no curiosity about the exten-
> sion of our knowledge is more disadvantageous than that which always
> wants to know the usefulness of investigations in advance, before one
> enters on them, and before one can have the slightest conception of this
> usefulness, even if it were put before one's very eyes. However there is
> one sole advantage, which can be made comprehensible and at the
> same time of consequence even to the most recalcitrant and reluctant
> novice in such transcendental investigations, namely this: that the un-
> derstanding which is only occupied with its empirical use, that does not
> reflect on the sources of its own knowledge, can to be sure get on very
> well; but there is one thing it cannot do, namely, determine for itself the
> limits of its use, and know what may lie within or outside its total
> sphere; for that just the deep investigations that we have instituted are
> required. But if the understanding cannot distinguish whether or not
> certain questions lie within its horizon, then it is never sure of its
> claims and its possessions, but should only count on frequent repri-
> mands, when (as is unavoidable) it incessantly oversteps the limits of
> its domain and goes astray in mirage and delusion.[13]

Insofar as Kant wants the understanding to know its own limitations, he
wants the same thing Hume does, as is made clear by the following passage
from Hume:

> While a warm imagination is allowed to enter into philosophy, and hy-
> potheses embraced merely for being specious and agreeable, we can
> never have any steady principles, nor any sentiments, which will suit
> with common practice and experience. But were these hypotheses
> once removed, we might hope to establish a system or set of opinions,
> which if not true (for that, perhaps, is too much to be hoped for), might
> at least be satisfactory to the human mind, and might stand the test of
> the most critical examination.[14]

Hume's notion of "the most critical examination" and Kant's are not exactly the same. Hume is a minimalist as well as an empiricist. He tries to explain our idea of necessary connection in the simplest possible way, without
anything as complex as Kant's categories of the understanding, transcendental aesthetic, or the rest of the conceptual apparatus that Kant brings to
bear. It may well be that Hume's empirical explanation of the foundations
of science and of morality – "empirical" because it denies innate ideas –
does not suffice. Since it is only a hypothesis, if it seems incorrect or inadequate, we can just try another until we get a more satisfactory result.

Kant does insist that Hume's explanation of our ideas of necessary connection, the nature of the mind, morality, etc., is inadequate and incorrect. For example, Hume maintains that what we call "necessary connection" is just a belief founded on habit and the constant conjunction and resemblance of sense-impressions. Kant says no; we have a notion of necessity, and it is a strong notion, and it simply could not have come from the senses. Therefore, it must already have been there in the mind.

This is the standard argument for innate ideas that goes back to Plato. To say that some of our ideas are "innate" or inborn does not mean that we are conscious of them from birth, but that at some point when we examine the contents of our minds, we discover ideas that could not have come from experience. Therefore, they must already have been present in the mind when the mind came to be. To state the argument more formally:

> In regard to all of our ideas, they come either from the senses or from the mind.
> Certain ideas do not come from the senses.
> Therefore, they come from the mind.

Virtually everybody would accept the major premise, that there are only two possible sources of our ideas, so the argument depends on establishing the minor premise, namely, that certain ideas do not come from the senses. Plato, for example, argues that the abstract concepts of number and figure in mathematics simply could not have come from the senses. Therefore, they must already be contained in the mind. We do not so much *learn* them as *recollect* them.[15]

Without getting into this age-old controversy, I will simply observe that a plausible argument for innateness depends on showing that what we get from the senses really is impoverished. That is exactly what Kant says about the phenomenalism/skepticism/dualism he inherits from Locke, Berkeley, and Hume. Hence, he can make a serious case for his own version of the doctrine of innate ideas.

Take, for example, the question of the unity and substantiality of mind. On this issue, Hume states:

> For my part, when I enter most intimately into what I call *myself*, I always stumble on some particular perception or other, of heat or cold, light or shade, love or hatred, pain or pleasure. I never can catch *myself* at any time without a perception, and never can observe anything but the perception. . . . If any one, upon serious and unprejudiced reflection, thinks he has a different notion of *himself*, I must confess I can

> reason no longer with him. All I can allow him is, that he may be in the right as well as I, and that we are essentially different in this particular. He may, perhaps, perceive something simple and continued, which he calls *himself*; though I am certain there is no such principle in me.[16]

This is too cute by half. Some of us are walking around under the illusion that they are substantial beings, but I, David Hume, know better. Ha, ha, ha. Hume is mocking Descartes, who states that the substantial unity of the mind is a self-evident idea. He doesn't know how to explain it, but it is intuitively clear. Hume's response is simply to deny that it is self-evident, giving the argument at the beginning of the foregoing passage.

This is one of the arguments in Hume that shocked Kant and helped rouse him from his dogmatic slumbers. Hume says, "I can never catch myself without a perception." But who or what is the "I" making the assertion? Furthermore, just because we can never catch ourselves without a perception doesn't mean that all we are is perceptions. That is an obviously fallacious argument. Similarly, speaking of the doctrine of the mind as a substantial unity, Hume says, "I am certain there is no such principle in me." But what is it then that is capable of being so certain? Just a flow of perceptions? If Descartes was wrong that he cannot doubt that he is doubting (as Hume would maintain), how can Hume be certain that he is certain? One can imagine Augustine and Descartes in the afterlife reading the foregoing passage and being very much amused by it. The question is, whom is the laugh really on?

In response to Hume, Kant asserts that the mind has to be a unity, that it is inconceivable and unintelligible otherwise. This is one of the most important positions Kant takes in *The Critique of Pure Reason*. As noted in the previous chapter, his insistence on this point helped me spot the argument for the unity of mind in Aristotle. However, what Kant actually says is that since, as Hume maintains, the unity cannot be found in the perceptions, it must be there as a *condition* of the existence of mind. In other words, Kant does not discuss this question psychologically, except in a marginal way. What he really is talking about is necessary preconditions.

But how far away is Kant from Hume? Hume's own minimalist hypothesis of the self (*i.e.*, of the mind) does not rule out a stronger one, and he was not a dogmatic thinker, as the following makes clear:

> Human Nature is the only science of man; and yet has been hitherto the most neglected. It will be sufficient for me, if I can bring it a little more into fashion; and the hope of this serves to compose my temper from

that spleen, and invigorate it from that indolence, which sometimes
prevail upon me. If the reader finds himself in the same easy disposi-
tion, let him follow me in my future speculations. If not, let him follow
his inclination, and wait the returns of application and good humour.
The conduct of a man who studies philosophy in this careless manner,
is more truly sceptical than that of one who, feeling in himself an inclination to it, is yet so overwhelmed with doubts and scruples, as totally
to reject it. A true sceptic will be diffident of his philosophical doubts,
as well as of his philosophical convictions; and will never refuse any
innocent satisfaction which offers itself, upon account of either of
them.[17]

Although Hume might well entertain a stronger hypothesis such as Kant's,
the unity of mind that Kant presupposes would be just another hypothesis or
"fiction." While Kant seems to be claiming more than Hume, we have no
direct perception of ourselves as noumena, so what does Kant's claim really
amount to? How does Kant know that the presupposition is necessary, that
it is an innate component of our minds? The outcome seems to hinge on
how strong a case Kant makes for the innateness of the transcendental ideas.

But think about those so-called "transcendental ideas." We don't know
where they come from. Their "necessity" is totally subjective. Their only
function is to combine with the raw data of the senses to create our experience, and we only presuppose them. Yes, they might be innate presuppositions, or they might be strongly held beliefs – how much difference does it
really make?

By the same token, if we have a deep need to believe in them, and if we
find them present in all mankind, and if they seem to have the force of necessity – well, perhaps they are innate.

My aim is not to try to settle this issue *per se* but to show that when you
look carefully at what Hume and Kant have to say about it, their differences
become smaller and smaller. What is it that the transcendental ideas transcend? Just a straw man version of phenomenalism. And Hume "transcends" that as well, so how much disagreement is there between them?

Nor is it just in their epistemologies that Hume and Kant very nearly co-
incide. Even their ethical theories, which appear at first to be irreconcilable,
on closer inspection seem surprisingly alike. Hume founds his ethics on the
passions, but his calm and long-lasting passions sound suspiciously like
reason, and the central concept of *sympathy* is framed so universally that it
calls to mind the Kantian kingdom of ends. By the same token, Kant, who

tries to found his ethics purely on principle, has difficulty maintaining its purity and brings in consequences in spite of himself.

When we look closely, the differences between Hume and Kant seem to fade away like the Cheshire cat in *Alice in Wonderland*. This is not to say that they all disappear. Significant differences remain, but they must be viewed in light of all that Hume and Kant had in common. We get a very different view of "the history of philosophy" than that of Rorty and his colleagues when we see the most radical empiricist and the most thoroughgoing rationalist saying almost the same thing.

Randall does point out the similarity between Hume and Kant.[18] In my judgment, his chapters on Hume are among the best he wrote. However, he fails to draw the general conclusions about "the history of philosophy" and the nature of "philosophy" that follow from this and other similarities.

We are close to concluding our discussion of these two writers, but several questions remain. The first is, if the basic ideas of Hume and Kant can be simply and clearly stated, why are Kant's writings, particularly *The Critique of Pure Reason*, so complicated and so hard to follow? The answer is that Kant gets tangled up in his own distinctions. At every turn he has to distinguish the empirical from the transcendental and keep the two from getting mixed up with each other. He has the noumena, beings of reason standing behind our phenomenal selves. Underlying the other natural phenomena are equally unknowable things-in-themselves. Then there is our own experience, which is a composite of the various transcendental ideas and the phenomena. We need to understand exactly what transcendental ideas we have, how they combine with the phenomena, why we mustn't mistake the phenomena for the things-in-themselves, what we can and cannot say about things-in-themselves, what the limits of our knowledge are, and so on. The task he sets for himself is difficult, and he is painstaking and thorough in completing it.

As a result, *The Critique of Pure Reason* is an enormously complicated book. The reader can tell from the endnote citations in this essay what it takes to make a proper reference to any passage in it. A brief look at the *Critiques*'s table of contents, with its parts, divisions, books, chapters, sections, and sub-sections, will confirm the impression. It is truly labyrinthine in its construction. A better name for it might be the Labyrinth of Pure Reason.

Then in light of the phenomenalist and the Newtonian assumptions Kant starts with, as well as the faculty psychology and logical categories that he took from textbooks of his own time, we must ask, is it really *pure* reason? It is more like the Critique of Impure Reason. Or perhaps we should call it the Labyrinth of Impure Reason. Indeed, the book is so complicated and the style so convoluted that German students are said to prefer reading it in English because it is less incomprehensible to them in that language than in their native tongue.

The assumptions are questionable, the reason is impure, the transcendental ideas don't transcend – as if all that were not enough, the elaborate analysis of the human mind and perceptions that Kant provides isn't really psychology. It is mostly a mass of presuppositions, limits, constraints, possibilities, and conditions. This makes it even more confusing, because with all the talk of concepts, perceptions, intuitions, ideas, reasoning, judgment, etc., it certainly *sounds* like psychology. In this respect, Kant is comparable to Noam Chomsky, who also argues that certain of our ideas are innate. When Chomsky put forth his ideas on universal grammar and deep structures, from which, he said, the actual sentences we utter are derived, his critics questioned whether any such structures existed. Chomsky has had to admit that he is not giving us psychology, but linguistic *competence*, what is logically presupposed in order to generate actual sentences. By and large, this is similar to what Kant was doing.

Kant wants to develop what he calls *rationale Seelenlehre*, a rational doctrine of the soul. But is it possible to do this in abstraction from real psychology? This is the same objection that is made to Chomsky. Furthermore, Kant's analysis is based, at least in part, on a real psychology, the phenomenalism he inherits from his predecessors and the Euclidean perceptual framework that he presupposes. Thus, at best it is only partly a rational doctrine of the soul.

With all these discouragements, we might be tempted to throw up our hands and confine ourselves to Kant's "popular" works, which are hardly light reading in themselves. To be sure, many have done that, and many have done less than that. However, there is a way to make Kant more accessible. It is the one I already have spoken of, namely, allowing the great writers of the tradition to shed light on each other. It is Aristotle who best performs this function for Kant, as he does for the whole of "modern philosophy."

Whereas Kant, like Descartes, has to resort to a dualistic explanation in an effort to escape the quandary his own assumptions land him in, Aristotle avoids that predicament because he has a different set of assumptions. The gap between the primary and secondary qualities, the atomism of perception, dualism, materialism – Aristotle avoids all of these pitfalls. When one has worked out his brilliant psychology/epistemology and theory of the organism (*i.e.*, the *psyché* or "soul"), one has something to compare with the flawed epistemology of the moderns.

If Aristotle is right, "the problem of knowledge," the epistemological difficulties of the "modern philosophers," simply vanish. They are pseudo-problems. Mind and human values have a place within nature. We do not have to find another realm in which to give them safe haven.

I have already compared Aristotle's ideas with those of Hobbes and Locke. The comparison with Kant is more complex and detailed. Maybe Kant's impure reason is still pure enough to call Aristotle to account. Perhaps the latter's argument for the unity of mind, which seems to withstand the criticisms of Hobbes, cannot stand up to Kant's *rationale Seelenlehre*. In other words, maybe it is, as Kant would say, merely a subjective, empirical unity. Or maybe not. Does Aristotle's naturalistic psychology explode Kant's rational, transcendental doctrine of the soul? Does Kant's impure reason turn out to be fatally impure, so that it collapses when measured against Aristotle's naturalistic model? Whatever the outcome, it is clear that Aristotle and Kant are indeed addressing the same set of problems. Indeed, this already is apparent from what has been said about the interrelationships among the "modern philosophers" and their relationship to Aristotle.

Once a proper comparison between Aristotle and Kant is made, and we have a standard by which to judge *The Critique of Pure Reason*, it becomes, to borrow the words of Pope, "a mighty maze, but not without a plan." We have an Aristotelian thread to guide us through the Kantian labyrinth, and we no longer fear being devoured by the Minotaur of Impure Reason. Since we have a way out of the maze, we don't worry where it will lead us.

Now that we have acquired a taste for Kant, it is both enjoyable and rewarding to read him in the original. His folksy style, while convoluted, is charming and conveys his deep absorption in his enterprise. This quality is almost lost in translation, as is the loving way he examines every *Bedingung, Möglichkeit, Einschränkung, Begrenzung, Begriff, Vorstellung,* and *Anschauung.** His pursuit of conditions, limits, and possibilities, of schemata, rules, principles, axioms, and concepts takes on a life of its own. It may be far-fetched to compare *The Critique of Pure Reason* to a mystery

---

* Condition, possibility, limitation, boundary, concept, idea, and intuition.

thriller, but there is an element of suspense as we get caught up in the architecture of Kant's thought. This magnificent display of intellectual energy and acumen could not be for nought, yet we wonder what the outcome will be. Those German students who read him in English just don't know what they are missing.

On the other hand, without being able to make the comparison with Aristotle, the foregoing experience is possible only for the hardy few willing to devote the time and energy to explore the esoteric reaches of Kant's thought. Indeed, that is the problem not just with Kant but with the whole "history of philosophy" until we grasp how much of a cooperative enterprise it is.

The writers in the tradition illuminate and complement one another. This dual relationship exists between Hume and Kant. One way of viewing Kant's "critical philosophy" is that he is subjecting a set of ideas that Hume did not choose to investigate to "the test of the most critical examination" that Hume called for. In like manner, Aristotle, Hume, and Kant stand in a multifaceted relationship to one another. For example, like Hume, Aristotle asserts that it is impossible to think without mental images derived from sense-perceptions. We have no imageless thought. Hume describes in detail the relative strengths and weaknesses of the mental images, a quantitative analysis that is only implicit in Aristotle. Thus, Hume fills a gap in Aristotle's thought. Aristotle's qualitative analysis of mental images in turn provides what is missing in Hume.

We could pursue this discussion at much greater length, showing, for example, how much Aristotle's and Kant's ethical theories have in common and how the differences can be reconciled. "Naturalizing" Kant's ethical theory as we naturalize his epistemology does not eliminate duty and moral principle. They are to be found in Aristotle as well as in Kant. Just because Aristotle does not emphasize them as much does not mean they are not there. In light of Kant we are more aware of their presence in Aristotle. In light of Aristotle, it appears that Kant goes overboard in emphasizing moral principle. He makes it too rigid and more abstract than it really is or needs to be. We can still have it without getting into the difficulties that Kant gets into.

There is little danger that by combining the ideas of Aristotle and Kant or Aristotle and Hume or Hume and Kant we will produce an intellectual monstrosity. In all likelihood, we will get something far more powerful than we now have. In short, not only do the writers in "modern philosophy" profoundly reinforce each other, but the whole "history of philosophy" is much more positive and constructive than the conventional view would have us believe.

D. Further Reflections on Similarities and Differences between Thinkers.

Hume and Kant provide a dramatic example of two thinkers who seemingly are very different, but whose ideas almost converge. At other times, two writers may have more in common than was previously suspected, but key differences remain. The question then is how significant are those differences.

Take, for example, Randall's statement that Hume and Spinoza were opposites both in philosophy and in life.[19] At first blush, this seems right on the mark. For Hume, on the one hand, our experience is made up of atomic sense-impressions, with no necessary connection among them, no ground underlying them, and no proof of their permanence and reality except recurrence and relative strength and weakness. Hume exalts the passions over the reason and explains human behavior and belief in terms of the former. He delights in puncturing dogmatism and playing the role of a skeptic. In his personal life, Hume was a hedonist.

For Spinoza, on the other hand, the ground of our being, which he calls "God or nature" (*Deus sive natura*), is so omnipresent that everything in the world is fully grounded in it and happens by universal necessity. He even models his chief work, the *Ethics*, after Euclid's *Geometry*, and he logically derives all of our ideas and experiences from God or nature. He identifies human freedom with the submergence of individual passions in the sublime rationality of the universal divine nature. In his personal life, Spinoza is thought to have been an ascetic. In short, Randall's statement seems like one arrow hitting two bull's-eyes, cutting through to the essence of two major thinkers in one pithy aphorism.

However, on closer examination things turn out to be not quite so clear and simple. When we read Hume carefully, we see that he was no skeptic. This is evident from his description of an occasion on which he has been carrying on refined metaphysical speculation:

> The intense view of [the] manifold contradictions and imperfections in human reason has so wrought upon me, and heated my brain, that I am ready to reject all belief and reasoning, and can look upon no opinion

> even as more probable or likely than another. Where am I, or what?
> From what causes do I derive my existence, and to what condition shall
> I return? Whose favour shall I court, and whose anger must I dread?
> What beings surround me? and on whom have I any influence, or who
> have any influence on me? I am confounded with all these questions,
> and begin to fancy myself in the most deplorable condition imaginable,
> environed with the deepest darkness, and utterly deprived of the use of
> every member and faculty.

Then what occurs?

> Most fortunately it happens, that since reason is incapable of dispelling
> these clouds, Nature herself suffices to the purpose, and cures me of
> this philosophical melancholy and delirium, either by relaxing this
> bent of mind, or by some lively avocation, and lively impression of my
> senses, which obliterate all these chimeras. I dine, I play a game of
> backgammon, I converse, and am merry with friends; and when, after
> three or four hours' amusement, I would return to these speculations,
> they appear so cold, and strained, and ridiculous, that I cannot find in
> my heart to enter into them any further.[20]

When Hume writes of his friends and of the activities shared with them, it is
evident that he regards them as real, not phenomenal. Hume was an ironist,
and doubtless was amused at being misunderstood and misinterpreted by
superficial readers. To be sure, he believes that the *ground* of nature and of
our experience is unknown, and may be unknowable, but we can obtain scientific knowledge of the world of our experience. He casts his theory of human nature along Newtonian lines, elaborately analyzing the relative
strength and weakness of our ideas, our passions, and our social interactions
as if they were Newtonian forces. This hardly sounds like a skeptic. Just as
Newton formulated mathematical relationships to describe the motion and
attraction of bodies, but did not say what the underlying causes of these relationships might be, Hume took a similarly minimalist approach. He tried
to show how much of our experience is explicable in quantitative terms.
This does not mean that nothing more can be said about it. If we think of
Newton's remark that we are like children playing on the shores of the
ocean of knowledge, we can better understand Hume's supposed
"phenomenalism." What Hume wants to avoid is excessive dependence on
metaphysical hypotheses or fictions. He wants us to recognize them for
what they are.

Spinoza too was an adherent of mathematical science. He lived before
the publication of Newton's *Principia*, but he was strongly influenced by

Descartes. He wrote his chief work, the *Ethics,* in the form of a treatise in Euclidean geometry. In his epistemology, Spinoza was a realist. The mathematical understanding is not of appearances, but of God or nature itself. Yet at the same time, Spinoza tells us that God or nature has infinite attributes, only two of which are known to us, thought and extension, and that He/it is infinite things in infinite ways. This means that our knowledge is very limited and incomplete.

While Spinoza is conventionally thought to be a realist and Hume a skeptic and a phenomenalist, Spinoza's realism is diminished by his statement of the limitations of our knowledge. Hume, on the other hand, while a phenomenalist in principle, is very much a realist in practice. They both accept the world of science and want to lead a life of moderation within it. While Hume elevates the passions over reason, his commitment to them is very mild and reasonable.

Another important point is that Spinoza, like Hume, denies the substantial unity of the individual mind. This precludes a belief in innate ideas, for how could a mind that is not a substantial unity have them? Spinoza is an empiricist, but a rationalistic one: The world is rational because it consists of attributes of the one substantial being, God or nature. Our minds, limited though they be, can grasp the rationality of God or nature and be uplifted by it. For Hume, however, there is no substantial being, no ultimate ground of rationality. That is the critical difference between them, the one that remains after all the similarities have been pointed out. Nevertheless, they both reject subjectivism and solipsism. For Spinoza, the reality of God or nature sweeps away metaphysical doubt; for Hume, it is the society of others, the company of friends.

Parallels exist in the lives of Hume and Spinoza. Neither of them were academics. Spinoza turned down the offer of a professorship at the University of Heidelberg because he did not want to have to teach students and was afraid his ideas would cause religious controversy. His "asceticism" seems to have been largely a desire for peace and quiet so that he could pursue his work. He had a circle of friends, corresponded and had dealings with the leading scientists of his day, and may have been acquainted with the DeWitts, the *Stadtholders* or chief executives of the Netherlands. He lived in various cities of the Netherlands during the *gouden eeuw*, the golden century or golden age, the heyday of Dutch cultural, economic, and political influence.

Another difference between Hume and Spinoza and in addition to the one mentioned was Hume's passion for literary fame, which, after initial disappointments, he achieved. Yet another difference was that Hume had a sense of humor; he enjoyed provoking his critics with his irony, whereas Spinoza was more retiring. Later in his life, Hume entered the diplomatic service and spent a number of years in Paris, thereafter returning to Scotland. Hume's "hedonism" was Epicureanism in the true sense of the term, *i.e.*, the enjoyment of refined, civilized pleasures – friendship, books, the arts, etc. Both men were bachelors, both incurred the displeasure of the clergy and the devout, and both died of wasting illnesses, conducting themselves till the end with the same equanimity and good humor they had shown throughout their lives.

Although there are a number of similarities between Hume and Spinoza that are overlooked or underemphasized, the central difference between them remains, Hume's "radical empiricism" versus Spinoza's rationalism. Hume is unconcerned to discover any ground for our perceptions, whereas for Spinoza, the presence of that ground, which he calls *Deus sive natura*, is so great that it fills and exalts the rational mind. The mind discovers its own limitations and the mathematical grandeur of nature with overwhelming conviction. Once we perceive the order and beauty of the cosmos, it floods in on us and our own meager being is subsumed into it. In this connection, we think of Galileo's remark that mathematics is the language of God, and we are reminded as well of Plato and Einstein.

Spinoza's vision of the universe is magnificent. He takes what in normal terms is atheism and transforms it into something so grand that we are forced to question our conventional understanding of the nature of the divine. He has been called a pantheist, and in a sense, he deifies nature, yet the brilliance of his vision breaks out of the narrow confines of this conventional concept.

But just as Plato has been compared to the intoxication of the night before and Aristotle to the hangover of the morning after, when we pass from Spinoza's exalted rationalism to Hume's sobering critique of the reality of our experience, it is not so clear who is right. The doubts increase when we consider the puzzlements raised by twentieth-century science.

A difference such as this is sharply focused because Hume and Spinoza start from the same mathematical, mechanistic world of modern science, and neither posits the unity of the mind or innate ideas. Yet they draw diametrically opposite conclusions about the foundation and the nature of human knowledge.

How can we settle such a controversy? First of all, we can put it into perspective by identifying both the similarities and the differences between the parties. We recognize that there is more to Hume and Spinoza than just this issue, central as it is. While it dominates Books I and V of Spinoza's *Ethics*, the other three books are mainly psychology/epistemology. In the *Tractatus Theologico-Politicus*, Spinoza applies his ideas to politics. The same comment can be made about Hume, who, together with the central issues, devotes much attention to the mind, the emotions, politics, history, and social relations. Both Hume and Spinoza have important contributions to make to psychology and the social sciences. However, a group of people calling themselves "philosophers" claim proprietary rights to these texts. By ignoring their similarities, exaggerating their differences, and downplaying their interdisciplinary character, these so-called "philosophers" make them largely inaccessible to researchers in other fields. They do this not just with Hume and Spinoza, but with the whole tradition.

By taking a more balanced view, we can better identify the critical differences and at the same time give proper attention to the commonalities. Some basis for the distinction between rationalism and empiricism obviously exists, principally the difference of opinion about innate ideas. At the same time, both the "empiricists" and the "rationalists" firmly believe in science. It may be that the issue of where the science comes from is less significant than the fact that we have it. We can get a perspective on this issue by recalling the way it was debated in the days of Plato and Aristotle. In the dialogue *Meno*, Socrates questions a slave boy about geometry and explains that what others call *learning* from experience he regards as *recollection* of innate ideas. In either case, whether the slave boy "learned" it or "recalled" it, he still has a knowledge of geometry. Aristotle in turn, who denies the innateness of ideas, has to explain the rational structure of reality, and then how we discover that rationality with our minds. In order to do this, he posits a divinity that is pure thought. In short, the belief in science is a belief in rationality and order, in *cosmos* rather than *chaos*, regardless of where that order came from or how we discover it. The debate on this issue is like a philosophical debate within any other scientific field. It is "philosophical" in the ordinary sense of the word, and it does not presuppose the existence of a field of study called "philosophy," whose purpose it is to study philosophical questions.

A brief look at controversies in the history of science may shed further light on this discussion. In the mid-eighteenth century, shortly after the lightning rod was invented by Benjamin Franklin, a controversy erupted as to its proper shape. The adherents of Franklin and those of Wilson, another pioneer in the field, disagreed about whether the tip of the rod should be round or pointed to better attract the lightning. At least one person was electrocuted in the course of experiments to determine the superiority of one or the other type of rod. Eventually, people realized that it does not make much difference because the lightning originates far away in the clouds. However, until that time, the controversy was carried on with much vehemence by the proponents of both sides. Are we to say that they were engaging in a philosophical debate that was part of a minor branch of philosophy called philosophy of lightning?

A more profound controversy in the history of science was the one between Newton or Huygens over whether light exists in the form of particles or waves. It turns out that sometimes it behaves like the one and sometimes like the other. Again, was this a philosophical difference between Newton and Huygens, and were they discussing the philosophy of light?

In ordinary language we commonly and correctly speak of *philosophical* differences – differences of principle or fundamental differences for which equally good reasons can be offered. The issue of empiricism versus rationalism may well be one of this kind, but then again, it may not. How can anyone know beforehand and absolutely whether or not a given issue can be resolved? Even in so-called "normal science," where we think questions are cut and dried, surprises constantly occur. Why insist on calling rationalism versus empiricism a philosophical issue and not do the same thing for a great many undecided questions in science? If any unanswered question for which the discovery procedure is not obvious, including those that have been around for centuries, is a philosophical question, then a whole lot of issues in "science" are "philosophical." Thomas Kuhn has a point in distinguishing between "normal science" and "paradigm shifts," but the purview of the former is a good deal less than we might at first think. Paradigms on all levels are constantly being questioned. In short, "science" is much more "philosophical" than is commonly believed.

At the same time, "philosophy" is much more "scientific" than it is generally understood to be. Differences such as those between Hume and Spinoza can be compared to the differences between Newton and Huygens as well as to other scientific controversies. The wave theory of light and the particle theory do not so much oppose as complement each other. Under some conditions, light behaves as if it were waves, and in other circumstances, as if it were particles. In like fashion, given all the similarities be-tween Hume and Spinoza and the ways in which their differences are qualified, it is not immediately apparent how much of a difference their dif-ferences make. The "cash value" of their ideas (in William James' phrase) is constantly shifting. In the end, the issue may be resolved by a third party, Aristotle.

In the case of Hume and Kant, we have both convergence and comple-mentarity. Descartes and Augustine also shed light on one other. Aristotle and the "modern philosophers" oppose, illuminate, and complement each other. In each instance, the relationship varies. But when we look at the dif-ferent ways the members of the tradition interact, we see clearly that they were part of a common enterprise not distinguishable from science. There is no special field called "philosophy" that studies philosophical questions. Were there such a field, it is highly unlikely that issues like rationalism ver-sus empiricism could be decided by it, that is, in the abstract. If such issues are to be resolved, in all likelihood it will be by something we will learn from one or more of the special sciences – unless somebody really turns "first philosophy" or "metaphysics" into an independent superscience. The history of ideas suggests that that will not happen. The best way for us to make progress is to grasp the unity of "the history of philosophy" and let it fulfill its natural role as part of science.

E. "Modern Philosophy" since Kant

If Aristotle and the early "modern philosophers" illuminate each other, does the same relationship hold with the writers since Kant? Having begun a rad-ical rethinking of the fundamental ideas of "modern philosophy," I now will survey the major writers in the tradition up to the present day. What follows is not a detailed account, but merely an attempt to see whether the latter fit into the framework I have outlined.

After Kant, as before, the tradition was dominated by people who either saw a close connection between their ideas and science or were trying to create a new science. Georg Wilhelm Friedrich Hegel and Karl Marx spring first to mind. Hegel tried to fit the whole of human knowledge into one stu-pendous synthesis controlled by a set of "metaphysical" principles that he developed from various concepts in the tradition, notably the One in Plato's dialogue *Parmenides* and Aristotle's concept of the divine, the Unmoved Mover. The logical and historical development or unfolding of these con-cepts he called the *dialectic*, another concept that he took from Plato. Because the process was controlled by an idea or set of ideas, his theory can be described as "dialectical idealism." Marx, partly inspired by Hegel, adopted the notion of an all-encompassing dialectic operating in history, but believed that human history and behavior are dominated by material, economic forces. Hence, he called his theory "dialectical materialism."

As explained earlier in Chapter 3, Hegel thought he had worked out a superscience, which could be judged by its explanatory power, as any science is. However, his central metaphysical thesis remains speculative and unproved, and the least satisfactory part of his thought was the attempt to fit natural science into his dialectical system. The more acceptable part, centering on the notion that there is a logic and an order to history, has had a lasting influence. For one thing, it led later in the nineteenth century to the systematic study of intellectual history called "the history of philosophy," which for all its limitations has been an important step forward. Along with history and "philosophy," Hegel exercised his greatest influence on nineteenth-century economics, most notably on Marx and Marx's followers.

The notion that history is *not* chaotic or random is an intriguing idea. On the other hand, if we all are prisoners of historical forces, we have no freedom. Hegel was jocularly described as eating "a breakfast of brass tacks," because when he awoke in the morning, he rejoiced at the thought that the world is rational. Even if we are persuaded that, broadly speaking, some kind of order does exist in history, it is very hard to say how much and very easy to try to fit historical events into an artificial and oversimplified framework. When we consider Hegel's own version of history, we wonder whether it really had to go through all the stages and dialectical oppositions he thinks it did. In other words, he has too narrow a view of historical necessity and is insufficiently open to the variety of possibilities that obtain.

The same fundamental criticism can be made of Marx, who may well have been right that the tendency of mankind is toward a more democratic and less stratified society than has existed through most of human history. However, his conception of the process by which this development would occur also was too rigid: there had to be certain clearly defined stages before social conditions could generate the class consciousness that would cause the workers' paradise to come into being. There is some evidence that Marx was taking a more flexible view of things in the decade before his death in 1883. Still, it is ironic that a man who considered himself a materialist should cling to so rationalistic an explanation of history and fail to see the variety of ways by which the desired goal might be reached. But Marx lived before the age of television, jet planes, and computers, so he can be pardoned for not foreseeing the extent to which advances in technology might of themselves cause a raising of consciousness. In any event, neither Hegel nor Marx were "philosophers" in the narrow, skeptical, twentieth-century sense of the word.

Another group of scientifically-oriented "philosophers" were the Utilitarians, a group originating with the social reformer Jeremy Bentham, who developed a far less abstract set of principles than Hegel's in his effort to produce a universal social science. John Stuart Mill, who followed Bentham, also maintained the practical and scientific orientation of the movement.

Still another important nineteenth-century approach was the *positivism* of Auguste Comte, who, like Hume, tried to develop social scientific principles free from metaphysical abstractions.

There is no need in this brief survey to enumerate all the nineteenth-century thinkers and movements ranging over what still were undefined or loosely defined fields. During this period science was extending what it already had achieved in physics, mathematics, and astronomy and making great advances in chemistry, biology, and geology. Efforts also were made to establish the social sciences as entities comparable to the natural sciences. By the last quarter of the century, these developments had progressed to the point where a wide variety of researchers started to think of themselves as belonging to distinct disciplines. They founded professional organizations, and the highly departmentalized university that we know in the twentieth century came into existence. During the time when the specialized disciplines were being formed, "philosophy" tried to define itself as one of them, a new discipline using an old name.

The gestation and birth of this specialized form of "philosophy," along with that of other disciplines, deserves a book in itself. We have an approximate idea of when and how it happened, but not a very precise one. Late in the nineteenth century, when the various disciplines we know today were beginning to constitute themselves as such, a subset of the academic community decided that they were "philosophers" as distinct from the various other professional groups that then were forming. However, from the moment of its birth "philosophy" experienced an identity crisis, and it has been an enduring one. The "philosophers" had a very difficult time deciding what precisely they were doing and what made them distinct from the other disciplines. William James defined philosophy as "the residuum of questions left unanswered," but it was obvious to anyone who looked that much of "the history of philosophy" did not fit that definition. He might just as well have said it was the residuum of questions no one else was interested in, or the residuum of texts no one else wanted to study, or the residuum of scholars who had no other discipline to join. Actually, these definitions are not wholly accurate either, but that only shows how artificial the distinction was to begin with.

The perennial identity crisis of "philosophy" was hard to resolve because things were less clear and straightforward than they had been in the seventeenth and eighteenth centuries. The writers from Descartes through Kant had a direct connection both with Newtonian science and with Aristotle. Now the connection with science was more uncertain, as science itself became more complex, and now the problems of the seventeenth- and eighteenth-century writers themselves became a barrier to a close connection with Aristotle.

"The history of philosophy" had never been studied in such detail before. Its very complexity precluded comprehensive understanding. The skeptical and problematic elements in the thought of the "modern philosophers" were seized upon and turned into the heart of the new discipline. The great irony is that the model for this development was Kant. Kant, who had awakened from his dogmatic slumbers to combat skepticism, wound up being the model for a discipline that became the very embodiment of skepticism. Indeed, to sum up the history of twentieth-century "philosophy" in one sentence, we could describe it as the unsuccessful attempt to find a satisfactory form of neo- or post-Kantianism to fit the changed circumstances of twentieth-century thought and life.

This description, together with the explanation that preceded it, can help us understand why a plethora of schools of thought have arisen within "philosophy" during the twentieth century: pragmatism, analytic philosophy, logical positivism, process philosophy, phenomenology, existentialism. All of these twentieth-century movements, whatever their surface differences, start from the post-Kantian or neo-Kantian relativistic framework of "the history of philosophy" and skeptical epistemology. Thus, they are not nearly as different from each other as they might claim to be or as their terminology and content might make them appear. In one way or another, all of them have had fairly close ties to science. This is true even of existentialism and phenomenology: Heidegger was interested in linguistics, psychology, technology, and the nature of time. Furthermore, they all confront the same fundamental problem that the early modern writers did: reconciling human values and experience with science and nature. This task has been made especially difficult by the upheavals of the twentieth century.

The gap or dualism in modern life and thought has only grown wider than it was before. Thus, the twentieth-century "philosophers" have had a harder job than their predecessors in the seventeenth and eighteenth centuries. They have made elaborate attempts to escape the problems of the earlier writers, but they have insufficiently questioned the assumptions that caused the problems. Their oft-repeated claim that they have broken free of those assumptions should not be believed. The proliferation of schools of thought is a reflection of this failure. They are nearly all variations on more or less the same theme of neo- or post-Kantianism with a new wrinkle, or several new wrinkles, or perhaps an entire facelift. A partial exception is Whitehead, who could be described as neo-Leibnizian, but his thought too reflects the problems of the earlier thinkers.

Because the early "modern philosophers" had a close connection both with science and with Aristotle, they produced a body of theory that will survive. However, twentieth-century "philosophy" has a weaker connection with both; its foundation is the assumptions and problems of the early "modern philosophers"; and it tends to be prolix and diffuse. Thus, we cannot be sure at this point how much of it will survive the test of time. One who will stand up well is William James. Unlike many of the others, he resisted the prevailing tendency of disciplines to split apart from each other; he was not long-winded; and he was an excellent writer. By contrast, it is harder to evaluate Charles Sanders Peirce, because his writings were so diffuse and incomplete. Certainly his contributions to linguistic theory and logic will endure.

The advances in logic that have been made over the past century and a half obviously will endure, as will the contributions of the "philosopher" J. L. Austin to linguistics. But on the whole, when reading the twentieth-century writers, one must go through a lot of low-grade ore to extract the gold and discard the dross. In doing that, we should keep in mind Whitehead's observation that the history of philosophy is a series of more or less extended footnotes to Plato and Aristotle. Whitehead's own writings should be included under that rubric. While the relationship with Aristotle is not so deep or direct as in the earlier thinkers, it can be found in the latter-day ones as well.

However, the "footnotes" to Aristotle often are superficial and/or inaccurate. John Dewey, for example, grossly misstates Aristotle's ideas in Part II of *Human Nature and Conduct*. He portrays Aristotle as having a fixed and inflexible concept of ends, and his account reads like a parody of the real thing. Surely Dewey read Book II of the *Nicomachean Ethics*, where the concept of moral virtue is so flexible that Aristotle can almost be mistaken for a relativist. Assuming Dewey was familiar with those passages, one wonders what he was thinking about when he made his criticisms. Something similar occurs in the chapters on value in *Experience and Nature*, Dewey's chief work. In the vast, cloudy expanse of his prose, he repeats, if not every cliché ever written about Plato and Aristotle, at least a good many of them. While Hobbes and Locke, Leibniz and Spinoza contradicted Aristotle in rebutting his ideas, they did not misrepresent him. This is different. On the other hand, while Dewey did not make good his escape from the dilemmas of "modern philosophy," he well understood their consequences. His critique of dualism and his description of its bad effects throughout our civilization may be his most enduring contribution.

Whitehead, for his part, was a much better writer than Dewey. In *Process and Reality*, his major work in "philosophy," he tries to develop a scientific metaphysics that avoids the mistakes he sees both in the thinkers from Descartes through Kant and in Aristotle. However, he spends many more pages on the former than on the latter, to whom he makes periodic, but only brief and superficial references. In presenting Aristotle as a rigid formalist, he makes a straw man out of him, as if Aristotle had developed a concept of form without ever uttering a word about function. Whitehead gets caught up in dealing with the mistakes of the modern writers without giving any sense that he has ever considered the possibility that a solution to their problems might exist in Aristotle. (Presumably he made his comment about Plato and Aristotle and the history of philosophy at some time *after* writing *Process and Reality*.) Such a solution might actually harmonize with Whitehead's "process philosophy" and also help him avoid what look like Heraclitean errors.**

** The pre-Socratic thinker Heraclitus said "*Pánta hreî*": "Everything flows" or "Everything is in flux." This has been interpreted to mean that nothing is fixed or stable and that there cannot be any science. Such a viewpoint could be characterized as a dogmatic functionalism, as contrasted with a rigid formalism. But Aristotle was always very careful to find a middle way

As for Ludwig Wittgenstein, he and Aristotle have a lot to say to each other, but Aristotle has a great deal more to say to Wittgenstein than Wittgenstein does to Aristotle. To be sure, Wittgenstein continues the critique of realist epistemology (*i.e.*, Aristotle's) carried on by his predecessors in "British empiricism," but unlike Hobbes and Locke, who speak directly to the texts in Aristotle, Wittgenstein writes as if he were on a desert island, or another planet, or as if Aristotle were in some other universe and Wittgenstein were communicating with him through a space-time warp. There he is, Ludwig Robinson Crusoe Wittgenstein, Captain Ludwig Spock Wittgenstein, working out a nominalistic, phenomenalist epistemology that speaks, point by skeptical, solipsistic point, to Aristotle's, yet Aristotle is never mentioned, and not the slightest hint is dropped that Aristotle ever existed. The mirror imagery (to borrow a phrase from Rorty) is so complete that it is as if the two of them were in the same room, not speaking to each other, but each expounding his respective viewpoint (remember that the Aristotelian texts are lecture notes). There is Aristotle, doing his *peripatetic* thing, (*i.e.*, walking about and lecturing), with his students following dutifully, and there is Wittgenstein, addressing his own coterie of students. They take diametrically opposed positions on the same set of issues as if they were debating each other, but in fact they are not. Still, it is as if they were communicating by Ouija board, or telephathically. Or perhaps it is another of Leibniz's pre-established harmonies. No moderator is there controlling their respective discourses, so while we can perceive their diametric opposition, we have to make the effort ourselves to pin it down, point by point. If one is unfamiliar with Aristotle's epistemology/psychology – and many of Wittgenstein's followers are not – one might conclude that no coherent alternative to Wittgenstein exists. However, Aristotle anticipated many or most of Wittgenstein's arguments, because he spoke to similar arguments put forth by skeptics and solipsists in his own day.

The question remains whether Wittgenstein will survive in the way and to the extent that the earlier British empiricists will – by raising objections that any realist epistemology must answer. Did Wittgenstein really do this in more detail and with more imagination than his predecessors or is he mostly giving a rehash of their views? It is easier to see that Hobbes will pass the test, because he speaks so directly to the Aristotelian writings.

---

between these two extremes, but it is not clear whether Whitehead did – or Leibniz.

As noted earlier, when you see the tradition as a unity, even the losers in the argument tend to look better. To put Wittgenstein to the test, you would have to make a close comparison of his writings with Aristotle's. However, to the best of my knowledge, no one has yet made a point-by-point comparison. This is not surprising when there are so many clones of Rorty running around in "philosophy" telling us that the history of philosophy is really "a series . . . of quite different sets of problems."

By and large, the foregoing comments about Wittgenstein apply to the "analytic philosophers," a group of which he was the most famous member. They like to make discrete points, in the manner of Wittgenstein. It is worth the trouble to go through their writings to discover what is of value, but I suspect that a great deal of it is a wordy, skeptical, superficial repetition of the earlier British empiricists and will not survive.

To conclude this rapid survey of major figures and movements in twentieth-century "philosophy," I will make a few comments about Edmund Husserl, who called his thought "phenomenology," and Martin Heidegger, who was both a phenomenologist and the chief theorist of existentialism. Husserl says he wants to make philosophy into a rigorous science, a goal I certainly agree with, and he asserts that our knowledge is knowledge of essences. So far, so good. But he grounds knowledge not in the objective world, as both Aristotle and modern science do, but in a "transcendental subjectivity" that at times seems more extreme than earlier idealist theories, and at other times like a complex, prolix rehash of them. Like other twentieth-century "philosophers," he has a good deal to say about the early "modern philosophers," and little, if anything to say about Aristotle. Yet Aristotle's ideas provide the best objective standard – a standard of, so to speak, nontranscendental objectivity – against which to judge Husserl's ideas.***

In contrast with the other twentieth-century figures, Martin Heidegger did read Aristotle very carefully, in Greek; he was critical of the subjectivism of the modern epistemologists; and he wanted to include science in his synthesis. Thus far, Heidegger's aims and those of this essay are in accord, and having this much in common with a writer of his stature lends support to what I am proposing. However, there are some critical differences. First of all, while Aristotle's writings are cited many times in Heidegger's chief work, *Being and Time*, there is only one brief reference to the *De Anima*.

***Husserl's chief work is called *Ideas*.

This may be surprising, but on the other hand, in the long tradition of commentary on Aristotle, the area that has been insufficiently studied is his psychology and biological theory. The main emphasis of the tradition has been on his metaphysics and logic. The "modern philosophers" are a partial exception to this statement, but in the context of materialist science, they studied him either to rebut him (Hobbes and Locke) or to make something different out of him (Leibniz).

However, in Heidegger's case the explanation is more complicated, and we need to look into his relationship to Aristotle a little more closely. In one of Heidegger's works, *Die Grundbegriffe der antiken Philosophie* (*The Basic Concepts of Ancient Philosophy*), Aristotle's writings are closely examined, but the chapter on *De Anima* is a mere six pages and consists of a summary of the work together with very brief analyses of key points. There also is an Appendix with five pages on the *De Anima* and the *Nicomachean Ethics*.

We may well ask, why did Heidegger show so little interest in Aristotle's psychology or at any rate place so little emphasis on it when he seems to have had a detailed knowledge of it?

The answer is that both Plato and Aristotle are part of a metaphysical tradition that Heidegger wants to undermine and rebuild on a different foundation. He is rethinking modern philosophy not in terms of Aristotle as I am doing, but in terms of the pre-Socratics. He works out a doctrine of being that combines the pre-Socratics with his own phenomenological/existentialist ontology and his analysis of time. His theory is founded on the concepts of *Dasein* (existence, *i.e.*, in the special way he understands it) and *Angst* (anxiety, dread). It is *Angst* about *Dasein* that gets the metaphysical/epistemological ball rolling and keeps it going.

The word *Angst* sounds psychological, but Heidegger uses it in an *ontological* sense. The question is, what does he mean by this distinction and is it a valid one?

Furthermore, why doesn't he consider Aristotle's psychology in detail when he specifically describes it as ontological?

> Aristoteles hat die ersten Grundzüge einer Ontologie des Lebens vorgelegt in seiner Abhandlung *Perì Psychês*. Es ist vollkommen irreführend, wenn man darin eine Psychologie sieht oder sie so benennt.

> Aristotle laid out the primary features of an ontology of life [*i.e.*, living

beings] in his treatise *Perì Psychês* [On the Soul]. It is completely misleading if one sees therein a psychology or so designates it.[21]

By "psychology" Heidegger means something subjectivist like the psychology of Descartes, the British empiricists, and Kant. But Aristotle is *not*
subjectivist. Not only is he an epistemological realist, but his treatise on the
psyché is much broader than "psychology" in the twentieth-century sense.
It deals with the nature of living beings and their powers and functions, especially the highest power, mind. We saw earlier that the word "philosophy" is used ambiguously, and now we see that so is "psychology."
However, when I speak of Aristotle's psychology, I mean it in the broader
sense of the term.

In the paragraph preceding the one just cited, Heidegger makes clear
our debt to Aristotle in this area:

> Auch hier ist zu betonen, daß uns heute vieles geläufig ist, was gerade
> durch Aristoteles den Phänomenen erst abgerungen werden mußte
> gegen schon bestehende dogmatische Theorien darüber oder
> ungenügende begriffliche Fassungen.

> It must be emphasized here that much today is familiar to us that had to
> be wrested from the phenomena precisely by Aristotle against already
> existing dogmatic theories about it or inadequate conceptual formula-
> tions.[22]

This makes it all the more puzzling why Heidegger did not investigate the
De Anima, Aristotle's *ontological* treatise on biology/psychology, in
greater depth and detail. On the other hand, because it was so closely associated with Aristotle's metaphysics, which was part of the traditional metaphysics Heidegger was trying to overcome, maybe he just didn't see the
need.

In my opinion, by not doing so Heidegger made a big mistake. It is precisely that part of Aristotle's thought upon which I rely most heavily in
Chapter 8 in attempting to show that Aristotle anticipated and solved the
problems of "modern philosophy": the mind-body dualism, the so-called
problem of knowledge, etc. The foundation for that project has been laid in
this chapter. As the reader will see, I outline an Aristotelian phenomenology
of life and mind. Had Heidegger done something similar, would he have
come to different conclusions than he did?

While answering that question is outside the scope of this essay, in

Chapter 8 philosophy and science are reunited and the dilemmas of modern philosophy are overcome with the help of Aristotle. Heidegger tries to do this in terms of the pre-Socratics. Since he is fluent in Aristotle's lingo and he wrestles with Aristotle's ontology, it should be possible to compare the results.

Aristotle's central concept is "substance" or substantial being, which is analyzed in great detail in *The Metaphysics*. But the best *example* of substantial being available to us humans is the *psyché* or "soul," *i.e.*, the substantial unity of the living organism. Let us suppose that we have worked out Aristotle's "psychology" or theory of the *psyché* in all of its brilliance and with all its powers, especially its highest power, mind. Now we see Aristotle in a way we have not seen him before, at his most cogent, at his best.

Heidegger sees the uniqueness of Aristotle's psychology compared with modern psychology, yet he bases his argument on *Angst* and *Dasein*. Surely there is a parallel between Heidegger's ontological *Angst* and Aristotle's ontological psychology. Is the *angstliche* way to being correct, or is Aristotle's? Apropos of this question, Randall once commented, "There's a lot in Heidegger, if you can just knock the *Angst* out of him." If you do that, the question is, what is left? Maybe not much, but on the other hand, maybe Aristotle's solution to the problem of the nature of being.

It is not just a matter of comparing Aristotle with Heidegger, but with the whole tradition. The unity and coherence of the writers in "the history of philosophy" is such that their combined efforts form a conceptual framework within which to judge individuals. Even if the claims I shall make for Aristotle turn out to be incorrect or remain unproven, at least we will know that different theories within the tradition can be compared and carefully evaluated.

These remarks complete my survey of "the history of philosophy" from the seventeenth century to the present. Again I emphasize that this was not meant to be a detailed account. I am trying to make a *prima facie* case for a new view of "philosophy" and its relation to other disciplines.

Notes

1. Strictly speaking, the famous statement "I think; therefore I am" occurs only in the *Discourse on Method* (Part IV) and not in the *Meditations*. Descartes says it there in French, not Latin: *je pense, donc je suis*. For some rea-

son, it is most familiar to us in its Latin form, *Cogito, ergo sum*, and people often refer to the whole argument, including all of Descartes' explanation of it, simply as "The *Cogito*." The argument is essentially the same in both treatises, but is developed more in the *Meditations*.

2. St. Augustine, *Of True Religion*, tr. J. H. S. Burleigh (Chicago: Henry Regnery, 1959), pp. 69–71.

3. St. Augustine, *Confessions*, VIII, 8–9.

4. For example, in a letter to R. P. Arnauld, Descartes acknowledges the dilemma of explaining how an incorporeal entity, the mind, moves a corporeal entity, the body, implying, as Randall remarks, that he doesn't take his own explanation of how this happens seriously. He then asserts that it does happen because we observe it happening all the time. However, this is a dogmatic assertion, not an explanation, and Descartes certainly was acute enough to recognize it as such. (See Randall, *The Career of Philosophy*, Vol. I, p. 394.)

5. Randall's allusion occurs in the following passage:

> In mathematical physics, as the entire truth about the world, the whole structure depends upon the initial ideas. There is thus needed a criterion for the truth of those ideas. So Descartes seeks one by inquiring into what it is that makes an idea indubitable. His metaphysical doubt does not arise from any genuine scepticism on his part; probably there never lived a more self-confident mind than Descartes. . . . His aim is to take a typically indubitable idea, and by an examination of its character as beyond doubt, to derive therefrom a criterion of certainty. So he turned to the time-honored and recognized example of an indubitable truth, the stock reply to the sceptic since St. Augustine, repeated in most of the Augustinian schoolmen, "Cogito, ergo sum." Everyone recognizes that his own conscious existence is beyond all question. Why is this so? What is the mark of its validity? Descartes can find none save that the idea is clearly and distinctly conceived. It is just seen to be true, by a kind of intellectual vision. Descartes' "Cogito" is thus clearly an example to be analyzed to find a general logical rule of evidence. (*The Career of Philosophy*, vol. 1 [New York and London: Columbia University Press, 1962], pp. 386–87.)

It is an oversimplification to say that "probably there never lived a more self-confident mind than Descartes." The impression one gets at many places in Descartes' writings is that his doubts were genuine. For all of his self-confidence, he seems to have been as fully aware of human fallibility as was St. Augustine. The Cogito" is far more than just "an example to be analyzed to find a general logical rule of evidence"!

6. John Locke, *Essay Concerning Human Understanding*, Book IV, ch. iii.

7. Kant gives the following definition: "If by 'noumenon' we mean a thing so far as it is not an object of our sensory intuition, in that we abstract from our mode of intuiting it, this is a noumenon in the negative sense. But if we understand by it an object of a non-sensory intuition, we thereby assume a special mode of intuition, namely the intellectual, which however is not the one we have, and of which we cannot comprehend even the possibility. This would be the 'noumenon' in the positive sense." *Critique of Pure Reason*, B307.

The reader should note how narrow and limited this definition is. A noumenon or being of reason is something whose existence we presuppose, but have no direct knowledge of. This includes ourselves as beings of reason.

8. See *Critique of Pure Reason*, I. Elementary Transcendental Doctrine, Second Part: Transcendental Logic, Second Division: Transcendental Dialectic, Book II, Ch. II, Section 9, Sub-section III, "The Possibility of Causality through Freedom."

9. David Hume, *A Treatise of Human Nature*, Book I, Part III, Sect. xiv.

10. Immanuel Kant, *Critique of Pure Reason (Kritik der reinen Vernunft)*, I. Transcendental Doctrine of Elements, Second Part: Transcendental Logic; First Division: Transcendental Analytic, Second Book: Analytic of Principles, Third Chapter: On the Ground of the Distinction of All Objects in General into Phenomena and Noumena, A237. Author's translation.

11. David Hume, *An Enquiry Concerning Human Understanding,* Sect. XII, Part III.

12. Hume, *A Treatise of Human Nature,* Book I, Part III, Sect. v, "Of the Impressions of the Senses and Memory." Randall cites this passage in *The Career of Philosophy,* Vol. I (New York and London: Columbia University Press, 1962), p. 644. The interpolations in the passage are Randall's.

13. Kant, *op. cit.*, "Phenomena and Noumena," A237–38. Author's translation.

14. Hume, *op. cit.*, Book I, Part IV, ch. vii, "Conclusion of this Book."

15. See *Meno*, and *The Republic*, VI–VII, the allegory of the divided line and the myth of the cave.

16. Hume, *Treatise*, I, IV, vi, "Of Personal Identity."

17. Hume, *Treatise*, I, IV, vii, "Conclusion of this Book."

18. Randall, *The Career of Philosophy,* Vol. I, p. 648: "Kant's so-called 'answer' to Hume thus turns out to be in reality an agreement with Hume . . ."

19. *Ibid.,* pp. 630–31.

20. Hume, *Treatise*, I, IV, vii, "Conclusion of this book."

21. Heidegger, *Die Grundbegriffe der antiken Philosophie* (*Gesamtausgabe*, Vol. 22, ed. Franz-Karl Blust. Frankfurt am Main: Vittorio Klostermann, 1993), Ch. 5, "Ontologie des Lebens und des Daseins," p. 182.

22. *Ibid.*

6
The Intimate Relationship of Philosophy and Science

"The history of philosophy" is an interdisciplinary tradition, broader than the "philosophers" are willing to acknowledge. It is part of the history of ideas and the history of science. However, all these terms are used so loosely that it is hard to know exactly what they mean. I have tried to clear up the ambiguity in the use of the word "philosophy." Completing this task requires me to deal with the parallel looseness in regard to the word "science." This I will now do, in the hope of removing some of the artificial barriers between philosophy and science.

When we look at the way the word "science" is used, we note three current meanings:

a) a formalized body of knowledge, consisting of principles or laws together with observed or observable facts that follow from them;

b) the method of inquiry, a combination of theory and experiment, by which a) is obtained;

c) the persons and institutions that conduct b) to acquire a). While a) and b) are found in dictionaries, it is striking that c), a metaphorical extension of the word that is very much in use, is not.

"Science" comes from the Latin *scientia,* "knowledge," meaning either knowledge in the mind of an individual or an organized body of knowledge. For hundreds of years the English word "science" had both meanings. However, the first one is no longer current.

The words "science" and "philosophy" have coexisted for hundreds of years, but not precisely with the meanings we assign to them now. In the Middle Ages, "science" and "art" often were used synonymously. "The seven sciences" or "the seven liberal sciences" were alternative terms for "the seven liberal arts," the group of studies that comprised undergraduate education, the Trivium (Grammar, Logic, and Rhetoric) and the Quadrivium (Arithmetic, Music, Geometry, and Astronomy). The word "philosophy" had the meanings now ascribed to "science." In the medieval universities, it meant the more advanced areas of knowledge and research, to which the seven liberal arts were an introduction. Philosophy had three branches: natural, moral, and metaphysical, which were commonly called "the three philosophies."

"Natural philosophy" was what we now call "natural science." "Moral philosophy" was the study of human conduct, including ethics (comparable to modern social science and philosophy). "Metaphysical philosophy" was the closest to what we now mean by the word "philosophy," the study of the ultimate reality and its most general causes and principles. To study one of "the philosophies" meant to go to graduate school, and the highest degree one could earn was "Doctor of Philosophy."[1]

From the foregoing it is easy to understand why, for example, Newton called his chief work *Principia Mathematica Philosophiae Naturalis*, Mathematical Principles of Natural Philosophy. Indeed, when one scrutinizes the examples of the use of the words "science" and "philosophy" given in the Oxford English Dictionary, it is apparent that "philosophy" was used to mean what we now mean by "science" until roughly the middle of the nineteenth century, around which time "science" took on its current set of meanings.

It was also in this period that the word "scientist" was invented. Until that time, scientists were called "natural philosophers," or just "philosophers." Here again, the OED can help us:

> *Scientist* . . .
> 1840. Whewell. *Philos. Induct. Sci.* I. Introd. 113. We need very much a name to describe a cultivator of science in general. I should incline to call him a Scientist. 1840 *Blackw. Mag.* XLVIII. 273 Leonardo was mentally a seeker after truth – a scientist; Correggio was an assertor of truth – an artist. 1853 F. Hall in *Leslie's Misc.* II. 169 Atrabilious scientists. 1878 T. Sinclair *Mount* 13 They know that the sun is better where it is than under the scalpel or other instruments of the intense scientists.[2]

The following was added in the *Supplement* to the OED. One wonders if the "ingenious gentlemen" referred to was Whewell:

> scientist Add:
> 1834 *Q. Rev.* LI Science . . . loses all traces of unity. A curious illustration of this result may be observed in the want of any name by which we can designate the students of the knowledge of the material world collectively. We are informed that this difficulty was felt very oppres-

sively by the members of the British Association for the Advancement of Science, at their meetings . . . in the last three summers. . . . *Philosophers* was felt to be too wide and too lofty a term . . ; savans was rather assuming . . ; some ingenious gentleman proposed that, by analogy with *artist*, they might form *scientist*, and added that there could be no scruple in making free with this termination when we have such words as sciolist, economist, and atheist – but this was not generally palatable.

2. (Usu. with capital initial.) A Christian Scientist.

1875 M.B. Eddy *Science and Health* viii. 428 The Scientist sees more clearly the cause of disease in mind, than the anatomist can in body; the latter examines the body to learn how matter is committing suicide, and the former reads the mind to find what beliefs are destroying the body.

1902 "Mark Twain" in *N. Amer. Rev.* CLXXV. 763 Where can you purchase it, at any outlay of any sort, in any Church or out of it, except the Scientist's? 1903 _____ In *Ibid* CLXXVI. 509 The Scientist hastened to Concord and told Mrs. Eddy what a disastrous mistake had been made.[3]

It is not clear exactly when the word "scientist" caught on, but certainly many years after it was coined. For some time the word was associated as much with Mary Baker Eddy and Christian Science as with natural science. It is hard to believe that late in the nineteenth century or early in the twentieth researchers in physics, chemistry, etc., still called themselves "natural philosophers." Nevertheless, the foregoing examples suggest that the word "scientist" was at best only coming into general use. Maybe for a while there was no consensus about which term to use. This makes sense if we recall that in this very period the academic disciplines as we know them today were first being organized. People doubtless were expending some effort in deciding what to call themselves.

It may come as a surprise to realize how recently the term "scientist" came into widespread use. By way of comparison, listed below are the words for "scientist" to be found in bilingual dictionaries in several other European languages:

Naturwissenschaftler; Gelehrte(r)
Cassell's The New Cassell's German Dictionary

scientifique, savant(e) [N.B. *Scientiste* means a proponent of scientism or a Christian Scientist.]
Larousse Unabridged French-English/English-French Dictionary

savant(e), homme de science
Mansion's Shorter French and English Dictionary

científico, científica
Larousse Diccionario General español-ingles

ychënii [learned man, scholar, scientist], *estestvoispuitatel* [*ispuitatel*
investigator of *estestvo* nature]
Müller's English-Russian Dictionary

natuurfilosoof, natuurkundige; man van de wetenschap, geleerde
Kramer's Woordenboek Engels [Dutch-English, English-Dutch dictionary]

(natur)vetenskapsman, (natur)vetenskapare
Prisma's English-Swedish Dictionary

"Natural philosopher" does persist in at least one language, Dutch, which still uses the term *natuurfilosoof*. Furthermore, when we look at the words for "scientist" in the other languages, we sense that by and large they are taken from the words for "learning" and "knowledge" in those languages and seem to lack the connotations of the English word.

Connotations may be subtle, but they strongly influence the way a word is used. "Scientist" is an important word in our language, so it is worthwhile to explore the nuances of its meaning. As the OED tells us, it was coined by analogy with "artist." In the latter case, the suffix "-ist" is added to "art," and the result sounds fine. But merely adding "-ist" to "science" would produce "sciencist," which has three sibilants (s-sounds), is awkward to pronounce, and obscures the root word "science." Not only does "sciencist" echo oddly in our ear, but it calls forth negative associations, sounding like a combination of "cyst" and "sissy." It just won't do. Thus, a suitable substitute had to be chosen, and a "t" was inserted to create "scientist." Here too, the whole is something other than the sum of the parts. The very analogy with "artist" makes the suffix with its extra "t" stand out. And *voilà*, the way it stands out is with a faintly negative connotation. To be sure, a scien*tist* sounds like an advocate and champion of science, but also like a huckster and salesman of it.

Interestingly enough, one of the German words for "scientist," *Wissenschaftler*, also has a faintly negative connotation. The suffix *"-ler,"* the only one that can be attached to *Wissenschaft* to mean "a person who works in the sciences," connotes littleness, such as would be conveyed by "little professor" or "pedant."

Maybe I have my connotative antennae a little too finely tuned, but it seems to me that in more than one language, the word for "scientist" retains a negative connotation along with its positive ones. One might ask with Shakespeare, what's in a name? Would a rose by any other name smell as sweet? In truth, there is much in a name. A bad name for a rose *would* interfere with our perception of it, and a good name or description makes us see it better. "My luv is like a red, red rose" adds something positive to the meaning of "rose." Subtle modification of the meanings of words constantly occurs, and is as observable as any molecular process or chemical reaction.

"Scientist" has come to be a mighty word in our culture. It was not always so. It is hardly a couple of generations since the word connoted "mad scientist" to many people. Understandably, the scientists want to preserve and even increase the prestige now attaching to it. Thus, one could hardly expect them to welcome with shouts of glee the suggestion I am working up to, namely, that "natural philosopher" is just as good a name for investigators of nature as "scientist."

This would be more apparent if the pseudo-discipline now using the names "philosophy" and "philosopher" ceased doing so and joined up with the appropriate disciplines as recommended earlier. However, even if those developments occur, we can expect scientists to cling to their present name and emphatically reject any suggestion that they give equal place to their former one. They would point to all the positive connotations of the words "science" and "scientist": freeing the mind from superstition, adhering rigorously to the facts and to what can be experimentally proven, and so on. This is all true of course, but why doesn't "natural philosopher" stand for the same things? Partly because "philosophy" and "philosopher" retain their negative connotations, but mainly because of another important characteristic associated with the word "science."

One of the most striking features of science as a social institution is that it is ahistorical, or even antihistorical. For many scientists, the history of science is irrelevant or marginal to their concerns, a history of errors, a subject in which they have no interest. They are looking not toward the past, but toward the future. After all, approximately 90 percent of all the scientists who ever lived are alive today. There is much to be said for the conviction that science is the key to human progress, and that through it we can eliminate superstition and ignorance and build here on earth the heavenly city envisioned by the eighteenth-century *philosophes*. Particularly in the United States, the belief in the ability of science and technology to solve problems has always been very strong. In general, America has an anti-historical ideology and largely defines itself as breaking with the past. At its most enthusiastic and inspired, this spirit is well expressed in the following lines of Whitman:

> Have the elder races halted?
> Do they droop and end their lesson, wearied over there beyond the seas?
> We take up the task eternal, and the burden and the lesson,
> Pioneers! O pioneers!

> All the past we leave behind,
> We debouch upon a newer, mightier world, varied world,
> Fresh and strong the world we seize, world of labor and the march,
> Pioneers! O pioneers!

> . . .

> Do the feasters gluttonous feast?
> Do the corpulent sleepers sleep? have they lock'd and bolted doors?
> Still be ours the diet hard, and the blanket on the ground,
> Pioneers! O pioneers!

> Has the night descended?
> Was the road of late so toilsome? did we stop discouraged nodding on our way?
> Yet a passing hour I yield you in your tracks to pause oblivious,
> Pioneers! O pioneers!

> Till with sound of trumpet,
> Far, far off the daybreak call – hark! how loud and clear I hear it wind,
> Swift! to the head of the army! – swift! spring to your places,
> Pioneers! O pioneers!

"Philosophy" by contrast is obsessed with its own past, defining itself in terms of its history, overshadowed by it, unable to come to terms with it. Think of Rorty's description of the history of philosophy as "a series of quite different sets of problems." If "science" is a- or antihistorical, "philosophy" could be described as super- or hyperhistorical. These imbalances reflect and feed off each other. "Philosophy" is obsessed with its own problems, which it magnifies along with its imaginary differences from "science." In the end, it becomes a parody of itself. "Science," while a far more successful enterprise than "philosophy," also has developed its own mythology, ideology, and hang-ups. Albeit to a lesser extent than "philosophy," "science" too becomes at times a parody of itself. If it can present itself as ahistorical, *i.e.*, persuade us that its history is irrelevant to it, that its errors, its human failings are not really a part of it, then it can perpetuate the myth of itself as over and above the converse of ordinary human beings, more than human, transcendent. If something is an error, it is not science. This could be called the Dogma of the Infallibility of Science. Thus, it comes to resemble a religious faith.

Historically, the relationship between "philosophy" and "science" has been intimate. They are part of the same intellectual tradition whose origins antedate the ancient Greeks. The current imbalance in each of them is caused by their artificial separation from each other. I already have described the ill effects of this imbalance on "philosophy." Now I shall describe the further consequences of their separation and their imbalance.

Notes

1. *Oxford English Dictionary,* "Philosophy."

2. *Ibid.,* "Scientist."

3. *Ibid.,* Supplement, "scientist."

7
The Exclusion of Mind from Nature

The ahistorical viewpoint of modern science is epitomized in a famous couplet of Alexander Pope:

> Nature, and Nature's laws, lay hid in night.
> God said, "Let Newton be," and all was light.

This is hyperbole, but very much in the spirit of the mythology that science created for itself that led it to forget its origins in the Middle Ages and the ancient world. The mythology – or ideology – was partly a response to the attacks on it by adherents of religion who felt threatened by it. In particular, the scientists were reacting to medieval scholasticism, which embraced a host of metaphysical qualities and entities attributed to Aristotle, but which really were a medieval version of his ideas. The scientists also wished to exclude views they saw as erroneous, but seductive, like Aristotle's concept of *teleology* or "final causes," the notion that living organisms have natural ends or goals built into them. All of these things were excluded from science along with the mistaken Aristotelian-Ptolemaic theory of the heavens.

Minimizing the importance of its own history and marginalizing the story of its errors has left science prone to further errors and, in particular, has led to the greatest error of all, the exclusion of mind from nature. This is ironic, because science itself is one of the greatest achievements of the human mind. Nevertheless, it arose not by revealing truths about mind or human nature but about matter in motion. Its success was assured in the seventeenth century when it discovered mathematical laws that apply to the material world. Thereafter its field of inquiry ranged from subatomic particles to the greatest masses of matter, from the center of the earth to the farthest distances our telescopes can reach.

Mathematics and physics led the way, and it was well into the nineteenth century before great advances were made in biology. As for psychology and the social sciences, even now, late in the twentieth century, little has occurred to match the great achievements in natural science. This is not surprising, because from the time that modern natural science came into being, the question was raised whether its concepts and methods could be applied to the human sciences. Could these areas be brought under the same laws that govern matter? Many people were repelled and frightened by the idea that the human mind and human values could be reduced to nothing more than an adjunct of physics and chemistry, an offshoot of the material universe. Hence, they tried to preserve the integrity of human nature by assigning it to a different realm outside that of science, beginning with the "mind-body dualism" of Descartes. The "modern philosophers" of the seventeenth and eighteenth centuries were, as we have seen, a group of thinkers attempting to reconcile the conflicting claims of science and human values. While not all their solutions were dualistic, dualistic thinking predominated and has become a permanent feature of modern Western thought and life.

Indeed, it is not just a matter of theory. Dualism extends throughout our experience. We have often been told how great the contrast is between our scientific and technological prowess and our social and moral backwardness. We depend on science and technology and the conveniences of industrial society, but they bring with them a host of problems that we have not been able to resolve. The gulf between the sciences and the humanities in our education and cultural life is all too familiar. In developing what C. P. Snow called "The Two Cultures," we have institutionalized this separation, something we accept as the price of progress. Indeed, we can hardly imagine modern life in any other form.

Dualism is so much a part of our lives that we may not see its historical and intellectual basis until it is pointed out to us. The sources of dualism and its cultural and intellectual consequences were described at length by John Dewey, among others. But despite the efforts of many, the intellectual consequences are not fully appreciated, because they need to be viewed in a perspective broader than that of "modern philosophy," namely, the one I have tried to reach in this essay. It is absurd that we can know so much about matter and about remote areas of the universe and so little about ourselves. It is equally ridiculous that we cannot understand the relationship of the mind to the natural world it knows so well. In short, not only is the contradiction in our culture something we should not accept, but intellectually as well, dualism is a dilemma, not a solution.

Besides dualism, the other prevailing tendency in modern thought is to try to explain living processes, human nature, mind, and values in terms of the laws of matter and motion. This position is called materialism or reductionism. Materialist theories have been put forth since ancient times, and despite the far greater sophistication of the science now used to buttress them, they do not represent anything new under the sun. Their newest wrinkles are taken from such high-powered disciplines as molecular biology, genetics, neurology, and computer science, yet it remains to be seen whether the current crew of materialists and reductionists will have any more success than their predecessors.

In the eighteenth and nineteenth centuries, the attempt to find a materialist reduction was made in terms of the atoms and molecules that obey Newton's laws of motion. Now in the twentieth century, never mind that the physicists are knocking more and more holes in their own materialism as they make the explanation of the ultimate nature of matter and the laws that govern it ever more esoteric. What the physicists are tearing asunder, the molecular biologists, geneticists, neurologists, and cognitive scientists are busily putting back together again, trying to explain mind in terms of matter even as matter becomes ever more mysterious. It doesn't matter what matter really is – it is enough to explain mind! After all, what could mind be but highly complicated biochemistry and electric circuitry, the brain a complex bio-computer? Look at the steady flow of discoveries and devices – the robots, the gene-splicing, the ever more powerful and sophisticated artificial organs guided by computers, the computer programs that can mimic the brain. Just give them enough time. They'll do it!

If you take their word for it, the El Dorado, the Holy Grail is just around the corner – or maybe the next corner, or the next. Who knows? If not tomorrow, then in a decade or a generation, we may pick up the newspaper or turn on the TV and receive the startling news that mind finally has been reduced to matter.

To the best of my knowledge, no one ever has surveyed the scientists to find out how many of them are materialists. Surely not all of them fall into this category. Those that have religious faith and put their faith in a different realm from their scientific activities are dualists. Others may not be religious but still believe in free will and human values. They too are dualists. At least in regard to alternatives to the reigning scientific paradigm, the dualists are aligned with the materialists. They believe in mind, but they don't know how to reconcile that belief with their commitment to science. In addition to the scientists, it would be interesting to know what percentage of people in other professions, as well as members of the general public, fall under these different categories. Yet even without benefit of a survey, we can safely say that there are plenty of materialists around.

The materialists are committed to the idea that science will soon explain all the mysteries of mental activity in terms of electrical and chemical processes and computer algorithms. While the materialist millennium, the inbreaking of the reductionist kingdom, seems ever at hand, somehow it never arrives, even though they have been heralding it for centuries. But they are not deterred by failure. The stubbornness with which they persist in their belief is something to wonder at. It is like a religious faith. They are battling age-old ignorance and superstition, you see. They must fight to protect science against the forces of darkness that forever threaten it.

One can understand why medieval scholasticism was rejected, and why crude forms of vitalism are dismissed out of hand – vitalism being the theory that living organisms contain a "vital force" that is not subject to the laws of science. But any challenge to the reigning paradigm is regarded as if it were heresy. Consider the materialist "philosopher" Donald Davidson's comment that "Plato is not even wrong; he is out of the question." The attitude toward Aristotle is similar. The materialists do not want to consider even the possibility that an alternative to materialism exists. The depth of their commitment to their beliefs is akin to religious dogma, as if they had their own Apostle's Creed: I believe in materialism, the One, the True, the Apostolic. I believe in the Second Law of Thermodynamics. I believe in Maxwell's equations. And so on.

At the height of Marxism, critics observed that it was atheism transformed into a religion. I am not trying to suggest that scientific materialists are Marxists, merely that there is a parallel. We are familiar with the Marxists' commitment to their view of human history, their indignation at social injustice, and so forth. The question is, why are the scientific materialists so stubborn in their faith? Partly for legitimate reasons. Natural science constantly has had to battle ignorant and wrong-headed theories and has emerged from each test stronger than before. But its materialist adherents have overreacted. They simply have gone too far. Furthermore, the lack of interest in its own history prevents science from gaining a proper perspective on its assumptions, and the "philosophers" have not given it much help. Thus, the materialists have fallen into the trap of thinking that no rational alternative to their fundamental position exists.

Nor does it come as a surprise that they can dismiss Platonism out of hand. The Platonists – and there are some around – are as contemptuous of the materialists as the materialists are of them. After all, Platonism, with its emphasis on mathematics, inspired modern science, and if the materialists don't appreciate the significance of that, it's their problem. In any event, Platonism does not present a direct challenge to materialist science because it never was developed into a science. Thus, the two are not on a collision course and aren't especially interested in going head to head with each other.

Aristotelianism, however, *is* a form of science, and for a time its ideas contended with those of modern physical science. In the name of the geocentric theory and their armamentarium of dubious metaphysical entities, the medieval scholastics used their version of Aristotle to try to block modern science. Hence, the questionable views of the scholastics are lumped together with true Aristotelianism, and the latter looks guilty by association. Not only the modern scientists, but the "modern philosophers" from Descartes through Kant were – either openly or implicitly – criticizing Aristotle's ideas and attempting to replace them.

What makes Aristotle even more of an anathema to the materialists is the fact that he provides a thorough and carefully stated refinement of the common-sense view of things. He believes in free will and the substantiality of the mind and that life is not reducible to inanimate processes. He finds a place in nature for human values. It is not surprising that his viewpoint has had great appeal. Materialism, on the other hand, is rejected by most people precisely because it denies all these things.

Aristotle appeals to many because he is grounded so solidly in common sense and the values people hold most dear. However, in the eyes of his critics, this only makes things worse. It looks to them as if he is using the plausibility of ordinary experience as the basis for highly unacceptable, unscientific dogmas.

As far as the materialists are concerned, Davidson's saying about Plato applies even more strongly to Aristotle. They are more defensive about him and are at greater pains to make him a straw man, to rule him out in advance, to make it impossible to be seduced by his ideas. They do this by clinging ever more tightly to their mechanist, reductionist paradigm of science, to which the most obvious alternative is the seductive heresy of Aristotle. To them he much more than Plato is the Great Satan.

At least the "modern philosophers" of the seventeenth and eighteenth centuries, particularly Hobbes and Locke, spoke to the issues Aristotle raised. An alternative to materialism might be mistaken, but at least it was plausible. Aristotle might be wrong, but still his views required rebuttal. However, contemporary materialists are unwilling to concede this. If they did, they would have to look at him more carefully and question their own paradigm, something they are unwilling to do. Thus, Aristotle's views are not just wrong; they are *implausible*.

If Aristotelianism turns out to be implausible, it should at least be intelligible. However, the materialists deny even that. If one takes literally the view that *nature consists solely of atoms and molecules in motion*, Aristotle's concepts seem *unintelligible*. To the materialists, the idea of a *natural being – i.e., a living organism –* that is more than just atoms and molecules is a self-contradiction. If that being has the ability to *act upon* atoms and molecules, the idea is even more self-contradictory. How can something immaterial (*i.e.,* the soul or the mind) act on matter? This is just vitalism. It is an unintelligible position, and we want none of it in science! Thus, Aristotle's ideas are subject to a double banishment. They not only are cast out of nature, but expelled from our very *conception* of nature. As a materialist might say, Aristotle is not even wrong; he is out of the question.

The psychology that follows from this position is straightforward: What we call "the mind" is a flow of images connected by chains of association, acting on each other like physical forces and lacking any substantial unity. Human behavior is completely determined by whatever combination of mental forces proves to be the most powerful. If we know all the causes, we can predict all the effects. There is no free will. Underlying the mental phenomena are the more obviously physical and chemical processes of the body. In cruder forms of materialism, the latter directly and powerfully influence the former. In behaviorism, a more refined version of determinism, "operant conditioning" by positive and negative reinforcements (rewards and punishments) shapes our character and actions. Whatever form it takes, if determinism is correct, we are not responsible for our actions. We lack both freedom and dignity.

Materialist psychology purports to explain the nature of mental activity and human behavior, but what insights into our behavior has it provided? Keep in mind that this theory has been around for a long time. If it were correct, it would have achieved something by now. But it clearly has not, despite the promises of its adherents. It survives because of their inability to think of an alternative, which is reinforced by their refusal to look for one. They are trapped by their own anti-Aristotelian propaganda. The hopes of the materialists are fed as well by the continuing advances in science and technology. To hear them tell it, someone soon will invent a computer program that makes fluent translations from one language to another, or one that outdoes Shakespeare, or another that composes music as beautiful as Beethoven's. Soon there will be a robot that outsmarts human beings, a machine that truly acts human, like the computer HAL in the movie *2001*. Don't underestimate American technology. Before long we will have machines to read each other's minds. In truth, yesterday's science fiction is today's fact. Today's science fiction may well be tomorrow's fact. No wonder the advances that constantly are being made feed the faith of the materialists.

Still, it is remarkable how little of that faith has been realized. With all that has been and is being accomplished in technology and science, we should long ago have seen the triumph of materialism. Yet somehow the millennium never arrives. For all the marvelous ability of computer programs and robots to mimic human actions, they are just cleverly designed algorithms and machines, not minds. Consider the things the "cognitive scientists," the "psychologists," and the "philosophers" are unable to tell us. Except in the most limited way, they cannot explain how the mind performs its various functions, among them memory, reasoning, and the creation and use of language. They have at best a crude explanation of how the mind is connected to the body, how it moves the body, and how it moves itself (*i.e.*, how it thinks). They offer no clear and coherent explanation of consciousness or of unconscious mental activity. They can tell us little of value regarding the nature of intelligence, the emotions, personality and its development, mental illness or its treatment, or mental health. They cannot agree on the nature, genesis, and role of ethical beliefs and standards. While free will and moral autonomy are presupposed in our legal system, our religious beliefs, and in our everyday lives, science, when it is not denying them, doesn't know what to say about them because it has no coherent view of man or human nature. The "philosophers" offer the scientists no help, because they too cannot achieve a consensus on this issue. In light of how little modern psychology and "cognitive science" actually know, it is paradoxical that Aristotle's views in those areas should seem incorrect and inadequate to anyone.

Furthermore, materialism is unable to explain satisfactorily the nature of living organisms, merely asserting that living processes eventually will be understood totally in terms of physical and chemical processes, and that this explanation will extend to all mental phenomena. But they never have fulfilled this promise, and the likelihood that they will do so is not in the offing.

Whether advocated by Hobbes in the seventeenth century, or La Mettrie and the *philosophes* in the eighteenth century, or the Darwinists in the nineteenth century, or the molecular biologists, geneticists, cognitive scientists, behaviorists, and materialist philosophers in the twentieth, materialism is still the same old position. Its adherents believe it is on the cutting edge of science and its opponents will be swept away before it. For decades we have been told the mind is really a computer. The latest rage is genetics, as now this gene, now that one is declared to cause this or that psychological characteristic. However, the materialists have been making the same promises or threats for centuries with no noticeable effect, so that we can feel justified in being skeptical about the latest bees in their bonnet.

Consider the most widely known of the current materialists, Daniel Dennett. In *Consciousness Explained* he does the same thing that Hobbes does – he flat out denies the unity of mind. That is the central thesis of the book. But whom does he hold up as his chief antagonist? Descartes, who, as we saw in Chapter Five, is the weakest representative of this position. Reading Dennett, you wouldn't know Aristotle existed. (I believe he is mentioned in a footnote somewhere.) The denial of the unity of mind is accompanied by a tidal wave, deluge, or monsoon of trendy cognitive science jargon and accompanying rhetoric: hard-wired brains, evil neurosurgeons, conscious robots, heterophenomenology, informavores, etc., etc. – as if an army of cognitive scientists were assiduously filling in any and all gaps that Hobbes *et al.* had left incomplete. It is an impressive display of verbal showmanship that lasts for hundreds of pages. But for all the hoopla, it is less than what Hobbes offers the reader. Hobbes after all was speaking to the arguments of Aristotle. Nevertheless, reading Dennett is fun, especially if you don't take it too seriously. It just needs to be relocated to a different section of your local bookstore from where it now can be found – *i.e.*, to the science-fiction section.

While in dealing with atoms and molecules science has done wonders, the perennial effort to extend it beyond that realm has been a failure. What is even worse, apart from its success in explaining matter, science has actually regressed! Dualism, for example, is not an advance; it is a giant step backwards. It makes the presence of mind in nature unintelligible and it turns knowledge into a problem. Materialism does essentially the same thing. In general, the account of mind that modern science gives us is crude and simplistic – and that statement includes modern "philosophy." The modern scientists and philosophers have primitivized the concept of mind; they have rendered it unintelligible; and in so doing, they have all but excluded it from nature.

The following anecdote will make clearer what I mean. At a conference on memory held at the Johns Hopkins Medical School in the spring of 1992, Stephen Kosslyn, Professor of Psychology at Harvard, was describing a machine that is capable of detecting images in the brain. He described one instance of it picking up a spatial pattern in the visual cortex of an animal. The pattern bore the same shape as an object the animal was looking at. In other words, a machine exists that can actually detect and record our thoughts – or at least some of them. In describing this incident, Kosslyn did not hide his own wonderment, exclaiming "I find this technology absolutely awesome!" Certainly it is impressive, but I remember thinking at the time, Yes, the technology is awesome, but the science is primitive.

At first blush, it seems marvelous that a machine can actually peer inside our brains and observe the workings of our minds, but is that really superior to what we ourselves can do? If there is *any* area of investigation to which we have privileged access, it is our own minds. Since we know perfectly well that the seat of the mind is the brain, and that our thoughts are not disembodied, but occur somewhere, somehow in that organ, then we know that the shapes and forms we see with our eyes are recorded there. Hence, if someone invents a machine that can detect them, it may be a great technological advance, but it is hardly a surprise to find them there. Where else would we expect to find them, and what else would we expect to find?

Furthermore, when you think about it, even the technology is not very awe-inspiring. Once the concept of electromagnetic radiation was understood – and that *was* a marvelous scientific advance – the development of technology based on it is impressive, but not astonishing.

However, Stephen Kosslyn is not alone in being awe-struck. Millions of people would share his amazement. This is not just because of the modern-day worship of machines and technology, but more particularly because the subject of the mind and consciousness is a *terra incognita*, an area of mystery to us. Yet it was not always thus. The mind was *rendered* mysterious by modern science. Once you get into your head the idea that everything that goes on in the universe can be understood only by reducing it to the movements of atoms and molecules, and you adamantly deny the possibility of any alternative, it is no wonder you find yourself in a pickle when you try to explain mind.

Perhaps not all readers are convinced that the modern concept of mind is as primitive as I say it is. To be sure, the materialists are not. However, I strongly suspect that the latter are greatly outnumbered by the dualists, and dualism, as noted earlier, is not a solution, but a dilemma. This is generally recognized. The list I gave of mental phenomena that modern science cannot explain is not something I thought up, but is common knowledge. We have a chasm running through our intellectual lives and through our civilization as a whole.

The situation brings to mind Woody Allen's motion picture *Sleeper*, in which the hero, played by Allen, is put into suspended animation in a time capsule and, waking up in the twenty-first century, discovers that the world has changed in unexpected ways. Science and technology have progressed in some respects and regressed in others. While attempting to adjust to the changes, the hero has a series of escapades with the evil powers-that-be in the not-so-brave new world.

Sleeper is an excellent allegory for the history of Western science, which has advanced in some respects and retreated in others. We have made extraordinary progress in our knowledge of matter and have largely forgotten what the ancient Greeks knew about mind. I say this after having studied Plato and Aristotle and reflected a great deal on their ideas about mind and soul. Even readers who are not materialists may not be convinced. Still, Chapter 5 gives some sense of the kind of criticism of the modern thinkers that can be made, and Chapter 8 contains a description of Aristotle's key ideas in this area. Thus, the reader should obtain a reasonably clear conception with which to evaluate this proposition.

Instead of the twenty-first century, we can imagine Woody Allen put to sleep, say, in the third or second century B.C. in Alexandria and waking up in the twentieth century – or even better than that, imagine Aristotle himself put into suspended animation in the fourth century B.C. and revived in our time.

Aristotle was a scientist through and through, and we can be sure he would be duly impressed with the marvels of our science and technology, which in all likelihood would be the first things to engage his attention. But before long he would discover how little our knowledge of our own behavior and of our minds has kept pace with our knowledge of matter. He would be equally astonished at how greatly biology has advanced, so far beyond where he was able to go, while denying or making irrelevant the substantial unity of the organism, which was so apparent to him. In particular, he would be amazed at the way we have turned mind into something unintelligible, or barely intelligible.

Our scientists have invented the most amazing machines, some of which peer inside our brains and see the physical traces of the activity of our minds. But when they try to go beyond the images on the machines to explain what lies behind them, it is obvious that they have only the foggiest idea of what they are talking about. Yet we need not resign ourselves to this unsatisfactory state of affairs. Looking at the modern world through the eyes of Aristotle, we can gain a new perspective on ourselves. In the next chapter, I will present a sketch of his view of the nature of mind and the soul in the hope that the reader may share that perspective and get a sense of what it promises for ourselves and our civilization.

8
Putting Mind Back into Nature
with the Aid of Aristotle

A. *Aristotle vis-à-vis Modern Science*

The simple-minded materialism and simple-minded vitalism described in the preceding chapter feed off each other. Similarly, the more sophisticated versions of the two positions tend to converge on a few narrowly focused questions. This seems to happen with many controversies, and it is almost enough to make a Hegelian out of one as one watches the thesis and the antithesis converge into a synthesis. On the other hand, a synthesis may not occur, as the two sides of a controversy go round and round in their respective circles, often for centuries.

For the most part during the modern period, the materialists have been on the offensive. The adherents of mind, free will, and human values have had to defend their views from the encroachments of science. The materialists appear to have all the advantages in the debate, but the contest may not be as one-sided as it seems. Indeed, one wonders why the scientists do not reflect more on some of their own pronouncements. Neurologists, for example, are fond of saying that the human brain is the most complex object in the universe. If that is so, what about the mental activities the brain supports? They must be of comparable complexity. Consider the most important one, language. Our linguistic ability is so central a part of our nature that, paradoxically, we take it for granted and seldom stop to reflect on how wonderful it is. Here too we are blinded by prejudices engendered by our awe of science. We think of mathematics as a model of precision, compared to which ordinary language seems rough and imprecise, but we never could have created the former without the latter. Most of us have no idea of the brilliance of human language and how well it compares to that of science and technology.

The psychological processes by which we create, learn, and use language are one of the wonders of nature, as marvelous as anything going on in distant galaxies, in the innards of matter, or at the center of the earth. On the one hand, we are not conscious, except very intuitively, of what we are going to say until we have actually said it. Yet on the other hand, no sane person would argue that we are zombies and the words just come out automatically. Our speech is *under our voluntary control, yet we don't know how we do it.* We direct a set of processes that seem to function just below the level of consciousness. This suggests an order of *mental* complexity that reflects the complexity of the brain with which the neurologists are so greatly impressed. Would that our behavior as moral beings matched our capacity for speech! If we cooperated as much in all of our activities as we do in the creation and use of language, the world would be a much better place.

I spoke earlier of Chomsky, who has swum against the materialist tide. In revealing the complex processes of language, he has partially deprimitivized the concept of mind. The mind that controls these processes must be very powerful. Indeed, it must be a substantial unity. To the best of my knowledge, Chomsky does not actually go so far as to speak of the mind as such, but he does call his theory "Cartesian linguistics," after Descartes, who most certainly did posit the substantial unity of the mind. He further compares his own ideas to those of Kant, who did so as well. In 1959, in his famous review of B.F. Skinner's *Verbal Behavior*, Chomsky scathingly criticized the behaviorist/materialist theory of language and mind. In short, Chomsky took several giant steps toward restoring to mind what modern science had taken from it.

Chomsky's mind ranged back to the seventeenth century to help bring about this restoration. Had he gone as far into the past as the fourth century B.C. to the thought of Aristotle, he would have discovered a great deal more. At one point in his writings, he seems to recognize the opportunity he is missing:

> [A]s a question of science . . . we ask how comes it that human beings with such limited and personal experience achieve such convergence in rich and highly structured systems of belief, systems which then guide their actions and interchange and their interpretation of experience.
>
> In the classical tradition, several answers were suggested. One might argue, along Aristotelian lines, that the world is structured in a certain way, and that the human mind is able to perceive this structure, ascending from particulars to species to genus to further generalization

and thus attaining knowledge of universals from perception of particulars. A "basis of pre-existent knowledge" is a prerequisite to learning.
We must possess an innate capacity to attain developed states of
knowledge, but these are "neither innate in a determinate form, nor developed from other higher states of knowledge, but from
sense-perception." Given rich metaphysical assumptions, it is possible
to imagine that a mind "so constituted as to be capable of this process"
of "induction" might attain a rich system of knowledge.

A more fruitful approach shifts the main burden of explanation
from the structure of the world to the structure of the mind.[1]

The quotations in the foregoing passage are from the conclusion of *The
Posterior Analytics*, one of the key chapters in Aristotle's writings. Whatever Chomsky's reasons were, he took the road more traveled and stuck to
the modern period with only a nod in the direction of the ancients.

Through whatever combination of luck or skill by which it happened, I
came upon a previously undiscovered route back to the ancients. As noted
earlier, one of the people who guided me was Chomsky. But Chomsky only
went part of the way. My aim in this chapter is to show that there *is* genu-
inely an Aristotelian solution to the problems of "modern philosophy," and
to present it in as straightforward and uncomplicated a way as I can. I will
provide enough detail to make the case properly and, I hope, satisfy scholars
– or maybe I should say, displease scholars, *i.e.*, the ones whose applecart
would be upset by the emergence of a neo-Aristotelian paradigm. At this
point, I am not trying to convince the reader that Aristotle was right, just
that his position is both intelligible and plausible. If I succeed in doing at
least that, I will have shown that Aristotle cannot be dismissed out of hand,
and that his ideas on psychology, language, the social sciences, and the nature and origins of life, *inter alia*, are worthy of serious study.

It may be hard to believe that the ideas of someone who lived nearly
2,400 years ago could address so many contemporary issues, especially
someone who was mistaken in several key areas. Modern science corrected
Aristotle's mistakes, but it made some errors of its own, and now he can return the favor. Some of the errors are embodied in "modern philosophy,"
which is not some mysterious discipline distinct from science – in large
part, it is just incorrect science.

Not only do Aristotle's ideas solve the problems of "modern philosophy," but they offer a solution to the difficulties the scientists are facing in
trying to explain life using a mechanistic, reductionist paradigm. Like the
"philosophers," they too are neo-procrusteans, but not in the same respect.

The former try to *squeeze* "the history of philosophy" onto the short and narrow bed of epistemology and chop off its interdisciplinary legs when it fails to fit. The latter try to *stretch* materialism to fit the facts of life.

Doubtless the materialists would respond by accusing Aristotle of being a vitalist, as if that would suffice to end the discussion. However, if Aristotle is a vitalist, he is a sophisticated, not a simple-minded, one. *Living organisms are substantial beings. At the same time, existing within nature, they obey the laws of physics and chemistry.* This may sound like squaring the circle, but it is not, as I shall show. To get some purchase on this seeming contradiction, consider the following, from the contemporary French biochemist Martin Olomucki:

> At the different stages of molecular organization, the first structures to appear were relatively simple and few in number. But it is the highly varied combination of these basic elements that led to the development of new structures and new functions of striking diversity. The advent of life, this remarkable event which occurred in the Universe, thus cannot even be considered a miracle of chemistry. In fact, chemistry did no more than to produce molecules whose appearance at a given point in time under specific conditions obeyed simple laws. The subsequent emergence of "living" structures of infinite complexity appeared to be more like a recombination phenomenon within the framework of *a progressive self-organization of matter tending to higher degrees of order* [emphasis added].[2]

The question is, what precisely is "self-organization"? Just what is "a recombination phenomenon within the framework of a progressive self-organization of matter tending to higher degrees of order"? Practically every word in this definition of life is loaded with ambiguities. At least Aristotle gave an unambiguous definition. It is that the self-organization of living matter is based on the presence of a substantial unity called the *psyché* or "soul." The operations of the *psyché* are *subject to all the laws of nature*, yet at the same time the organism is a higher order of natural being than non-living objects.

Kant presupposed this kind of being, but because he had no way to explain its causal activity within the Newtonian framework of molecules in motion, he had to locate it *outside of nature*. As we saw in Chapter 5, other modern writers had to go through similar intellectual contortions. The very idea of dualism is dubious. Why should the world be split up in this arbitrary way?

Aristotle avoids these problems by means of a set of concepts that I now will explain. They are 1) form and matter, 2) the four causes, 3) substantial being, and 4) the soul and mind. I will give a brief exposition of the first three, and spend more time on the soul and mind. It should already be apparent that my approach is much broader than is normally the case in "philosophy." The exposition will freely combine various passages in Aristotle's writings with ideas from modern science. The reader may be surprised at how easily this can be done. However, if we cast away the stereotypes of Aristotle passed down to us since the Middle Ages, we will see that his ideas and those of modern science fit together hand in glove.

The task of comprehending Aristotle's ideas is made more difficult by the nature of the texts. They are not essays or treatises, but lecture notes, presumably Aristotle's own. Some scholars believe they were made by his students. If so, he had some awfully good students or at least some very good note-takers. In any case, as might be expected of this type of writing, the texts are very concise. Aristotle often packs a wealth of ideas into what looks like a deceptively simple phrase or brief passage. If we fail to read him carefully and with imagination, we will overlook much of what is there.

This kind of explication and extrapolation is hard to do if one does not have at least some Greek. Aristotle had a remarkable way of using ordinary language with technical force, of preserving the vigor of everyday speech while adding technical precision. In general, the translations lose this unique quality, making him sound dry, abstract, and "metaphysical." Hence, I have done my own translations of most of the passages from his works cited in this essay, being as literal as possible, inserting brackets where needed to fill out elliptical comments. My aim is to give the reader an idea of what is actually there to be explicated. I have tried to give a sense of a man talking so that we can hear the voice of the speaker coming to us across the centuries. One way of doing this is to translate colloquial expressions with expressions of today that have comparable force. Take for example the phrase *kaì gár*, which Aristotle uses frequently. *Kaì* means "and," *gár* means "for" (*i.e.*, the conjunction "for"), and together they comprise an idiom meaning "for truly." It is an emphatic rejoinder, as in the sentence "For truly, Empedocles cannot be right!" On the other hand, while such a rendering of *kaì gár* might have been just fine in the seventeenth or eighteenth centuries, who in the late twentieth century says "For truly"? We have to think of something more up-to-date.

Apropos of this problem, a colleague in Classics with whom I used to be acquainted was sitting one evening in a bar in Seattle talking with a colleague in the same field. The latter was saying, "Do you know what *kaì gár* really means? Don't tell anybody I told you this, but it really means 'Shit, man!'"

If every time Aristotle used the expressions *gár* or *kaì gár*, we rendered it into English with one or another of our everyday expletives, the translation that resulted might curl the hair of an Oxford don, but it would capture the vigor of Aristotle's discourse. But maybe I am underestimating Oxford dons. They might not be as stuffy as some people think and might appreciate the virtue of translating colloquial Greek into colloquial American English. This would be one more way of demonstrating that Aristotle was speaking to us and not just to the people of his own time.

The foregoing is not the only linguistic problem. To begin my exposition with Aristotle's concepts of form and matter, I will first have to clear up the verbal confusion that attends the use of these words owing to the fact that we are all accustomed to the terminology of modern science. From that standpoint, we think we have a clear idea of matter, whereas form is very hazy. The world is made up of atoms and molecules – they comprise what we moderns mean by "matter," the primal stuff out of which everything else is made. But "form"? What's that? It sounds like something abstract and metaphysical. Nevertheless, matter is subject to mathematical laws, and it has physical and chemical structure – thus, it has mathematical, physical, and chemical *form*. In other words, "form" is synonymous with "structure." It doesn't just mean *external* shape, but whatever structure anything has, both internal and external.

Every object that exists has structure. It is hard to imagine what a structureless, formless object would be – a contradiction in terms, I suppose. Even motions and processes have structure or form. The motions may be erratic and irregular, but that is still form. In short, form is not a hazy concept at all. It is always in there pitching (so to speak), and we could not exist without it.

However, despite the reliance science places on certain kinds of form, matter is taken to be the ultimate reality accessible to it. Form is regarded as a property of matter. To think otherwise, in science's view, is to believe in the metaphysical abstractions of the scholastic Aristotelians of the Middle Ages whom science overthrew.

Unfortunately, the excesses of many of the scholastics gave Aristotle a bad name and caused people to overlook his highly sophisticated discussion of form and matter. For Aristotle there is no such thing as pure matter because nothing in the universe is totally without structure or form – at least nothing that we know of. Strictly speaking, "matter" is a relative term. A given thing is *matter* for anything more complicated than itself that is made out of it. Sub-atomic particles are the matter out of which atoms are formed. Atoms are the matter out of which molecules are formed. Inorganic molecules are the matter out of which organic molecules are formed – and so on. The object that is created at each stage of the process is *a composite of form and matter*; it in turn is matter for the object at the next stage, which is a more complex composite of form and matter – and on and on all the way to the most complex objects in the universe.

While Aristotle's way of talking about matter is more precise than that of modern science and easily could have been retained without embracing any of his other ideas, virtually everyone speaks of sub-atomic particles, atoms, and molecules as "matter." Our clinging to this way of speaking reflects the materialist, reductionist bias of modern science, the notion that everything in nature really is atoms and molecules. If you consider any object whatsoever, it *really* is *whatever it is made out of*. This is the opposite of the process described in the preceding paragraph, where you go from the simplest to the most complex objects in the universe. To the materialist, the most complex objects in nature ultimately are reducible to the simplest. Hence, the fact that every material object has form may be interesting, but is irrelevant. The people who still believe in form and its highest manifestations (mind, values, the soul, free will, etc.) have to find a place for them *outside of* nature.

Aristotle is not left with this undesirable alternative. For him, both form and matter have a place *in nature*. He explains how they interact by means of the doctrine of the "four causes." Whether or not he is right, once again he will prove to be the one who is stating the issues precisely and the materialists will be the ones that are slovenly in their language.

In modern science, to speak of one thing *causing* another means some kind of physical or chemical process is occurring; causation is just matter in motion. Aristotle calls the matter out of which anything is made the "from what" and the processes it undergoes the "by what." This simple way of talking was rendered into Latin as the *causa materialis* and *causa efficiens*, respectively, from which we have in English *the material and efficient causes*. The Latin terminology is formidable, but so far, Aristotle and modern science are in accord. Causation in the modern sense is equivalent to the first two of Aristotle's four causes. However, he then speaks of the *formal and final causes*, which modern science rejects. The formal cause is the structure or form of whatever object or objects you are talking about. To us moderns it may seem strange to speak of the form of anything as being a *cause*, but again, this just reflects our materialist bias. In fact, if we monitored our own usage, we might be amazed to learn that we speak of formal causes all the time, although without using Aristotle's name for them. For example, because a fertilized human egg has a certain genetic structure, it develops into a human being, not an elephant or rhinoceros or a chimpanzee. The structure or form of a full-grown human being is there potentially in the egg. In order for the human to develop, it has to be that structure and no other. This is what Aristotle means by the "formal cause." Scientists might be shocked to learn that they are speaking Aristotle's lingo in another form, but they most certainly are doing so.

In any event, the real sticking point is final causes. This English term is a translation of the Latin *causa finalis*. Aristotle's Greek is more literal: *héneka toû*, for the sake of which. The "final cause" is that for the sake of which anything exists, the built-in goal or end that controls the functioning of all natural objects. An acorn exists "for the sake of" becoming an oak; a chicken's egg exists "for the sake of" becoming a chicken; a fertilized human egg exists "for the sake of" becoming a full-grown human being. From the Greek word *télos*, meaning end or goal, this doctrine is called "teleology."

The modern objection to teleology is that the end or goal doesn't control anything. The form of the full-grown organism may be potentially there in the egg or seed, but so what? The fully developed organism is *a result, not a cause*. Living organisms are just complex sets of physical and chemical processes that have evolved over the course of the last billion and a half years or more. It may be impossible for us to discover every single genetic variation that occurred to cause the evolution of species, but we can be certain that only physical and chemical processes were operating, and that there were no final causes.

The foregoing seems a clear statement of position, as the moderns try to wash their hands clean of Aristotle. Yet even here they do not fully succeed. While denying teleology in principle, science constantly talks about organisms in teleological terms, *as if* they really were organized to fulfill some natural end or goal. The rationale is that this is just a convenient way of speaking. Over the eons, by natural selection, organisms have evolved with such a wealth of adaptations that it *looks as if* they had controlling ends or goals. This, however, only reflects the marvelous complexity of matter, which can mimic final causes without the latter actually existing. To put it in Kantian terms, teleology is a *regulative* principle, not a *constitutive* one: We can *talk* about nature as if it contained ends or goals, but they are not really there. So Kant concluded in "The Critique of Teleological Judgment," the second part of his last major work, *The Critique of Judgment*. Aristotle, on the other hand, would insist that it doesn't just look as if the ends and goals exist in nature. They really do.

At last we have got down to the nitty-gritty. We started off with crude versions of materialism and vitalism, which are very far apart and, ironically, feed off each other's weaknesses. Even highly intelligent people defend these positions in an unsophisticated way. However, once past the cruder disagreements, we recognize that the ultimate differences between modern science and Aristotle are highly sophisticated. On this level, as we saw in other controversies in the history of ideas, the opposing sides turn out to have a lot in common. Their positions tend to converge on one or more clearly focused issues. In this instance, we again find that Aristotle helps us do the focusing. It is he who is speaking precisely and modern science, together with the materialist "philosophers," that is sloppy in its use of terms. Aristotle's treatment of matter and form is more accurate, and so is his formulation of causes in nature. In the end, it all boils down to the question of substantial form, the unity of the soul and of mind, and final causes, a set of closely related issues. As William James would say, that is the "cash value" of the difference, or as we would put it today, that's the bottom line. Therefore, let us go ahead and consider these issues.

B. Substantial Being, Soul, and Mind

Asking whether or not final causes exist is equivalent to asking whether substantial beings exist, for only the latter can have built-in ends or goals which they strive to attain, *i.e.*, final causes. In order to consider this question, I first must explain what Aristotle means by "substantial being."

Employing Aristotle's superior terminology, we can say that every object in the universe is a composite of matter and form. Aristotle calls this composite an *ousía*, a word that can be translated as "being" (its literal meaning in Greek), "substantial being," or "substance." It is hard to find a single English word that adequately translates *ousía*. If you say "substance," as is normally done, it seems to mean non-living physical objects.

If you translate it as "substantial being," it seems to mean living organisms. In fact, Aristotle means both. Everything in the universe is either an inanimate object or a living organism or some property or attribute of inanimate objects or living organisms. The universe is composed of *ousíai* ("substances" or "substantial beings") in various kinds of motion or change and producing motion or change in other *ousíai*.

What differentiates one *ousía* from another is having a certain kind of essential form. Perhaps this sounds abstract and "metaphysical," but all it means is that everything that exists has a certain nature or "essence" that can be expressed by a defining formula. The substantial being of anything is its essence or nature, which we try to discover and state in a definition, concept, mathematical formula, or law, or some combination of the same.

Aristotle calls the substantial being or essence or nature of living beings the *psyché* (pronounced "psü-khéh"), a word that is translated as the "soul." Here as before there are linguistic pitfalls we must avoid. "Soul" has largely religious connotations. While *psyché* also is used in the context of religion, it is basically a biological word, and Aristotle employs it as a scientific term. He does not, for example, believe in the immortality of the soul. In English we have the word "psyche," which we have taken from the Greek, but it denotes the mind and the emotions without the broad biological meaning of its Greek original. Hence, to avoid confusion, I will continue to speak of *psyché*, not its English counterpart, and I will put quotation marks around "soul," unless the context is clear enough to make them unnecessary.

The reader may not feel that Aristotle has clarified things very much when he asserts that "it is obvious that the *psyché* is the primary substantial being, and the body is matter, and the human being or the living creature is the combination of the two . . ."[3] But think of it this way: The body considered all by itself is just inert matter, like a corpse. A corpse isn't a biological creature, except if we are speaking ambiguously. Properly speaking, the biological creature is the *living* creature, so its essence or nature is whatever made it alive, in other words, the *psyché* or "soul."

Modern biology doesn't use words like *psyché* or "soul." It would say that what makes us alive is a set of biological processes that the body supports and that could not occur without it. Why then should we call this collection of processes "the soul"? First of all, because they are not any old processes loosely strung together. They are highly integrated and organized. Even materialists recognize that. Moreover, the processes that constitute an animal are, broadly speaking, different from those that comprise a plant, and human processes have special features that make them different from those of other animals, and so on. In other words, there are essential characteristics and essential differences that can be identified and defined.

Fine, but does even a highly organized, discretely definable set of processes add up to a "soul"? It does if it is sufficiently unified, that is, if the processes constitute a real or substantial unity – in other words, if there really is a controlling principle for the sake of which the activities of the organism take place.

To try to decide this question, let us look at what Aristotle has to say about the nature of the soul. Here is how he actually defines it:

> . . . Soul is the first actuality of a physical body potentially having life. And such is any body having organs."[4]

Once again, the reader may find Aristotle's terminology less than crystal clear, but we can restate it in more familiar language. "An organic body" or "a body having organs" just means the organism considered as an anatomical object, a set of organs. He is speaking of it not as a corpse, but in the abstract, apart from whatever it is that makes it alive. What brings it to life is precisely the *psyché* or "soul," and that is the "first actuality" of a body with organs.

He then clarifies this definition by comparing the sleeping and the waking organism. The sleeping state is the first actuality of the living body, and the waking state is the second or full actuality of the organism. He makes an analogy with an axe and with an eye. An axe has a certain shape and composition that enables it to cut, just as an eye has a certain structure that enables it to see. This structure or shape is the first actuality, and the cutting or seeing is the second or full actuality. He concludes: "The waking state is actuality in the same sense as the cutting and the seeing; the soul is actuality in the same sense as the power of vision or of cutting."[5] In other words, the "first actuality" of an organism or its "soul" is what keeps it alive during its sleeping state, *the primary set of processes by which the organism maintains its existence*. In the twentieth century, with our far more detailed knowledge of physiology, we speak of the autonomic nervous system and the centers in the brain that control it: the cerebral cortex, the hypothalamus, and the medulla oblongata. These keep the heart beating and the lungs breathing and maintain other vital signs. The maintenance of vital processes is often called *homeostasis*. The question remains whether these processes comprise a kind of Gestalt that functions as a substantial unity, or whether they simply are a set of reflexes, a biological machine.

In the *Metaphysics*, Aristotle equates unity and substantial being. Since the soul is the *ousía,* or substantial being, of a living organism, it must be a unity as well.[6] But he gives no specific argument or other direct evidence for the unity of the soul as such. What he does provide is an argument for the unity of *mind*, the highest power of the soul.

But will the argument for the unity of mind shed light on the question of the unity of the soul? In Aristotle's account they clearly are related. "Soul" is an overarching concept encompassing a variety of interconnected powers. To begin with, all organisms have the ability to take in food, grow, and reproduce. This set of powers Aristotle groups under the heading of "nutritive" or "vegetative" soul. In addition, many organisms have the power of sense-perception and self-movement. They have "animal" soul. Man, the *logikòn zôon*, the animal with reason, has "rational" soul. This does not mean that man has three souls, but simply that human beings have these three sets of powers. This conception is different from that of Descartes, Kant, and other modern writers, for whom the body is a machine governed by the laws of physics, in which, somehow, the mind dwells. For modern dualists it is difficult, if not impossible, to explain how the mind interacts with the body. However, it is not a problem for Aristotle. Our power to think is naturally connected to our other biological powers.

Since soul and mind are closely related, we can expect them to shed light on each other. Since we seem to have reached an impasse in deciding whether or not the "soul" really exists, I will consider what Aristotle has to say about the unity of mind and the mind's other properties, and then reconsider the question of the soul in light of what has been established about the mind.

The four basic components of Aristotle's concept of mind and consciousness are 1) the unity of mind, 2) the blank tablet, 3) the formal identity of the mind with its objects, and 4) the mind as a form of forms, together with the concept of *epagogé* or induction. They are stated in Book III of the *De Anima*, except for *epagogé*, which is treated in the *Posterior Analytics*.[7]

The unity of mind is the foundation of the whole Aristotelian psychology. It plays the same role there as the transcendental unity of the apperceptions does in Kant's epistemology and the *Cogito* in Descartes'. Here I will simply summarize the argument. Readers who wish to follow it in more detail may consult the Appendix.

In Greek the key proposition of the argument runs: *deî dè tò hèn légein hóti héteron* (it is necessary for one [thing] to say that [any two other things are] different).[8] In other words, for the mind to distinguish any two or more items it is thinking about, it itself must be a unity. The individual ideas cannot distinguish or compare themselves. Furthermore, if the mind thinks them separately and doesn't combine them, how can it compare them? It has to be a unity both in order to distinguish them and in order to combine them. Otherwise, its operations become unintelligible. Indeed, it cannot exist.

At the same time, the mind cannot be identical with any particular item that it thinks. While it has the capacity to perceive and to think an enormous number of things, it cannot be permanently identified with any one of them because it then would lose its ability to think the others. Aristotle likens it to "a tablet on which nothing is actually written."[9] This is the famous doctrine of the mind as a blank tablet. If it seems too metaphorical, think of it in more modern terms as the cerebral cortex without any mental activity occurring.

But if the mind is a blank tablet, even if it is a unity, how can it exist all by itself? It needs something to perceive or think about in order to exist. As Aristotle says, the mind is nothing until it thinks.[10] Thus, the mind cannot be conscious of itself without being conscious of some object. In a way it becomes identical with it.[11] On the other hand, if it is totally focused on the object, it enters a hypnotic state and falls asleep. It must constantly withdraw itself, so to speak, from the object in order to become conscious of it. At the same time, in unifying and distinguishing its various objects, the mind becomes aware of itself performing this activity. This is entirely natural because the mind per se is nothing but an abstract unity. How could it be aware of its objects and not be aware of itself? Consciousness, in order to exist, must constantly move from one object to another while distinguishing itself from all of them.

To be sure, there is no reason why all mental activity has to be conscious. Clearly, a good deal of our thinking takes place below the level of consciousness. Our minds could not perform their normal functions without the aid of unconscious mental processes. However, the unconscious processes – at least the ones associated with our everyday mental activity – are under the control of conscious mind, and unconscious thinking seems to have all the characteristics of conscious thought, except of course consciousness. In the next section, I shall consider the nature of unconscious thought and its relation to conscious thought.

It is important to understand that the blank tablet is a limiting concept. So long as we are alive, the tablet never is completely blank. The mind is always working, at least a little bit, even when we are asleep. On the other hand, the tablet never becomes 100 percent full. It is always partly blank. The mind becomes formally identical or identical in form with the various things it thinks and perceives, but not completely. This is true of consciousness from moment to moment and also speaking more broadly. In a real sense, we become the things we know; the musician becomes his music, the artist becomes his art, and so on.[12] We see the world through the lens of what we know and from the perspective of our experience, but this is not an absolute identity. The mind remains distinct. As long as we are alive and conscious, we retain the ability to have fresh experiences.

We can understand the foregoing even better when we consider the last basic element in Aristotle's concept of mind, the mind as a "form of forms." In the passage containing this definition, he uses the word "soul," but it is clear from the context that he means its highest power, mind. I will translate so that the voice of the speaker comes through loud and clear:

> "So the soul is just like the hand; shit, man [kaì gár], the hand is a tool of tools, and the mind is a form of forms, and sense-perception is the form of perceived objects."[13]

This may sound as if Aristotle is talking in riddles, but in fact he is making a brilliant analogy. As frequently occurs in his writings, the passage is highly condensed, and it repays the effort to unpack it. First of all, what does he mean by saying "the hand is a tool of tools"? This is partly a play on words. The word for "tool," órganon, also means "organ." If we overlook the double meaning, we lose the analogy: The hand qua organ of the body is a tool belonging to the mind. The mind operates the hand, and by means of the hand, it makes and uses other tools.

That is clear enough, but what does he mean by calling the mind a "form of forms"? To understand this, we have to start with sense-perception. When we perceive objects by means of our senses, we do not have the objects themselves in our sense organs, but only their form. We recognize physical objects and distinguish them from each other by their sensory form. (Aristotle uses the word eîdos, which literally means the *visual form* or shape of an object, to refer to the perceptions of all five senses.) This means that sense-perception itself is low-level thinking. The process continues when we give names to the things we perceive, thereby putting them into categories, analyzing, and defining them, etc. Now we really are thinking because we are on a higher level of abstraction than mere sense-perception.

In other words, the expression "a form of forms" implies a scale of perception and thought, from the lowest to the highest level. We proceed by abstraction from one level to the next. Each level is more abstract than the one before it. At the highest level is mind. But mind, as we just saw, abstracts itself from any given set of perceptions. Thus, the mind itself is a kind of abstraction, a "form of forms." It has no specific content. Its only characteristic, its empty unity, is precisely what enables the mind to perform all its wondrous operations. Far from being a defect, this is its great virtue because it can become identical in form with whatever it knows and perceives, and yet through all the vicissitudes of experience, it retains its integrity, its unity and substantiality. Thus, we have a self-identity that persists through time.

To be sure, each of us is intimately associated with his or her memories. Certain memories define us more fully than others because they are more deeply rooted in our personalities. To a considerable extent, we are defined by our experience, yet we retain a capacity to rise above it.

The *scala naturae* or ladder of nature that is implied in the "form of forms" passage is made explicit in another key passage in Aristotle's writings, in which several other important concepts are introduced that shed light on the nature of mind:

> [All animals] have an innate power of discrimination, which is called sense-perception. While sense-perception is present [in all animals], in some it persists, and in some it does not. . . . Those in whom it does persist retain it in the soul. If this happens often, already a distinction arises, so that in some reason comes into being from the persistence of the perceptions, and in others [it does] not. Thus from sense-perception arises memory . . . and when the same thing occurs often [we have] experience; for the memories, while many in number, comprise one experience. And from experience – or the universal when it has quite come to rest in the soul, the One alongside the Many, the one and the same thing that is present in them all – [comes] the starting point of art and science; in regard to [things that] come to be [and pass away], of art; in regard to facts, of science. Thus these are neither innate, determinate mental states, nor do they arise from other, more highly developed mental states, but from sense perception, just as in battle, after an army has been put to flight, when one man stops, another stops, then another, until [the army] returns [to what it was] at the outset [*i.e.*, until the original formation is restored]. The soul is so constituted that it can undergo this [process].
>
> What was just said was not said precisely, so let's say it again. As soon as one of the individual percepts has come to a halt, the universal

> is first present in the soul (shit, man, it perceives the particular thing, but the perception is of the *universal*, for example, "man," not "a man, Kallias"); again [and again] [one or another] among these [percepts] stops, until the indivisible [categories] and the [ultimate] universals are established: for example, a particular species of animal [and on] until [the genus] "animal" [is there], and so on. It's clear then that we must know the primary [premises] by induction, because, fuck it, sense-perception introduces the universal in this way.[14]

Is nothing sacred! Perhaps the reader is shocked at my language, as if I had mistaken Aristotle for Aristophanes. Imagine translating the entire corpus this way, using expletives or other equally emphatic up-to-date expressions every time Aristotle says *kaì gár* or *gár*. It would make a rousing translation many a hesitant reader would be unafraid to try. We could call it *The Unexpurgated Aristotle*. Some scholars would have fits, but these are not holy texts that are being profaned. I am simply letting the voice of the speaker come through to us across two and a half millennia.

The foregoing passage is in the final chapter of Aristotle's treatise on the nature of science, *The Posterior Analytics*. He is asking where the axioms and presuppositions that underlie science come from. They arise from sense-perception, which we share with the other animals. In explaining how this occurs, he provides a biologically based scale of intelligence from the ground up. All animals have the capacity to receive sense-impressions, but we humans can manipulate the perceptions that come to us through our senses and recreate the world in our minds. To borrow a line from Goethe, *Im Innern ist ein Universum auch* (there is also a universe within you). The outcome of this inner creativity is art and science. Each increase in mental power that Aristotle describes presupposes a corresponding increase in "wiring," as we would say today. We are free to update his primitive anatomy and physiology to supply what he lacks in those areas, but on the other hand, his conception of the nature and development of the mind is superior to our own.

The passage just quoted not only presupposes what was said earlier about the nature of the mind, but it adds some further points. The metaphor or analogy of the army in rout is what nowadays is called Gestalt psychology. Aristotle's version of it is much more inclusive than the modern one because it goes beyond mere sense-perception to the action of the mind.

Equally important is the concept of "induction" or *epagogé* mentioned at the end of the passage. Normally, the word "induction" means generalizing from particulars. *Epagogé* (pronounced "ep-a-go-géh") includes that and more. It operates from the lowest levels of intelligence to the highest and explains why the mind is a "form of forms": The mind "induces" itself as a unitary blank tablet from the perceptions. Presumably, mind exists at all levels but is hard to recognize at the very lowest ones because it is so limited. On our level, it is much more highly developed because we have more wiring, *i.e.*, more association neurons, to support it.

This completes my account of the elements of Aristotle's concept of mind. It is worth pausing for a moment to compare his view of mind and consciousness with that of Hume, cited in Chapter 5: "I can never catch myself without a perception; therefore, I am nothing but the perceptions." Even though the mind cannot think without a mental image derived from the senses – Aristotle and Hume agree on this point – it still must be something distinct from the mental images. Otherwise, it is unintelligible. How can one perception be conscious of another? Or how can a stream of perceptions be conscious of anything? What is the "I" Hume is talking about that is doing the catching?

In describing the mind as an empty unity, a blank tablet, a form of forms, Aristotle may at first seem to be mouthing meaningless abstractions. It turns out he is giving a rational account of the human mind. His explanation is no more abstract than the concepts of mathematics or the laws of chemistry and physics. Why should the mind that can discover and understand the latter be any less grand than they?

C. Conscious and Unconscious Thought

While Aristotle wrote two short treatises on dreams, and speaks of dreamlike behavior in one important chapter of the *Nicomachean Ethics*, his writings have nothing specifically to say about unconscious thought and its relationship to conscious thought.[15] Nevertheless, the existence of unconscious thought is strongly implied by his account of mind and its operations. Hence, what follows is an extrapolation both from the texts and from the development of them I already have made. Since habit is one of Aristotle's key concepts and habitual activity obviously crosses the threshold of the unconscious, that is a good place to begin.

Much of our activity and behavior is habitual, containing many individual actions that are performed without our being specifically conscious of what we are doing. For example, in typing, as I am doing now, I am conscious of moving my fingers, but I am not aware of every single letter as I type. I have a Gestalt, an overall view of the keyboard before my mind, and because it is so familiar, I don't have to focus on the individual letters. To say it in Aristotelian lingo, I am formally identical with the keyboard. A part of my blank tablet is taken up with this Gestalt. My mind is, so to speak, doing it for me. Yet there is no question that the movement of my fingers over the keys is under my voluntary control.

In short, a boundary exists between conscious activities and those just below the surface of consciousness, one we constantly cross. The most dramatic example of this movement is provided by language. As noted in the third paragraph of this chapter, we don't know exactly what we are going to say until we have said it, but we certainly do have an intuitive idea of what we are going to say. A large part of that intuition seems to be of linguistic material that is subliminal, below the threshold of consciousness but nevertheless under our conscious control.

How can we explain this unconscious activity and relate it to the characteristics of mind already described? One way is to think of it in terms of the energy needed at different levels of functioning. There is only so much energy available to the mind from the nervous system. Much of it is required for the mind to be conscious of itself. What the mind gains in self-consciousness, it loses in operating power, and vice versa. In the conscious state, the mind is keenly aware not only of itself, but of what it is doing. When it wants to scrutinize something, it shines the light of consciousness on it and examines every nook and cranny. But when it wants to perform a series of rapid operations – linguistic, mathematical, musical, athletic, or whatever – it has to give up most of its self-awareness. Playing a musical instrument provides a particularly good example of this process. When we play a piece from memory, it almost seems as if there is a direct connection between our unconscious mind and our fingers, but in fact we are not human tape recorders or player pianos. We do not temporarily become robots. The voluntary control may be largely subliminal, but it *is* voluntary control. We still have to concentrate on what we are doing, even if we cannot observe the connection between our intuition and the movements of our fingers.

Would we be better off if we were more aware of the subliminal processing? Surely we would not want to clutter our consciousness with irrelevant details. However, the ability to hold an extraordinary number of the more interesting details before consciousness is a sign of genius. Doubtless the Mozarts and Einsteins of this world have such an ability.

At the beginning of the Sixth Meditation, Descartes observes that not only can we *think* of the concept of a triangle, we can hold an image of it before our minds, but we cannot visualize a chiliagon or thousand-sided polygon. While it is unlikely the mind can do the last-named even subliminally, it can – presumably – hold more complex figures before itself and do more complex calculations in that state than it can consciously do, and thus we accomplish much of our thinking.

This raises a further question. If thought does not need to be conscious, can living creatures exist entirely without consciousness? The answer clearly is yes. Plants do not have it (it would be a big surprise to learn that they do). On the other hand, animals, by virtue of having sense perception, do have it. Even when it is rudimentary, as in the case of insects, it still is consciousness.

Granted that it is problematical to call the reactivity of one-celled organisms rudimentary consciousness. Still, whatever the precise level of complexity at which consciousness recognizably emerges, relatively low on the scale of animal life it is there. Moreover, it seems that unconscious thought exists for the sake of conscious thought. Since animals have the power not only of sense-perception, but of self-movement, they could not decide how to move their bodies if they lacked consciousness. Even in a Hobbesian deterministic world, where one desire overcomes another without benefit of the unity of mind, if the desires were not conscious, they would not be desires. Consciousness, then, is the highest power of mind, and it goes hand in hand with unconscious thought. The more a creature has of one, the more it seems to have of the other. We need the ability to screen out distracting details, an ability that unconscious thought supplies.

Granting the existence and the importance of unconscious thought, we still must ask, how extensive is it and how deep does it go? If it is possible in the first place, why should it not extend itself beyond subliminal cooperation with conscious activities? The mere fact of dreaming is evidence that this is so. Even though dreaming is a form of consciousness, it occurs while we are unconscious and presupposes what Freud calls "dream-work," *i.e.*, creative subconscious activity, to produce it.

Besides Freud, the nineteenth century Romantic writers believed in the creativity of the unconscious, and Freud can be considered part of that tradition. While Aristotle is not regarded as a Romantic, at least his ideas imply a significant role for the unconscious mind. Moreover, both Aristotle and Freud had a high regard for Sophocles' tragedy, *Oedipus the King*. As in the case of the characters in Sophocles' play, an idea can take a long time to develop and surface. It may be repressed or it may simply be inchoate. One does not have to accept the whole Freudian theory of the unconscious to believe that profound thinking can occur subconsciously. We do not know how deeply subconscious thinking goes or how much it influences our conscious experience. In this regard, consider what Aristotle has to say about the forces that most profoundly shape us:

> But suppose someone says, "Everybody strives for what seems good to them, and they are not masters of their own imagination [*i.e.*, they cannot control how things seem to them], but [depending on] what sort of person each one is, so his goal [in life] appears to him. If therefore each person is responsible for his own character, he will in a sense also be responsible for his imagination [for what appears to him to be good]; if not, no one will be responsible for doing evil things, but will do these things through ignorance of the [proper] end, thinking he will obtain the greatest good through them. However, the end [in life] he aims at is not of his own choosing, but he must be born having, as it were, vision, whereby he judges well and will choose what is truly good; he is well-endowed by nature who is well-endowed in this. For the greatest and noblest thing, that one cannot obtain or learn from another, but is something one has by nature, such a thing he will have; and to be well and nobly endowed by nature in this respect is to be well endowed in the full and true sense of the word."[16]

The thing that most influences our character is a kind of vision that goes to the very depth of our being. We do not know where or how we acquired it. What we do know is that each of our personalities is largely formed early in life. The buried experiences that formed it are lost to memory. It is something we do not choose.

However, this hardly means we are helpless in its grasp. Precisely because it is largely buried and highly intuitive, we must heed the injunction of the Delphic oracle, *Gnôthi seautón*, Know thyself. Nor is there any set way to achieve self-knowledge. It is not necessarily a matter of lying on a psychoanalyst's couch and free-associating in an effort to dredge up one's hidden self. Of course we need to be reflective and self-aware, but in addition, our true being comes out in the fullness of experience, whatever that may be for each of us. Self-knowledge may come from combining thought and action. Thus, we must be careful in interpreting Aristotle's statement that the *bíos theoretikós* is the highest kind of life. While this phrase usually is translated as the speculative or contemplative life, I suspect that he means something more than merely the life of the scholar or scientist, and that it includes a life of action. The motto of the Jesuits, *In actione, contemplatio* (In action, contemplation), expresses, I think, its essence. We do not know under what circumstances the highest level of self-knowledge may be achieved, and so we must keep our minds open to new possibilities. Normally we can expect that greater self-knowledge will improve our behavior and increase our chances for happiness.

One further issue should be addressed before concluding this section. Modern science has often raised the possibility that our personalities and behavior may be strongly influenced by our genetic make-up. While individual humans obviously differ in their physical endowments, Aristotle is disinclined to believe that any of our ideas or personality traits are directly shaped by heredity. However, he was far too much an empiricist not to change his mind on any issue in light of strong evidence, so let us simply say that the evidence for direct genetic influence would have to be very strong to convince him.

D. The Conscious Operations of the Mind

Once we have a general idea of the way in which the activities of the conscious mind depend on subliminal or unconscious processing, we can go on to consider key human functions like the creation and use of language, which depend very much on what is occurring below the surface. I now will briefly describe our use of mental imagery, spatial organization ("mental space"), and categories to create an array of symbolic abstractions, of which the most important is verbal discourse. Language, as we shall see, is the product of a kind of collective genius.

Not everyone has a high opinion of mental imagery. Plato, for example, wanted to escape the world of the senses, and doing so meant, among other things, learning to think without mental images or phantasms. Like Plato, Aristotle believed that the mind elevates us above mere sense-perception, but he denied that imageless thought is possible, and so did the British empiricists long after him. Both assert that we cannot think without using mental images derived from our senses. However, Aristotle understood these phantasms differently from the way the British did. To him they are much more than "decaying sense" (in Hobbes' phrase), or "weak ideas" (in Hume's). Looked at merely as mental images, and compared to the strength of the perceptions from which they are derived, they are indeed weak, but at the same time, they represent *ideas*. These seemingly weak mental phantasms are *symbols* that stand for abstractions, and as such they are very powerful. As Aristotle puts it, "the abstractions are [contained] in the sensible forms."[17] We human beings live in a world of symbols and abstractions. Through our ability to create and use language, our inner world of mental images is expressed and developed. With this ability, we go on to reshape the world around us.

As Chomsky reminded us, language and mind are closely related. A theory of mind has to explain language, and a theory of language must equally concern itself with the phenomena of mind. Moreover, verbal language is not our only mode of symbolic expression. There is the language of art, of music, of mathematics. These too depend on and reflect the nature of the mind.

Our mental activity is a flow of phantasms, and it is not necessarily dream-like. There is a certain amount of free play, but in general it is highly ordered. Our particular human ability is to combine the mental phantasms and pack a lot into them. In explaining this ability, Aristotle distinguishes between what he calls the sensory imagination (*aisthetiké phantasía*), which we share with the other animals, and the deliberative imagination (*bouleutiké phantasía*), which we alone have – so far as we know:

> Sensory imagination . . . is present in the other animals, but deliberative imagination in those that have reason; whether [someone] shall do this or that is already a matter of calculation; and it is necessary to measure by one [standard], for he pursues the greater [good]. Therefore he can make one image out of many.[18]

The key statement in the foregoing passage is *hóste dúnatai hèn ek pleiónon phantasmáton poieîn*: So [the animal with reason] can make one image out of many. The complex images that we fashion are the engines that drive our thinking.

An excellent example of this phenomenon on a very high level can be found in Mozart's description of the way in which he composed music:

> [P]rovided I am not disturbed, my subject enlarges itself, becomes methodised and defined, and the whole, though it be long, stands almost complete and finished in my mind, so that I can survey it, like a fine piece or a beautiful statue, at a glance. Nor do I hear in my imagination the parts *successively*, but I hear them, as it were all at once

(*gleich alles zusammen*). What a delight this is I cannot tell! All this inventing, this producing, takes place in a pleasing, lively dream. Still the actual hearing of the *tout ensemble* is after all the best. What has been thus produced I do not easily forget, and this is perhaps the best gift I have my Divine Maker to thank for.

When I proceed to write down my ideas, I take out of the bag of my memory, if I may use that phrase, what has been previously collected into it in the way I have mentioned. For this reason the committing to paper is done quickly enough, for everything is, as I said before, already finished; and it rarely differs on paper from what it was in my imagination.[19]

This is an example on the level of genius of what we do all the time. Genius is ordinary human ability writ large, and we can glean from Mozart's description of the creative process details of the power of the mind to combine many phantasms into one and then break them down again.

Note the difference between this ability and animal intelligence: Animals tend to be very literal-minded and territorial, marking off specific areas as their territory and finding their way around within it. Humans, by contrast, create symbols, and use them to reshape the objects they encounter and reorganize the world in which they live.

Besides using mental images as symbols, human beings arrange them relative to each other in what can be called "mental space." Consider Aristotle's analogy, cited earlier, between an army re-forming itself after being routed and the way we organize our perceptions. We not only group images together, but we do it in a *Gestalt* (shape, form, pattern) within a mental field. In the ancient world and in the Renaissance, when people did not have the conveniences of modern technology to make them lazy, they were much more aware than we are today of the spatial manner in which the mind organizes information. An "art of memory" existed, in which people who wanted to memorize speeches or other material broke it down into little portions which they associated with locations within buildings that were very familiar to them.

The fact that such an art could exist and flourish suggests that our minds organize data in spatial form. By this means, we have a large capacity to store and retrieve information. While compared to computers, our storage capacity is not very great, we have it all over them in our ability to recombine and reshape the contents of our minds.

Together with a) combining mental images and b) organizing them in mental space, we are able c) to categorize information and arrange it into hierarchies. These three abilities make it possible for us to create, acquire, and use language. They explain the marvel of language that I spoke of at the beginning of the chapter.

Behaviorists like the late B. F. Skinner maintain that language is just "verbal behavior," a disorganized collection of habits developed by "operant conditioning." Dennett describes language as resulting from a "pandemonium" in the neurons. We are "hard-wired," he says, to produce it the way beavers are hard-wired to build dams – it is just instinctive behavior.[20] These people are dead wrong. Of course our brains and our speech organs are constructed in such a way that we can produce human speech. Yet at the same time a language operates by means of a system of categories and a memory system. In order to see this, we have to look at it more broadly than contemporary linguistics, with the partial exception of Chomsky, is willing to do. Aristotle does look at it in this way. He can help us not only to appreciate its ingenuity, but also to learn it faster and use it better than we now can do. As is the case with other areas of research, Aristotle's ideas about language fit hand in glove with the best of twentieth-century linguistics. He adds a dimension – maybe more than one – that contemporary linguistics simply lacks.

Discourse results not from a "pandemonium" in our brains, but from our intuitive grasp of the structure of whatever language we are thinking in, combined with our intuition of the situation we are focusing on. This is like the process of thinking described by Aristotle and Mozart. The "seeing everything at once," the complex image that Mozart speaks of is already highly organized! He simply unpacks it. Similarly, the *combination* of the complex images comprising our language together with our intuition of whatever we wish to talk about is linguistically organized. We *perceive* it in a certain syntactical order. This is easy to demonstrate if we compare, say, the syntactical patterns of Japanese and English, which contrast strongly. The arrangement of *words* represents patterns of *perception* or *thought*.[21] In short, whether it is Mozart composing music, Einstein thinking about physics, or ordinary folk engaging in everyday discourse, our minds have the intuitive capacity to combine discrete items of information into a whole and then unpack them.

If the complex image or intuition from which we form a sentence is already linguistically organized, then we have a proto-sentence just below the surface that is easy for the mind to convert into a finished sentence. The proto-sentence doesn't actually have to be expressed in discourse in the form of a "deep structure," as Chomsky would say, ready to be transformed into "surface structure." Aristotle's concept of the active intellect, that the mind is identical in form with what it knows and perceives, helps us understand why. The identification of mental images with the words that name them is so strong that the latter are close at hand without the mind having to ransack its own contents to find them. At the same time, the mind has a set of complex images of the grammar of the language. It intuitively unpacks that and turns the proto-sentence into a finished sentence. The whole process occurs quickly because the different components of it are all so closely connected and so intuitively clear.

In trying to comprehend how the mind works, we must beware of assuming that it functions like a computer. While Aristotle knew nothing of that modern-day invention, he certainly did know about calculation, and while the mind performs calculations, it is not primarily a calculating machine. Remember what was said in the last section about the chiliagon and the mind's ability to function more efficiently below the surface of consciousness than above. Intellectual intuition or *noûs* operates on that level as well. The mind is *not* performing a large number of computations to produce the sentences we utter. It operates primarily by means of *noûs*.

While what we say is largely produced subliminally, the emerging discourse clearly is subject to voluntary control. It doesn't come out *against* our will. Indeed, we have an overwhelming sense that what we say is what we intended to say. If occasionally we blurt something out,
it just means that one intention overcame another.

But how do I know that utterance and intention really do correspond? How do I know this isn't just an illusion or that my argument isn't circular? For one thing, most of the people most of the time are not surprised or shocked by what they hear themselves saying. Generally speaking, it seems appropriate to whatever it was they were talking about or doing.

Suppose, however, that a behaviorist like B. F. Skinner or a "cognitive scientist" like Dennett argues that it all happens automatically or haphazardly or by operant conditioning. But the thoughts expressed in speech make sense! They come out *as if* they were rationally planned. So these people are arguing, in effect, that the less rational part of our minds is doing what the more rational part can do much better.

What they really are doing is denigrating both language and mind, denying the rationality of the one and the substantiality of the other. In their view, the production of ordinary speech is no big deal to begin with, so that the processes involved can well require a relatively low level of mental activity. This kind of argument caused Chomsky to blow fuse after fuse in his famous review of Skinner's book *Verbal Behavior*. The Aristotelian objections to it should be clear from what has been said thus far in this chapter as well as from what follows. In light of Aristotle it is easy to rebut such simplistic views of language and mind.

Up to a point, the creativity that goes into a language resembles that of Mozart or Shakespeare – except that it represents the efforts of a group of people rather than one individual. A language is an enormous collective work of art, like the great medieval cathedrals. However, languages dwarf the cathedrals in their complexity and in the thousands or millions of people who contribute to them. The Homers, Virgils, Dantes, Shakespeares, Luthers, and Goethes refine and develop what they find, but what they find is something marvelous in itself.

A language is constructed on the basis of small differences in sound, grammatical form, and meaning. The small differences are able to carry a heavy symbolic load because of the ingenuity that goes into their creation. A language is hierarchically organized so that a relatively small subset of key features organizes large amounts of detail.

What are the key structural elements that we intuit and that enable us to produce coherent speech? First of all, the mind organizes reality into categories, and it appears to work on a fairly high level of generality. I know this because I have compiled a 56,000-word list of the non-technical vocabulary of English, which clearly reveals a pattern of organization resembling Aristotle's ten categories.[22] While the latter are very general, they can be branched downward as far as we wish, and thereby we capture the hierarchical structure of the entire vocabulary of a language. At different times in the history of linguistics people have attempted to do something like this – for example, in the Middle Ages – but Aristotle had the idea way ahead of them.

For practical purposes such as studying a language, the downward branching does not have to be carried very far – only 25–30 categories and subcategories are needed. The reader may be wondering, if so small a number of categories control all the meanings of a language, why do languages have so many thousands (or in some cases millions) of words? The answer is that there are a lot of details to name, a lot of fine distinctions to make. The crucial point, however, is that a set of categories derived from Aristotle's can be used to analyze thoroughly the lexicons of all the languages in the world.

Besides being organized in categories, each language contains a set of key features that form a skeleton of its vocabulary and its grammar. These include rules of word formation (for example, by means of prefixes and suffixes) as well as grammatical endings and syntactical rules. Taken all together, they constitute a memory system. Each language has one; it is unique and ingenious; and finding it is like solving a puzzle. If one then explains it to students, they can use it along with the category system to learn languages much faster than by conventional methods.

With the foregoing, I conclude the discussion of mind and consciousness and will now consider the way in which the mind moves the body.

E. How the Mind Moves Itself and the Body

Even if Aristotle is right about the unity and substantiality of the soul and mind, it still remains to connect his ideas with modern science. This can be accomplished only by giving a satisfactory solution to the mind-body dualism. The Aristotelian theory of soul and mind has to be able to solve that problem. As I am about to show you, it does exactly that.

This problem is famous and perplexing: How is the mind connected to the body, and how does it move the body? Even more to the point, how does a mind that is a substantial unity move the body without violating the Second Law of Thermodynamics? Since he was unfamiliar with the Second Law of Thermodynamics, Aristotle could not answer the last of these questions. Nevertheless, he had to deal with the materialists of his day, and he did consider the relation of mind and body. By explaining his ideas on that question, we will see that they also speak to the doubts raised by modern materialists regarding this one.

On the other hand, if you have a materialist, reductionist view of mind, as Hobbes, for example, does, there is no problem. The mind doesn't *act* on the body because it is *part* of the body. The operations of mind simply obey the laws of physics. The ideas have a certain quantity of *force*, and they influence each other just as bodies in motion do. The stronger ideas overcome the weaker ones – that is, in the literal, physical sense. To a reductionist, psychology becomes a branch of physics. Hobbes' *psychology* is contained in his treatise *De Corpore* (On Body). The behaviorists, following the lead of Watson and Skinner, have similar views, as do Dennett and Churchland and most of the "cognitive scientists."

The issue is more complicated if you are dissatisfied with the simplistic materialist view of mind and do not think mind can be reduced to matter. If at the same time you accept modern science's view of the universe, then you are a dualist like Descartes or Kant and you have to explain how mind and body are related. Descartes actually tried to make the connection, and his solution, via the pineal gland, satisfied nobody but himself. Locke got himself into similar difficulties, as we saw. Spinoza did not succeed by making mind and body two parallel attributes of "God or nature," nor did Leibniz with his pre-established harmony. Kant wisely refrained from trying to solve the problem as such. He understood that given the conceptual materials he had to work with, a solution was impossible. Instead, he produced a complicated framework of preconditions and presuppositions to deal with it that I dubbed "the labyrinth of impure reason."

A large part of "modern philosophy" is just false science, that is, incorrect theorizing that does not give a satisfactory explanation of the very problems it raises. The dilemmas of the seventeenth and eighteenth centuries became the basis for the twentieth-century discipline called "philosophy." This outcome is not surprising, given the rock-solid refusal of "philosophy" professors and scientists to grant the possibility that living processes and mind may be included in science on other than reductionist terms.

The heart of this intransigence is the denial that any rational alternative is even *conceivable*. Not even Aristotle at his most sophisticated will make them budge. How does mind, a "form of forms," a "blank tablet," a substantial unity that is not itself matter, *move matter*? Only matter can move matter! How can the *mind* move the voluntary muscles of the body? Indeed, how can it move itself? Thinking requires electrochemical activity in the central nervous system, just as muscular movement does. Hence, the same problem arises even for thinking!

According to the Second Law of Thermodynamics, bodies at different levels of excitation tend to approach an equilibrium. Thus, water does not run uphill; or if two bodies are in contact, the hotter one does not become hotter and the colder one colder: They reach a temperature somewhere between their initial temperatures. Eventually, this will happen to the entire universe, which will reach a state of *entropy*, or total equilibrium, where no energy will be available to do any kind of work – that is, if nothing interferes with this long-term process.

At first blush, it looks as if mind *qua* substantial unity is doing just what the Second Law of Thermodynamics forbids. It is moving nerve-currents without having any physical source of energy to accomplish the movement. It is "making water run uphill."

We think this because we have all been brought up with the mind-set of the modern period: Form is form and matter is matter, and never the twain shall meet. However, if we shed our inherited prejudices and use a little imagination, we shall see how easily they do meet. Following Aristotle's lead, let us start from the lowest identifiable state, and work upwards. We recall that beginning with the sleeping organism, he defined the *soul* as the primary actuality of a living body, meaning the complex of involuntary processes that keeps the body alive. The soul does this all the time but is easier to identify when the organism is functioning at the minimum level, *i.e.*, when it is asleep. The *full* actuality is the fully functioning organism, for example, a conscious human being performing the various activities that humans perform. The question is, how does the mind get from sleeping to waking? Clearly, its activity is supported by electrochemical processes. The brain has 25 percent of the body's blood supply and a goodly part of its energy, which produces the waking state we call consciousness. If something so fundamental required an effort, the mind would have little energy left over for anything else.

While the waking state occurs spontaneously, it still comprises a mental act, however basic. The energy that constantly is supplied to the cerebral cortex is focused into a unity. But to exactly what mental process does this correspond? Between sleeping and waking there is an intermediate trance-like state that we normally don't linger in but that nevertheless is identifiable. It usually is transitional – for example, as we fall asleep or when we awaken, we are at least momentarily in it. If at any time during the day, we let our thoughts lapse, we can linger in this condition, not focused on anything in particular, but we normally pass from it to the round of thoughts and activities that make up our daily lives. Can it really be that the mind *draws itself* out of this condition and in so doing does not violate the Second Law of Thermodynamics?

That is exactly what I am saying, but the answer requires a further understanding of the nature of the mind. Aristotle observes that thought by itself moves nothing.[23] It has to be accompanied by desire or appetite (*órexis*).[24] He uses the phrases *orektikòs noûs* or *órexis dianoetiké*, desiring mind or intellectualized desire: "Hence, choice is desiring mind or intellectualized desire, and such a principle [of action is] man."[25] In defining choice, these phrases also define the basic action of the mind. Another key sentence that sheds light on this question is the one that begins the *Metaphysics*: *Pántes ánthropoi toû eidénai orégontai phúsei* (all men by nature desire to know).[26] Aristotle's interpretation of the verb "know" is very inclusive, encompassing sense-perception as well as knowledge in the scientific sense. In other words, we human beings have a natural desire to be conscious, to be aware of the world around us, to think about things. The other animals have it too, but as beings possessed of reason, we seem to have it more than they do. Aristotle compares it to the divine, which he conceives of as pure intelligence.[27] Whether or not it truly is an imitation of the divine, it is a very special kind of desire, to be distinguished from the specific needs and desires of our daily lives.

In general, "the object of desire . . . although [itself] unmoved, moves [others] by being thought of or imagined."[28] Thus, as the mind emerges from the trance-like state, its desire to realize itself focuses it into full consciousness. Yet I find it hard to distinguish between imagining myself out of that state, desiring to leave it, and actually doing so. In this instance the object of desire, the desire, and the act of fulfilling it are almost identical, if not identical. The passage from one of these states to the next seems infinitesimally small. Because the mind is so abstract an entity, it is hard to make any distinction between them. The mind simply is realizing its own nature. It is simultaneously being acted upon and acting, and thereby it is moving matter (putting into motion an electrochemical process in the nervous system).

The self-actualization is repeated as the mind expands its horizons, thinking first about one thing, then another. Its initial act of consciousness is the same as or similar to its other acts. Indeed, since it can't think about itself in the abstract, without a perception, the two seem to be equivalent! But perhaps we can distinguish between the desire to know in general and the desire to know some specific thing. Either one may rouse us from the trance-like state. In either case, it is hard to distinguish between the object of thought, the desire to think about it, and the actual thinking about it. In both cases, the mind is acting, but the general case provides the purer example of its self-movement.

In becoming conscious of itself, the mind necessarily is conscious of something else, *and vice versa*. It recovers itself from the specific things it is thinking about. As Aristotle describes it:

> Life is defined for the animals by their capacity for sense-perception and for humans [by their capacity] for sense-perception and thought. . . . It seems then that life in the proper sense of the term is

sense-perception and thought. . . . The one who sees perceives that he sees, and the one who hears that he hears, and the one who walks that he walks, and likewise in all other activities there is something that perceives that we are doing them, so that whenever we perceive, [we perceive that] we perceive, and whenever we think, [we perceive that] we think, and the [perception] that we perceive or think [is the perception] that we exist (for existence [as we saw] is sense-perception or thought) . . .[29]

What do you know! Aristotle anticipated Descartes' *Cogito* by 2,000 years. However, this is part of a theory that is superior to Descartes'. On the one hand, "that part of the soul called the mind . . . doesn't actually exist until it thinks."[30] The blank tablet has to have something written on it. As Hume put it, I can never catch myself without a perception. On the other hand, the mind, both conscious and unconscious, cannot be *reduced to* its thoughts and perceptions. When Hume went one step farther and concluded that we are *nothing but* our thoughts and perceptions, he was mistaken. Knowing and being conscious of anything presupposes self-consciousness because it presupposes distinguishing oneself from the object. Otherwise, the concept of mind and consciousness is unintelligible. The mind could not be conscious; indeed, it could not exist because it would be locked onto some one or more of its ideas – it would fall into a hypnotic state in the true sense of the term. What we normally call a hypnotic state is really a form of sleepwalking.

It should be clear from the foregoing what makes the mind's action free, what keeps it from being machine-like and deterministic: The mind is a unity without any specific content. It is identified in part with what it knows and perceives, but only in part. It is always conscious of itself as something more than any finite perception or set of perceptions. It is constantly abstracting itself from them. The central nervous system has, so to speak, an excess of neurons that enable it to do this. The abstraction is a higher energy state. The energy the mind has *qua* unity is always greater than that of any particular thing it is thinking about, and because the mind is a blank tablet, the extra energy is free, *i.e.*, at the mind's disposal.

In being aware of itself, the mind is aware of other things as well. The tablet is never fully blank. There is always something written on it. When the mind actualizes itself through the desire to know, *i.e.*, when it thinks, the tablet becomes blanker. The stronger the desire to know, the harder it thinks, and the blanker the tablet gets.

When absorbed in various activities, it becomes partially identical in form with them. To the extent that it is under the influence of desire it is passive. If that were all there were to it, we would be zombies, pushed and pulled by desire. But clearly, we are not zombies. Because the mind is conscious of itself as distinct from any activity, it can choose not to do it and stop doing it once it starts. The acts of self-induction and re-absorption go on continuously. The more deeply absorbed in the activity the mind is, the more it draws upon the available energy and the more operations it can perform to further the activity. Yet it remains fully conscious of what it is doing, as the extra energy and the greater concentration produce a heightened awareness.

In understanding this process, we can fully comprehend Aristotle's concept of pleasure, which otherwise might seem obscure. While we can correctly speak of "a sensation of pleasure," the pleasure is *not* the sensation. The latter is a *symptom* of pleasure. Pleasure is the flourishing of the *activity*. Aristotle says that it "completes the activity" like an *epigignómenón ti télos*, a supervening end or goal or perfection, and compares it to the acme of someone in the prime of life.[31] In light of the preceding paragraph, we can see what he means. The mind in a sense becomes the activity, and as the activity is perfected, it also is exalted, as for example when one listens to a beautiful piece of music that is well performed.

We must remember that the unity of mind that is doing all this is not static, but dynamic. Its physical basis is some neural process centering on the cerebral cortex. There should be no more problem about how this can constitute a unity than how 24 frames a second produce a motion picture or a little dot moving 515 times a second across your TV screen creates a picture.

Moreover, the mind's activity occurs within a framework of mental space. The mind imagines a world of space and time and moves around in it. Whether it is retrieving memories from wherever they are stored on the neurons, or holding images before itself, or representing motion to itself, it is all the same fundamental process. Thus, I can mentally draw geometric figures; I can manipulate numbers, words, images; I can call forth memories, listen to music and speeches or compose them, reason, make judgments, in short, perform all the operations the mind is capable of.

Recalling what was said earlier about the role of subliminal processing, we recognize that only a part of mental action is conscious. We have no perception of how we retrieve memories or how we actually perform our mental acts. Look what has to go on in order for us to process speech. Every sentence we utter requires acts of memory and a set of operations that clearly are under our conscious control, but that we are barely aware of. The production of speech is highly intuitive. As noted earlier, what the mind gives up in consciousness, it more than makes up for in power to function.

But consciousness is needed to direct the process, and it would have no motive to do so if it did not enjoy the results. Now we see even more clearly how special consciousness is. It is mind at its acme, mind celebrating itself, an aesthetic property, whereby the mind can appreciate as well as control its own activity.

This section began by mentioning the Second Law of Thermodynamics. Thus far, the explanation has dealt with the mind as a formal entity operating within that law, and I have spoken of the energy involved only in passing. Now we need to look more closely at the mind in *material* terms, that is, as a neurological entity requiring energy in order to act. When the mind thinks about specific things and becomes identical in form with them, it draws on the body's store of available energy. The more it becomes absorbed in them, the more energy it draws – up to the body's limits. In so doing, it takes energy – and mental awareness – from other things. If I am fully absorbed in a piece of music or concentrating intently on a problem in mathematics, I am much less aware that my foot is asleep or my arm is itching. When the mind "goes blank," as it constantly does in moving from idea to idea, it stores up energy and then releases it when it once again thinks about some specific thing – or when it moves the voluntary muscles, a process that resembles thinking.

The analogy that springs to mind in known physical processes is the excitation of an electron in its orbit around the nucleus of an atom and its subsequent movement to a more active orbit; as it loses energy and returns to its original orbit, it releases a photon of electromagnetic energy.

However, we are not talking about electrons but about the free action of a substantial being driven by *orektikòs noûs*. I am trying to draw analogies with known physical mechanisms and processes, but it is uncertain which is the best one or the best type to choose. Perhaps a magnetic or an electromagnetic field is a better model. There too energy is built up based on certain structural characteristics of the field, and under the right conditions it is released.

We do not know the precise nature of the movement that is the physical basis of thinking, whether it is brain waves or nerve currents moving across groups of synapses or something of the sort. Clearly, our minds are not dis-embodied. They have their earthly abode in our nervous systems, and inso-far as they make use of the nervous system, they obey the laws of physics. As Archimedes said, *dós moi poû stô kaì tàn gân kináso* (give me a place to stand and I will move the earth). It is not a question here of moving the earth, but of bringing about small changes in electrochemical activity. The entire electrical output of the human brain would not suffice to light a 60-watt bulb. Something in the central nervous system serves as the *poû stô* (literally, "where I stand"), providing a fulcrum for the mind to initiate mo-tion.

In drawing analogies with physical processes to explain the mind's ac-tion on matter, it may seem I am in danger of being hoist with my own pe-tard and falling into reductionism and materialism. However, remembering what was said at the beginning of this chapter, we can avoid the terminolog-ical confusion that arose when science tried to rid itself of metaphysics. All so-called "material" processes have formal or structural characteristics without which they could not occur. "Matter" is a relative term. If the mind is "a form of forms," its *matter* is the forms (*i.e.*, the mental images) that partly fill up the blank tablet. It is true that those mental images are physical entities just as the mind itself is, but to admit this is *not* to reduce mind to matter, because it still is a combination of form and matter. What makes *this* combination of matter and form different is that it has the special character-istics of mind.

While we have only a vague idea of what the physiology of its action might be, the principle is clear: The mind is a unity, and thus it can act on the body. If we can satisfy ourselves on this point, the main difficulty is re-moved. The unity has a physical representation or analog that serves as the fixed point, the *poû stô*. Some neurological process or other should be discoverable to explain fully the physical details of the mind's action, of which I have given the merest sketch.

Perhaps this all seems too simple a solution to a problem that has befud-dled the best minds for centuries, minds trapped by their materialist and mechanist assumptions. At least it should be clear that in no way does the Aristotelian theory of body and mind contradict the laws of science. It is no more contrary to science that the mind can move the body than that opposite magnetic poles and electric charges attract each other and like poles and charges repel. Whatever transcendent properties mind may ultimately have, it is first of all a part of nature.

It is a little frightening to think of the mind as fully a part of nature, for that means we can take our high technology and study it as we do any other physical phenomenon. By making the connection of mind and body mysterious and incomprehensible, dualism has staved off this confrontation. Still, a moment's thought will banish our apprehension. What could be more familiar to us than our own minds? In our everyday experience we are constantly aware of their interaction with and dependence on the body. Learning the scientific details of this relationship should cause us no greater concern than before. Indeed, increased understanding should enhance our control over it and enrich our experience. For example, the path that Hindu fakirs have trod may be more fully explored and made available to all.

Having explained how the mind causes movement in that part of the body with which it is most closely associated, the nervous system, I have given Aristotle's solution to the mind-body problem. Now it is only a question of extending that explanation to show how it moves the voluntary muscles.

While the precise way the cerebral cortex supports thinking is unknown, the electrochemical process of muscular contraction is well understood, *i.e.*, as it proceeds from the motor nerves to the muscles. An impulse from the former stimulates the actin and myosin filaments of which the muscle fibers are composed, and the fibers contract. The electrical energy in the nerves is not enough to cause the contraction by itself. It triggers the release of the chemical ATP (adenosine triphosphate), which is stored in the muscle fibers and is rich in energy. ATP supplies the energy for the contraction.

But what about the mind that originates the impulse that travels down the motor nerves to the muscles? Here we have to turn to Aristotle. Instead of becoming formally identical with an idea or percept (or set of ideas and percepts), as it does when it is thinking, the mind becomes formally identical with one or more muscles, and thereby causes them to contract.

What does it mean to say that my mind becomes formally identical with my muscles? What is actually happening when I move them? It *feels* as if I am moving my own body. But how far into the body do "I," *i.e.*, the substantial unity of the mind, extend? The cerebral cortex contains the sensori-motor cortex, which is connected to the voluntary muscles. So at least we can say, I am in the cerebral cortex and I extend myself to the muscles via the nerves leading to and from the sensori-motor cortex.

The next question is, am I also located in the muscles? The Aristotelian theory suggests that I am. Note that this contradicts the primitive concept of the mind that prevails among the "philosophers," the "psychologists," the "cognitive scientists," and just about everybody else. But that concept doesn't leave many coherent options. Either I am a homunculus, a little self seated at a sort of console or switchboard in the central nervous system, sending and receiving nerve impulses to and from the rest of the body (the view stemming from Descartes), or else the self is a "pandemonium" of nerve impulses that doesn't have any center (Dennett). Either concept is problematic and self-contradictory, and is only accepted because people cannot think of anything better. Let us put them aside, at least temporarily, and see if Aristotle does not provide a more satisfactory explanation.

Consider once again the idea that the mind is a blank tablet on which nothing is actually written, but which, in order to become aware of itself, has to become temporarily or formally identical with whatever it knows or perceives. What is the thing with which this provisional identity occurs most? Why, one's own body, of course! The mind depends upon the body for its very survival. Thus, while it is an entity distinct from the body, it is intimately connected to it. The cerebral cortex communicates directly with muscles and flesh. The conventional wisdom is, if a motor nerve is stimulated at one end in the cortex, motion will occur at the other end in whatever muscle that nerve is connected to; *therefore*, the self is located in the cortex alone. But that doesn't follow. The mere fact of motor stimulation does not set any boundary for the mind. It is far more plausible to assert that "I" am located wherever there is a direct connection to the cerebral cortex. Thus, when I have a sensation in my sense-receptors, that's really me "out there" in the receptors. "I" am in the brain as well.

When I am conscious, I am always aware of my body, even if I am not concentrating on any particular part of it. The source of this awareness is the continuous impulses occurring both in the sensory and the motor nerves. I may not be concentrating on my limbs, but if one of them loses circulation and "falls asleep," I will notice it. If I totally lose sensation in a limb, I most certainly will notice it. Similarly, by reflex action some of the motor nerves are continually firing in every muscle, causing some of the muscle fibers to contract. The body thereby maintains muscle tone. Even if I am not moving my muscles, they are at the ready, waiting for me to move them. While I am sitting here typing, I might absent-mindedly, with a minimum of thought, move my arm, my shoulder, my back, my toes. Do we really want to say that the contractions of muscle tone are absolutely, positively not "me," and that the half-conscious movements I make *are* me? One set of contractions of the same muscle fibers is not me, and another set *is* me. That is cutting the mind-body dualism awfully fine. How close to the cortex does the reflex arc have to go before the movement is done by me?

All this is what "the formal identity with the body" boils down to in physiological terms. Then there is the mental side, with which modern science also does not know how to deal. Those who insist on the homunculus theory have to explain why the sensations appear to be "out there" in the body, but really are in the brain. If the pain I have in my foot is really in my head, why do I grab my foot and not my head? This is a silly notion, and is easy to dispense with when we see how sensible is the Aristotelian view.[32]

Besides the problem of the apparent *location* of the sense-perceptions, there is the question of their *nature*. In Chapter 5, I criticized Locke's arbitrary distinction between primary and secondary qualities and substituted the Aristotelian view that our sense-perceptions really do resemble their objects. The specialized receptors in our sense-organs by means of which we perceive hardness and softness, heat and cold, color, light and darkness, sound, taste, and smell are so structured as to capture these qualities of the objects. If sense-perception is not occurring *in the sense-organs*, but in the brain, we have to explain how a set of electrical impulses convey those qualities rather than the receptors themselves. If there were no alternative to the dualistic homunculus theory of perception, that would be one thing. But in fact, Aristotle provides us with a theory that not only is more coherent and more comprehensive, but also much more plausible. Furthermore, if the mind is located in the receptors and the motor nerves as well as in the brain, it is much easier to see how it moves the body.

To sum up the explanation thus far of how the mind moves the muscles: The most persistent formal identity each of us has is with our own bodies. Each of us is "out there" in the sense organs as well as in the brain. We move the muscles by a process that is essentially the same as thinking. As we imagine the action we are about to perform, we begin concentrating on the muscles, increasing their tone (*i.e.*, the number of fibers contracting), thereby tensing the muscles preparatory to moving them.

This model also helps us understand greater and lesser physical exertion. I imagine myself lying on a weight bench, about to press a barbell. Before I move the weight from the stanchions, I concentrate on what I am about to do, tensing the muscles I am about to use. I cannot feel the individual muscle fibers contracting, but I can feel the overall effect. The neurons are triggering the ATP, which is providing the energy for nearly all of the physical work. I say "*nearly* all of the physical work" because the mind, by concentrating on the muscles, is doing a small, but critical portion of it. Of course the mind doesn't move the body all by itself. It has the adenosine triphosphate and the muscle fibers to help it. Or as Aristotle puts it, "That a little change occurring at a source [of motion] causes many great differences far away is not hard to see, just as when a rudder shifts momentarily, a great shift occurs in the prow."[33] It *feels* as if I am doing all the work, but that is because I am formally identical with what I perceive in the sense-receptors. Part of me also is located there, so I perceive what I am doing.

This whole action requires most of my concentration, especially if it is strenuous. It is hard to think about Einstein's theory while you are pressing a heavy weight, and vice versa. (Somewhere in his writings Aristotle remarks drily that it is hard to think about philosophy when you are making love.) You have to concentrate to keep the muscles contracting even as the ATP is consumed and waste products build up, causing you to feel tired and making your formal identification with this part of your body more difficult. In strenuous exertion, we come close to using up all the available energy.

In talking about the mind being "out there" in the body moving our limbs, we ought not to forget the speech organs. They are very much a part of the body, but they are, as it were, much closer to home, and we are "wired" for talking a lot more than for the use of our limbs. Speech comes to us so naturally and is so closely associated with thought that we tend to forget it includes a complicated set of *physical* acts. The fact that we so readily gloss over this aspect of the mind's relationship to the body shows once again the inadequacy of "modern philosophy."

Exactly how the parts of the self that are spread out over the body communicate via the nervous system is a problem for further research, but at least we can grasp the basic idea of how the mind moves the voluntary muscles.

It may at first be hard to conceive that the mind, something that seems completely immaterial, can move the body, but Aristotle helps us overcome this difficulty. The *psyché* or "soul" is the form or primary actuality of an organism, "and the body is that which exists potentially."[34] In other words, a dead hand or leg or a dead body are only limbs or a body in an ambiguous sense. Until they are alive and functioning, they are not really a hand or a limb or a body.[35] The "soul" *is* the life of the body, the substantial unity that makes the body truly a body, and *mind is its highest power*. The mind, a form of forms, moves the hand, a tool of tools. It is no more strange that the mind moves the body than that the body is alive in the first place.

By casting off the blinders of dualism we have been able to discover a solution to this problem that vexed the "modern philosophers" as well as many others in the modern period. A careful comparison of Aristotle and the moderns makes the superiority of his psychology and epistemology manifest. We see how much science knows about the interaction of nerve and muscle while it knows almost nothing about the mind that operates along the nerve pathways to move the muscles. It is like a great superhighway that suddenly stops dead in the middle of nowhere halfway to its destination. This alone should lead us to take seriously the solution that Aristotle offers.

In the end, we should be able to rid ourselves of dualistic thinking and feel comfortable with the idea that mind is constantly acting, moving the body and thinking, and that all this occurs within the framework of science. We are essentially minds that exist in bodies, and the universe is something that has mind in it. Aristotle tells us that all living creatures imitate the immortal and divine in whatever way they can. Our rational powers bring us closer to pure intelligence than those of the other animals, yet the use we make of them is flawed and limited. When we understand the true nature of mind, and see how much it is influenced by the body and distracted by things alien to its nature, we can more readily grasp that it moves the body, and often for ill rather than for good.

F. The Mind and Ethical Behavior

Strenuous physical exercise provides dramatic examples of the mind acting on the body. But what about more mundane, everyday activities? In such cases, people don't use all or nearly all of the available energy. It is easier to go to bed when you feel tired than stay up most of the night and work, even though you would like to and know that you should. In these circumstances, a process of deliberation occurs – however brief it may be – before you decide to yield to the feeling of fatigue.

All movement that the mind initiates is by definition voluntary or free, but it may or may not be preceded by deliberation. Many bodily movements occur without hesitation, and we perform many of our daily activities with little or no reflection. Nevertheless, we are continually making decisions, large and small, and these require deliberation. Indeed, it often occurs where we might not expect it. When instant decisions have to be made, the process may be greatly accelerated. For example, I once listened to a police officer in New York describe shooting a burglar whom he came upon in a store or warehouse. The man had his back to the officer, who called to him loudly. The burglar turned around suddenly, pointing a revolver at the policeman, who fired all the shots in his own pistol, killing him. Later there was a hearing, and the attorney conducting it asked the officer, "Why did you fire six shots at the suspect? Wouldn't one or two have been enough?" The officer replied, "If I had had nine bullets in my revolver, I would have fired all nine. You had two weeks to think of that question. I had two seconds to decide what to do." He said he almost got in trouble for that answer.

In the two seconds, or whatever it was, between the time the suspect turned around and the officer discharged his entire revolver, did no deliberation take place? In answering this question, we should not mistake the noun "deliberation" for the adjective and the verb "deliberate," which have a connotation of proceeding slowly. The noun is more general, and includes any process of reasoning with regard to acting or refraining from action. In this instance, the decision had to be made very quickly, but it was a rational decision. Our minds can operate very rapidly when necessary.

During the period when I was in graduate school, I drove a taxi in New York and Denver and was held up three times. The first time the robbers had a switchblade; the second time I was shot at, and the third time, I was assaulted. These incidents happened more than thirty years ago, but I remember each of them vividly. On each occasion, I had to make very quick decisions, and the speed in no way detracted from their rationality. In fact, the exigency of the situation increased rather than diminished my acuity. There is no question that deliberation occurred. One of the clearest things I remember is what was going through my mind.

Some decisions are made in a very brief time. Others may occur after years of hesitation and indecision. Most are somewhere in between. In any event, free will does not mean arbitrary or chaotic action. This is true in all the various situations of our conscious lives, strenuous, stressful, or mundane. Although we do not always act rationally, we act for a reason, even if it is not a good one. Actions do not happen gratuitously. It may be impossible to know with total certainty what our motive is for any given action, but usually we can be fairly certain of it. It is not as if some mysterious outside force were moving us for which we cannot account. Most of the people most of the time wake up in the morning with a pretty good idea of the things they are going to do during the day and why they are doing them. Our lives are filled with a great variety of major and minor needs and goals.

It also is true that many of our actions are performed from habit. We normally think of a habit as an action done repeatedly and without reflection, but it is more than that. A habit is a *predisposition* not only to behave in a certain way but to view a given thing or situation in a particular way. Behavior follows from the mental state and conversely, by repeating the behavior, we can induce the mental state. Nevertheless, it is the latter that is paramount.

A habit in the proper sense of the term is more than a conditioned reflex. Even when our behavior is dominated by the most deeply engrained habits, we are not automatons. Nor is somebody twisting our arms or applying hot irons to our flesh. We still are conscious of what we are doing, and we can change our behavior, although often it requires great effort. To express this inclusive conception, Aristotle uses the word *héxis*, which is derived from the Greek verb meaning "have," just as the English "habit" is derived from the Latin verb "to have," *habere*. *Héxis* means a state of mind, a predisposition either to think or to act, a habit of behavior or a habit of thought.[36]

There are good and bad habits. Our virtues and vices are good and bad habits, respectively. Aristotle defines moral virtue as a *héxis prohairetiké*, a state of mind or predisposition or habit with respect to choice. Moral virtue is a dynamic balance or "mean" between two extremes. The extremes are vices, or bad habits. For example, courage is a "mean" or happy medium between recklessness at one extreme and cowardice at the other. Moderation (or "temperance" or self-control) is a happy medium between self-indulgence and asceticism. Aristotle offers a calendar of virtues and vices that fit this pattern, to which we can add others that he does not identify. Altogether we can come up with a long list of major and minor virtues and vices covering most of our behavior. Following is the calendar of virtues and vices to be found in the *Nicomachean Ethics*. In some cases, the virtue or vice does not have a name, so that a description must suffice.

EXCESS (Vice)	THE MEAN (Virtue)	DEFICIENCY (Vice)
recklessness	courage	cowardice
self-indulgence, wantonness	moderation, temperance	asceticism
extravagance	generosity, liberality	cheapness, stinginess

EXCESS (Vice)	THE MEAN (Virtue)	DEFICIENCY (Vice)
vulgarity	magnificence, suitable expenditure	cheapness, meanness
vanity, conceit, pride	magnanimity, high-mindedness, greatness of soul	pettiness, small-mindedness
excessive ambition	the mean in the pursuit of honors	lack of ambition
bad temper	gentleness, good temper	apathy, passivity
obsequiousness	friendliness, ability to get along with people	surliness, grouchiness, uncooperativeness
boastfulness	honesty, candor	excessive modesty, dishonesty
silliness, tactlessness, boorishness	tastefulness, tact, wittiness	lack of a sense of humor
bashfulness, shyness	modesty, a proper sense of shame	shamelessness
doing injustice	justice, acting justly	suffering injustice

Justice, the most important virtue, is at the bottom of the list simply because I followed the plan of the *Nicomachean Ethics*, where Books III and IV deal with the calendar of virtues and the whole of Book V is devoted to justice. Needless to say, while Aristotle's list is comprehensive, one might find additional virtues and vices to add to it.

To get from vice to virtue means changing our habits. Since virtue is in a mean between vices, we often miss the mean, erring toward one side or the other. The best way to correct our vices is to overcompensate. The degree of overcompensation needed varies with the vice. In the case of alcoholism, for example, there is no mean. You have to stop completely. In the case of smoking, the remedy is not quite so extreme. In other cases, such as getting over phobias or overcoming cowardice in general, the remedy may be less clear. In other words, the concept of the mean is very dynamic. It is not cut and dried at all. The concept of virtue as being in a mean provides a framework, but the individual has to find his or her own best adjustment, or nearest approximation to the ideal.

There is no question that in changing our habits, behavior is involved. We cannot just think our way out of our bad habits. "Indeed," Aristotle says, "those things that we have to learn to do, we learn by doing them."[37] This applies to arts and skills as well as to our moral behavior. Nevertheless, in order to overcompensate, to steer for the mean by "tacking," we have to do more than strike out blindly for the other extreme. Much of the time, it is not clear precisely what our bad habits are. Our personalities consist of complexes of habits of thought and behavior that usually are hard to disentangle. A certain amount of deliberation and self-analysis is required. Sometimes we can do this by ourselves and at other times we need the help of others. It doesn't have to be full-scale psychoanalysis. Most often it is a matter of trial and error: analyzing our mistakes, trying to correct our behavior by putting the results of the analysis into practice, and repeating the cycle as necessary.

In performing self-analysis and changing our habits, we also lay down rules to ourselves. These may be guidelines or principles stating what we should do to correct our behavior. The rules can be very specific or fairly general, depending on what the problems are. After all, we act from a variety of motives – habit, emotion, calculation, duty or principle. A large part of our decision-making is based on the latter two – calculation and obedience to rules and principles. Some of the principles are merely practical, stating what we have to do to change our behavior and attain our various goals. But there are also moral principles that we lay down or acknowledge and feel a duty to obey. Aristotle carefully defines moral virtue in general as well as the individual virtues and vices, and principles of behavior follow from the definitions. Furthermore, Book V of the *Nicomachean Ethics* is devoted to the highest virtue, justice, which is a universal principle. In fact, Aristotle conceives of deliberation as governed by what is called "the practical syllogism."[38] This process of reasoning applies to deliberation in general, which includes ethical deliberation. The practical syllogism consists of a general statement that such and such an action or goal is good and ought to be pursued (or is bad and should be avoided). That is the major premise. The minor premise is that some action or goal that is before one is an instance of the general statement. The conclusion (that the action or goal should be pursued or avoided) is the act. The reasoning can happen intuitively. The major and minor premises do not have to be stated in words.

Thus, in Aristotle's view of ethical deliberation, we are constantly laying down rules to ourselves. Hence, we can compare him with Kant, that great adherent of ethical principle and duty. As noted in Chapter 5, Aristotle much more than Kant sees principle in the context of experience. To be sure, we formulate ethical principles, and to some extent we act on them, but we also act for practical reasons. As Kant himself admits, we cannot know for certain that we do anything purely on the basis of moral principle.

It is often the case that we seem to be acting on either rational or moral principle, and our actions are consistent with principle. At other times we acknowledge that something is rational or right, but fail to do it, or even do what is wrong or foolish. On these occasions, we are *consciously disobeying* principle. Aristotle calls this *akrasía*, which means lack of self-control or moral weakness. When we are in this condition, it is as if we were drunk or dreaming or sleepwalking. We are aware of the principle, but we do not acknowledge it with our full mind. This condition is manifested in making both moral and practical decisions. A related area of irrationality familiar to us moderns is neurotic behavior. All these types of failure to obey principle are a form of sleepwalking or self-hypnosis that comes and goes. Certain critical stimuli to which we are sensitive put us – so to speak – to sleep and thereafter we wake up. If somehow we can keep our minds on the principle, we won't fall asleep. This can be compared to driving an automobile while you are tired and trying to keep yourself from falling asleep behind the wheel, but it is a more subtle sleepiness and wakefulness we are considering. We can understand *akrasía* better when we see it as a peculiarly human failing: "And this explains why animals cannot be morally weak or irrational: they have no grasp of the universal, but only mental images and memories of particular things."[39]

For Aristotle (as we recall) sense-perception is a low-level form of thinking. Animals cannot go beyond it. They cannot generalize the objects they perceive, and construct a language of symbols to discuss them and think about them. Hence, they are never morally weak or irrational because they have no universals in their minds to be overwhelmed by the particular object or situation before them. You cannot act irrationally or be morally weak if you don't have rational or moral principles to begin with.

I have already explained how the mind draws extra energy from the body in strenuous activity. Now in a more subtle example of the same process, I am asking how the mind motivates itself when the desire stemming from the situation immediately before it contradicts the principle it knows it should obey. How does it make itself do something it doesn't want to do? Or as Kant would say, how does it obey the maxim it lays down to itself?

We can be entrapped and ensnared by particular objects, goals, and desires. But we can rise above the particular thing before us and view it as only an instance of a universal. When Aristotle draws comparisons with drunkenness and soberness and waking and sleeping, he is doing more than making metaphors. I believe he means them literally. We humans have the power of reason, but often do not use it. We then are like sleepwalkers, dreaming with our eyes open. What then does it mean to say that the abstract idea, the universal, wakes us up? We cannot talk about being roused by an idea as if it were a physical force. The process may be compared to the actualization of the self, where the object, the desire for the object, and the attainment of it converge. The more the mind is already on the level of the universal, the greater this convergence is likely to be. Thus, some people wake up more quickly than others. We call them "smarter," but in evaluating people in this way, we should speak of their "moral IQ" as distinct from their purely intellectual one. Aristotle would support this way of speaking, since he distinguishes between moral and intellectual virtues.[40]

Unlike Kant, Aristotle doesn't use a lingo of duty and the moral law, laying down maxims to oneself and the categorical imperative, but a careful reading of the *Nicomachean Ethics* makes it clear that Aristotle has just as strong a sense of the role of principle and moral reasoning as Kant does. They both understand the importance of ethical principles, but Aristotle thinks vision is more important than discipline, and he has a much better sense than Kant of ethics in the context of experience. Unlike Kant, he has a real psychology as well as a social science, both of which Kant lacks.

In human life at its best, reason triumphs over the irrational, but it is a living, breathing reason that Aristotle construes very broadly:

> All men by nature desire to know; a sign of this is the affection [we have] for the senses; shit, man, apart from their usefulness, they are loved for themselves and most of all the sense of sight. For not only so that we may act, but even when we are not going to do anything, we choose sight, generally speaking, over all the others. The reason is that of all the senses, it helps us know something and reveals many distinctions.[41]

A sign of our desire to *know* is the affection we have for the *senses*! This is a very inclusive view. Knowledge is construed in the broadest possible sense, ranging from carnal knowledge and the other pleasures of the body to knowledge of other people through friendship and finally to the science leading us to knowledge of the divine.

The triumph of the universal over the particular, being guided by the more rational element in us – it sounds very elevating, but couldn't it still be given a Hobbesian interpretation? That is, the vision you have of the universal, of the moral principle, is just another mental image in your mind that has physical force. The universal is just the authority of the state or some other authority commanding us through fear, not through reason. It may be stated as a rational principle, but it would not affect us if it had no emotional force. Or take Freud's version of this idea: The universal is really the super-ego. I only *think* it is a rational principle commanding me. It's really my father or some other authority figure.

The answer to Hobbes, in addition to the arguments already advanced contradicting his views, is that you see reason at work, not only functioning independently of external authority, but also overcoming the irrational. You know it by its power to solve problems and to be a law unto itself, quite apart from any human authority. If that isn't reason, what could it be? Similarly, the Freudian superego may well be authority speaking in the guise of reason, but one of the standards of human development is the extent to which we free ourselves from blind obedience to authority and reason independently of it. Aristotle's view doesn't exclude that of Hobbes and Freud. We may indeed be motivated to obey reason out of fear of authority rather than by the force of reason alone. But we can and do strive to overcome our irrational fears, and at least some of the time we succeed.

Aristotle seems to have in mind a combination of self-analysis and behavioral development, done with imagination and discipline, and in the fullness of experience. You don't know what combination of reflection and behavior, of correcting bad habits and seeking new experiences, will help you to find the good in life. It is as if you constantly try to recreate yourself. Above all, it is a question of vision.

Each of us has a hierarchy of goals and needs, and they all lead back to our vision of the end or goal of life that Aristotle speaks of in the passage cited in Section C.[42] Human beings want happiness most of all, but opinions differ as to what will bring it about, and what sort of life is the happiest and best. Since we do not know for certain what our true good is, all we can strive for is *tò phainómenon agathón*, the good as it appears to us. The ability to discern the good most clearly comes from the kind of vision Aristotle calls the greatest and noblest of gifts. Our character and our personalities flow from this primal vision, and it may be that they are so fully formed at an early age that we can do little to change them. Thus, in the most important element in our nature we have virtually no choice. Once it is formed, there seems to be little we can do to change it.

Moreover, taking the larger view of ourselves, we can see all the other ways our freedom is limited. We have no control over when and where we are born, our physical endowments, our parents, our upbringing, the economic and political circumstances we find ourselves in – all the vagaries of fate and luck and chance to which we are subject. Although we can move our own bodies and have some freedom to regulate our daily lives and pursue our apparent good, we exercise these freedoms in the presence of so many constraints, one may well ask, why not resign ourselves to our lot in life and not make vain efforts to change it?

Yet though our freedom is qualified and constrained, without it we could not live as human beings. Precisely because it has so many limitations, it is all the more precious. Just struggling with the problems we all face, staying out of trouble, striving to get the most out of ourselves, taking advantage of the opportunities that are presented to us – we have plenty of choices to make all the time in our everyday lives. Although our deeper natures may not change much, relatively small adjustments in our habits and behavior can make all the difference between happiness or unhappiness and success or failure in life.

On the temple of the oracle at Delphi were written the words *Gnôthi seautón*, know thyself. That is exactly what we need to do. Knowing what we really are and what we really want is a never-ending pursuit. It can be carried out on the psychoanalyst's couch, but we are more likely to do it in the context of action and challenging experiences. As the Jesuit motto runs, "In action, contemplation."

The point is to see your apparent good better. It is a question of vision more than discipline. Even Kant, who may sound like a Prussian disciplinarian with all his talk about the categorical imperative and laying down maxims to yourself – even he had a vision. He was inspired, he said, by the moral law within and the starry heavens above. When you summon up all your energy and become fully involved in an idea or goal, when you are swept up by an informed and inspired vision – that's where the energy comes from. The more fully you are possessed and inspired by an idea, the more of your energy it naturally draws and the more you discover reserves of energy you never knew you had.

For Aristotle as for Plato, our vision of the good is what drives us. When we are possessed by an idea, we become identical in form with more things and we forget our hang-ups and problems. Some people are more single-minded than others and have a more sublime vision. Churchill, for example, describing his emotions on the evening when he became Prime Minister, said, "I felt as if my whole life had been a preparation for this moment." Even when our situation is less dramatic and our goals are more ordinary, we still can be inspired by the knowledge that we have freedom, that we have the power to change and more effectively pursue our apparent good. This realization alone may help us recognize our irrationalities and flaws sufficiently to modify them. When we actually get over our complexes and our bad habits, it is like awakening from a bad dream.

The struggle wakes us up and gives us the vision to overcome our bad habits. It follows that Aristotle's view of the good life is very balanced. Although he speaks of the *bíos theoretikós* as the highest form of life, he also says that in the fullest sense it is more than human. Hence, human life is one of activity and striving as well as knowing, and in it happiness is distinct from mere pleasure. The happiest life includes a full round of pleasures, but pleasure as Aristotle conceives it is more than just sensual gratification. Happiness depends on choosing your own course of action, pursuing your vision in spite of all the limitations and challenges you may face. Indeed, because of them it is all the more sublime. When you strive against odds, every victory you win is valued more. Happiness is not mindless contentment.

Fortunately, we do not have to depend on our own vision alone. Our personalities may have been formed at a stage in life that we cannot remember, but even then we were interacting with others. Other human beings influenced us then, and they continue to do so throughout our lives. Our primal vision may be modified by friendship, love, religion, or participation in some great enterprise, causing us to change our behavior or at least submerge our faults in some transcendent activity.

But what if everybody's view of his or her ultimate good conflicts with everybody else's? In that event the human race is doomed to a Hobbesian war of all against all and human society is possible only under the authoritarian constraints Hobbes envisioned, or the neurotic suffering described by Freud, or an eschatological world-view like that of St. Augustine.

Moreover, there are evil visions. Think of Hitler and Stalin and many others like them. It also may be that the human will is corrupt. This is an idea that has played a central role in Western civilization because it is part of Judaism and Christianity. Aristotle does not consider this possibility, but his psychology does not *ipso facto* rule it out if someone can bring forth evidence for it. That evidence may simply be religious doctrine, a different kind of evidence.

Despite the awful things that have happened in human history, we find in Aristotle a cautiously optimistic view of the ability of human beings to work together in worthwhile endeavors and overcome destructive tendencies. We have enough of a shared vision to make cooperation possible, and we have free will. We know from Aristotle's high regard for Greek tragedy his awareness of all the pitfalls that we encounter. There is no guarantee that human beings will not destroy themselves or simply make themselves miserable. Yet even in failing, the tragic hero has nobility, and we rely on an enlightened science to help us avoid dire eventualities. Barring acts of God or circumstances that overwhelm us, it is up to us to make something positive of our existence. Such an outlook not only is characteristic of the ancient Greeks, but also is very American. Randall used to tell his history of philosophy classes in the 1950s that Aristotle's ethics was meant for a prosperous, forward-looking people confident of its ability to shape its own destiny, "an ethic for President Eisenhower." However, Stoic ethics, he continued, was for a people who lacked such self-confidence. "It was an ethic of resignation, an ethic for Secretary Dulles."

In addition to being an optimist, Aristotle presupposes an objective standard of universal justice that transcends time and place. Thus far, I have been speaking of the definitions of the virtues and vices, good and bad, right and wrong, as if their reality could be taken for granted. But where do they come from?

Aristotle's ethics is based on teleology or final causes. This means the nature of a thing defines its end, which in turn defines its good. A thing and a good thing are essentially the same.[43] In other words, the more fully something realizes its nature, the better it is. Hence, if our nature is that we are rational and social beings, then our end is to realize these characteristics as fully as possible, and ethical principles follow as a consequence. Kant is in agreement with Aristotle on this point. The difference is that he *defines* nature more narrowly than Aristotle does, to include *only* the Newtonian world of atoms and molecules. Thus, he envisions a separate realm that he calls "the kingdom of ends." It is outside of the natural world, but the built-in ends are still there.

Wherever human nature is located, the question is, is there really such a thing? Do we really have a natural end or goal? Aristotle certainly thinks so. If indeed the human species is part of nature, surely we can be defined just as other species are. Hence, he defines mankind as the *logikòn zôon* and *politikòn zôon*, two formulas that must be translated and interpreted with care. First of all, they are interrelated, as he explains:

... [I]t is clear that the *pólis* [the city-state] is one of the things [that exist] by nature, and that man by nature is a *politikòn zôon* [an animal that lives in city-states]. ... And why man is more of a *politikòn zôon* than any bee or any herd animal is clear; for nature does nothing in vain, and man alone of the animals possesses speech [*i.e.*, *lógos*, rational discourse] ... and speech is for making known what is advantageous and what is harmful, and therefore also right and wrong; for it is peculiar to man as distinct from the other animals that he alone has perception of good and bad and right and wrong and the other [virtues and vices], and fellowship in these things makes a family and a city-state.[44]

Civil societies could not exist without language, and by the same token human language is very much a social product. Human beings do not create or learn it in isolation, as the examples of the few human children who have managed to survive in the wild clearly illustrate. Thus, the two defining formulas imply each other, and we must be careful how we translate and interpret them. *Logikòn zôon* is often rendered as "rational animal," as if we were rational all or most of the time. What it really means is "animal *possessing* reason," not necessarily using it or using it wisely and well. Moreover, *logikón* is the adjective derived from the noun *lógos*, which means both "language" and "reason," among other things. The instrument of reason is language, *i.e.*, the language of humans, in which meanings are assigned to clusters of sounds to make words and the words are combined according to rules. That is rational discourse. Similarly, *politikòn zôon* is usually translated as "political animal" or "social animal." The former rendering is too narrow and the latter too broad. *Politikón* is derived from *pólis*, which means city-state, the Greek form of political organization. What Aristotle really means by *politikòn zôon* is "the animal that lives in civil societies of which the highest expression is the Greek city-state or *pólis*." Aristotle was a Greek chauvinist, whose pupil Alexander the Great, through his conquests, spread Greek civilization over a large part of the world. It seems reasonable to generalize the notion of the city-state to include the nation-state and the empire. After all, the vast majority of human civilizations are centered in towns and cities.

Aristotle has a third defining formula for the human species, "featherless biped." Man is an animal that walks on two legs and lacks the hairy coat of other animals, in particular the apes. Since "nature does nothing in vain" and the first two defining formulas are interrelated, it is obvious that all three are closely connected. This raises another interesting point. While twentieth-century anthropology is still determining the details of man's evolution from the apes, we know that a crucial element was our ancestors' learning to walk on their hind legs. Acquiring this ability was closely connected with their rapid increase in cranial capacity and with the development of human speech. The conventional wisdom is that Aristotle was not an evolutionist, but did he really think that the human species existed as such from the creation of the universe or that it arose full-blown by spontaneous generation? The Aristotelian texts, a set of lecture notes from 2,400 years ago, do not speak to this question, but we can draw reasonable inferences from what they do say. Clearly, Aristotle is making the same kind of connection as modern anthropologists are between our biological equipment and our psychosocial development. The interconnection strongly suggests an evolution. Hence, Aristotle may have anticipated a key area of modern science, and in an important respect, he is ahead of modern science, for the three definitions imply each other. Together they form a unified concept of human nature that ranges powerfully over many disciplines. Such unity does not exist in these fields today.

The prevailing tendency today is to deny that there is any such thing as human nature. To persons who hold this opinion, the Aristotelian concept of human nature would seem hopelessly outdated, rigid, and dogmatic. However, it is they who are dogmatic. Their knee-jerk rejection of views like Aristotle's is one more symptom of the intellectual ills I have been describing. Unbeknownst to them, Aristotle was very precise in his use of language. He was as careful in framing definitions as modern scientists are in constructing mathematical formulas. The definitions of human nature, as well as other definitions like that of the soul, are verbal formulas, and are comparable to the mathematical formulas we are familiar with, like F=ma or e=mc^2. They are no more rigid and dogmatic than the latter. Henri Bergson once declared, "We cannot sacrifice experience to the requirements of any system."[45] Aristotle's formulas define our experience, but they do not confine it or exhaust it. His conception of human nature is both systematic and inclusive. Within it, individuals and cultures may vary enormously. This variation does not mean that the definitions are so broad as to be meaningless. They provide understanding in just the way modern scientific formulas do, and many details can be derived from them.

Establishing that there really is such a thing as human nature will do away with the skeptical "meta-ethics" pursued by the twentieth-century "philosophers," a turn of events that is long overdue. From the standpoint of common sense, it is ridiculous to render problematic something so essential to human life as ethics. Now common sense and science will come together again. We will avoid the pseudo-problems of "meta-ethics" because Aristotle gives us a scientific basis for ethics.

Still, this seems too good to be true because we are so used to the inability of modern thinkers to match in the human sphere the achievements of natural science in understanding and harnessing matter. It is hard for us to believe that we can have a science of human nature at all, let alone a non-reductionist one. On the one hand, human experience seems too chaotic to be reduced to a science, and on the other, we fear for its integrity should that be accomplished. Yet a careful and imaginative examination of Aristotle's ideas suggests that we can have our cake and eat it too – a science of man that really is a science, but that does not reduce human experience to something mechanical and non-human. We can have science *and* free will.

How can this be? First of all, the concept of free will remains secure because in Aristotle's view of things, experience is never sacrificed to the requirements of any system. No system exhausts it. At the same time, Aristotle fills a yawning chasm in twentieth-century social science. The problem with the latter is that it imitates the methods of natural science because it can't think of anything else to do, but unlike natural science, it lacks firm concepts on which to ground its analysis. Aristotle's conception of human nature and his concepts of soul and mind provide the necessary foundation. They do a much better job than is being done now of identifying which areas of our experience we can understand systematically and which ones we cannot. Thus they will help economics, political science, anthropology, and sociology, as well as psychology and linguistics, the two fields already discussed.

Take, for example, the concept of *philía* or friendship developed in Books VIII and IX of the *Nicomachean Ethics*. "Friendship" is understood very broadly to include a wide range of social relations that are voluntary and/or natural. It is based on three principles: the good, the pleasant, and the useful. The highest form of friendship is founded on *areté*, virtue or excellence, which means both moral virtue and other forms of excellence as well. (The English word "virtue" preserves this broader sense, as when we say this or that is "the virtue" of something, meaning the excellence of it. The word "virtuoso" also reflects the wider sense.)

In Books VIII and IX, Aristotle defines the essential nature of friendship, namely, two or more people wishing for and furthering each other's good, and then outlines a variety of friendly relations. By definition, friendship is mutual and equal, but great differences often exist between the partners. When he speaks of friendship between "unequals," he means people who are *different* from each other and *unequal* in regard to the specific qualities by which they differ. Mutuality and equality are achieved by compensating for the differences, often by an exchange of benefits and detriments. For example, parents support their children in infancy, and the children help their parents in old age. Children receive support from their parents, but must obey them. Parents love their children for their helplessness and (relative) innocence, and children love their parents for their help and support. Thus, mutuality and a kind of equality, *i.e.*, balance and equity, are attained. Perhaps in this brief telling, Aristotle's account sounds mundane, but the precision with which the relationships are described create a powerful framework for understanding them.

There are other forms of friendship between "unequals" that Aristotle touches on, but does not elaborate, including that between husband and wife (or man and woman). In the case of man and woman the differences are not as extreme as those between parents and children, but they are more subtle and harder to explain, particularly in regard to sexual attraction. However, the derivation of so many other friendly relationships from a set of principles is so precise that the possibility of satisfactorily explaining in detail the phenomena of sex and love is strongly implied. This includes both heterosexual attraction and the two main taboos, incest and homosexuality.

To work out the theory of sex and love implicit in Aristotle's concept of friendship is beyond the scope of this essay, as is a detailed account of other social relationships. The fact that Aristotle analyzes these relationships in quasi-mathematical terms is in no way reductionist. As with the definitions of the virtues, the defining formulas enhance rather than exhaust or destroy the richness of the particulars. They are the skeleton that is clothed with flesh and blood. In this fashion, finding the correct relationship between the abstract and the concrete can lead us to a true social science instead of the weak imitation of the natural sciences we now have.

The new social science will be allied with the arts. Sophocles' *Oedipus Rex*, which inspired both Aristotle and Freud, is an example of this kind of close connection in which the roles of the artist and the scientist converge.

Aristotle's theory of art and the connection between art and science are rich areas that have not been explored in this essay. Nor have I said much about his political theory, which is equally fertile. However, I am not trying to be exhaustive, merely to explain his central ideas and to give a sense of what they can contribute to our current concerns.

Consider how far we have come in relatively few pages: from the soul to the unity of mind, to the mind moving the body, to choice and free will, to the foundations of moral beliefs and the concept of human nature. That is a lot, but there is more ground to cover to finish what I set out to do at the beginning of this chapter. I now am ready to return to the question of the unity of the soul and the contribution Aristotle can make to modern biology.

G. The Mind and the Soul

Even if the reader is persuaded that Aristotle's view of the mind and its connection with the body is both intelligible and plausible, I still must explain its relationship to the soul. Indeed, for some pages now I have been talking about mind and body as if I had almost forgotten about the soul. It is time to look again at how the latter fits into the picture.

In everyday discourse, we are more comfortable talking about the mind than about the soul. The idea of *mind* seems intuitively clear to us, even if our attempts to describe it are limited and inadequate. Moreover, science reveals the direct connection that exists between the sensori-motor cortex and the voluntary muscles. The former is a key part of the cerebral cortex, the area of the brain where the mind, or at least the main part of it, is located. Hence, we readily see that some kind of connection between mind and body exists. *Soul*, on the other hand, is a vague word with religious connotations. We are much less clear about what it might mean.

This view of things did not arise by chance. It is part of our intellectual heritage. Descartes and his dualistic successors in the modern period – *i.e.*, much of modern Western thought – concern themselves with the relationship between mind and body. Descartes does use the word "soul" (*âme*), but for him this is just a broader term for the mind. The soul contains the passions, which are passive thoughts stimulated by the action of the body. It is the repository of all the different kinds of mental activity. In the Cartesian view the soul is not at all what it is for Aristotle: the primary actuality of the body, the unity of the processes that control the basic functions of the body and keep it alive. On the contrary, according to Descartes the human body is merely a machine in which the mind dwells. What is more, only human beings have minds. Animals do not have minds. They do not have reason, as we do. They are ruled by their passions, which are generated by the body, in Hobbesian fashion. They are just machines.

This leaves Descartes with the problem of explaining how the human mind got into the human body. To say God put it there is a pious answer, but unsatisfactory for a scientist, and Descartes is unable to give a better answer than that. His dilemma is that of modern thought. Kant is more cautious about invoking the name of God, but he has no better explanation of how the mind got there than Descartes does. This dilemma of the "modern philosophers" reflects the emphasis of Galilean-Newtonian science on atoms and molecules, and not on biological processes. It is hard to find a place for mind in a universe made up of little atomic billiard balls.

When in the nineteenth century science turned more of its attention to biology, the Darwinian theory of evolution provided an explanation of how mind arose. However, the scientists brought to the study of living beings the materialist and dualist mindset of the preceding centuries. As noted earlier, they might at times revert to teleological lingo in describing biological processes, but it was understood that this was just a convenient way of speaking. The ultimate explanation was assumed to be in physical and chemical terms, unless you were a dualist and put mind and values outside the realm of science. In any case, the soul in Aristotle's sense of the term was nowhere to be found.

We need not resort to Lincolnesque rhetoric – a house divided against itself cannot stand – to see how implausible any dualistic explanation is. We see the contortions Descartes, Kant, *et al.* have to go through to maintain it. Yet even if Aristotle avoids their difficulties, the connection between the mind and the voluntary muscles does not occur in a vacuum. It depends on many other bodily processes to support it. If the latter still constitute a biological machine, we have only partly solved the mind-body problem.

The discussion earlier of muscle tone and voluntary muscular movement illustrated the strangeness of the relationship between a mind that is a substantial unity and a body that is a machine. Respiration provides another example, but from an area of functioning that is more involuntary than voluntary. We have a breathing reflex that keeps us from suffocating while we are asleep or when we are preoccupied with less mundane activities than drawing breath. Of course we can consciously alter our breathing if we wish, making it deeper, faster, or slower, but most of the time it occurs by reflex action. Is the latter done by the body *qua* machine, while the voluntary breathing is done by the substantial unity, the mind?

Here is an even better example. The primary locus of the mind is the cerebral cortex. The latter has connections with many other parts of the brain, in particular the hypothalamus, which is located roughly in the center of the brain and is the chief area of the brain governing involuntary mind-body connections, such as increasing the heartbeat when one is excited or frightened. Indeed, the hypothalamus is part of the system that, together with the nerves, ganglia, and plexuses of the autonomic nervous system, maintains the stability of the body's basic functions. This control is exercised in the hypothalamus, the brain stem, and the spinal cord. Both in producing bodily symptoms of emotion and maintaining the body's basic functions – heartbeat, respiration, circulation, digestion, temperature, etc. – there is an intimate relationship between the cortex and these other parts of the central nervous system. In the contemporary version of this relationship, the hypothalamus takes over part of the role Descartes assigned to the pineal gland. However, the more up-to-date physiology only makes the relationship more problematic than it is in Descartes' conception. Where exactly are we to draw the boundary between the mind and the machine? On the way to the hypothalamus? In it? Just beyond it? Not only that, think of all the connections that exist between the cortex and other parts of the brain. What results is a mental Maginot Line meandering all over the brain separating the mind and the machine.

Still, a materialist might object, instead of an epistemological version of World War II or a Cartesian horror movie, couldn't there just be a set of reflexes that mimics a substantial unity? In other words, wouldn't a more sophisticated version of materialism suffice? Or is the latter subject to essentially the same criticism as the unsophisticated version? Let us consider the alternatives.

The simplest one is that the reflexes controlling the basic bodily functions operate independently of each other. They have their built-in parameters, and that's that. However, this seems simplistic. If one function or another is disturbed – particularly if it gets way out of whack – a variable response from some or all of the others would be needed that would have to be coordinated in some way. The question is, could the coordination be accomplished mechanically, by means of built-in parameters, merely constituting a more complex feedback loop?

The Aristotelian reply is that the foregoing account would not suffice, that the basic functions are actually directed and controlled by a substantial unity. But how do we know this is so? Since the mind and the soul are intimately connected, the mind being the highest power of the soul, and Aristotle gives an argument for the unity of the mind, could that argument apply to the soul? We ought to be able to extrapolate downward from the unity of the mind to the unity of the soul. We can imagine a replay of the Hobbes-Aristotle debate on this level, with the materialists saying no, the coordination isn't necessary, or it can be accomplished by reflexes alone.

Yet is the argument really the same? Recall the key lines: *Deî dè tò hèn légein hóti héteron* (it is necessary for the one [thing] to say that [two things are] different) and "As it speaks, so it thinks and perceives." But does the soul actually engage in some kind of mental discourse? There is no question that we engage in unconscious thought, but how far down does it go?

Can it be that the basic bodily functions are controlled in a way that is like the action of mind, but on a lower level? Since the parts of the nervous system that regulate these functions are closely connected with the parts in which mind is located, we can expect a significant degree of similarity.

Science is not yet ready to provide an observational or experimental test of either the Aristotelian or the materialist hypothesis, but let us see if it can shed any light on the issue we are considering. Indeed, the unity constituting the soul is less abstract and less complex than that of the mind. Therefore, it should be easier to trace physiologically – particularly as neurological research advances, and we realize what we are actually looking for. So far neurobiology has identified the individual nerve pathways regulating the vital functions, but has neither confirmed nor denied any unified central control. What is known accords with an Aristotelian view, even if it does not specifically confirm it. For example, the autonomic nervous system is divided into two subsystems, the parasympathetic and the sympathetic. These two balance each other, but, as a neurophysiologist explains, it is not a simple relationship of excitation and inhibition: ". . . sympathetic stimulation causes excitatory effects in some organs but inhibitory effects in others. Likewise, parasympathetic stimulation causes excitation in some organs but inhibition in others."[46]

It is not just the balance between the two subsystems that suggests an overall unity, but the fact that the balance is complex. Even without the complexity, one would not expect each reflex to act in total independence of the others. One would expect to see a variety of minor adjustments in individual bodily functions – fine tuning, so to speak – based not just on the individual reflexes by themselves, but on their interaction with the others. How could this interaction occur, particularly if it is complex, without some kind of coordination? It is clear that coordination must occur. The question is, could the parameters be built in? Is it a complex, but still mechanistic feedback loop?

This can be the case only if no perception is involved. Yet the control of temperature, heartbeat, blood pressure, breathing, digestion, etc., should involve some element of perception, even if it is unsophisticated when compared with the five senses. Why would the body be able to perceive the outside world and not its own primary functions? The latter kind of perception seems more essential than the former. Consequently, we can see an analogy with mind. The soul is another blank tablet, but less abstract than the mental one, and less complex. It is connected with the individual reflexes, and balances them. It is, so to speak, the means of communication between them. Consider the argument for the unity of mind. (The reader may wish to consult the Appendix.) In order to compare the perceptions coming in from two different organs, say, sweet and white, the thing comparing them must be one thing because how else could they be compared? Their respective organs cannot compare them, and they cannot compare themselves.

If there is perception on the level of soul, the same argument applies as on the level of mind. Since the individual functions cannot perceive each other, the thing that is coordinating them must do so. In order to do so, it must be a unity. That unity is called "the soul."

Lo and behold, it *is* a replay of Hobbes versus Aristotle. Moreover, the same answers to objections apply as in regard to the mind. Positing the soul is not espousing a crude vitalism; its activity does not violate the Second Law of Thermodynamics. Finally, all the other characteristics of mind should be found in the soul, but in a simpler and more primitive form.

Wasn't that easy! However, having solved one problem, another one immediately arises. If both the mind and the soul are unities, do we have two unities dwelling in each of us, and if so, how are they related? This question is well expressed by a poem of A. E. Housman:

> I lay me down and slumber
>   And every morn revive.
> Whose is the night-long breathing
>   That keeps me man alive?
>
> When I was off to dreamland
>   And left my limbs forgot,

> Who stayed at home to mind them,
> And breathed when I did not?
>
> . . . .
>
> – I waste my time in talking,
>   No heed at all takes he,
> My kind and foolish comrade
>   That breathes all night for me.[47]

Are there really two of each of us and not just one? While not exactly a case of Jekyll and Hyde, is it something like Siamese twins cooped up in each of our nervous systems?

It is understandable why one might think of the mind and the soul as two separate unities. While anchored in the body and dependent on it for existence, the mind is more distinct from the body than is the soul. It is a "form of forms," an abstract unity that can partially transcend its particular location in space and time. Especially when it experiences a vision of great beauty or truth, it rises to an exalted state and seems like an independent entity. Moreover, some individuals may use their minds to render themselves comparatively immune to the demands of the body, as in the case of Hindu fakirs walking on hot coals, or the indifference of Socrates to physical discomfort, as reported to us by Plato.

Because the mind is a unity with the power of reason, a kind of abstract entity, a "form of forms," and thereby has the power of partly transcending its limitations in space and time, we tend to conclude that it is totally transcendent. But it isn't. The mind inevitably is brought back to earth and reminded of its link to the body and to mortality.

In discussing Descartes, we saw the absurdities one can land in if one tries to make an absolute distinction between the mind and the body it inhabits. Yet even when we avoid this pitfall, it is no easy matter describing the connection, and the case is similar with the mind and the soul. Like the mind, the soul is a form of forms, but on a lower level. My soul is still me, but it is an inchoate me. Without positing a Freudian id, we see clearly that there is unconscious thought, and it goes down deep. Despite the flights of abstraction and fancy the mind is capable of, it has roots deep in the body, but we don't know how far down they go or how much the mind and soul are part of each other. At any rate, they are intimately connected. Even with its power of abstract thought, the mind only partly transcends its connection with the body. The action of the mind, especially conscious thought, is the

highest activity of the soul, and the other activities of the soul are unconscious thought or are very analogous to unconscious thought. It is as accurate to say that mind is a higher power of soul as that soul is a broader and
deeper form of mind.

What shall we say then? Are they two parts of the same unity? Can we
speak of higher and lower levels of the same unity? An answer like that
seems most likely. Working it out more precisely is a matter for further research. However, there is one topic we have not yet considered that sheds
light on this question, namely, the connection of mind, soul, and body via
the emotions. The latter exhibit this connection even more than the mind's
ability to move the voluntary muscles because here the mind is passive and
intimately related to the set of processes that are the locus of the soul.

H. The Emotions

If the mind somehow could exist without present in any other part of the
body except the nervous system and the sense-receptors, it would either
have no emotions or very circumscribed ones. But the mind *is* connected to
all the basic processes of the body, and consequently experiences a wide
range of emotions that it expresses in terms of the body. Indeed, the mind always is in some kind of emotional state, and the emotions are expressed not
only as ideas, but as physical symptoms. As noted earlier, the thing with
which the mind is most identical in form is its own body.

Consider what Aristotle has to say about the thought-content of emotions and their physical symptoms:

> It seems likely that all the passive states of the soul [*i.e.*, the emotions]
> are [associated] with the body: anger, mild-manneredness, fear, pity,
> fearlessness, and joy, as well as loving and hating – for simultaneously
> with them the body undergoes something [*i.e.*, experiences symp-
> toms]. . . . If this is so, clearly the emotions are formulas [rational ac-
> counts, forms] embedded in matter [*lógoi énhyloi*], so that their
> definitions must be suchlike [*i.e.*, they must be defined accordingly];
> for example, anger is a movement of such-and-such a body or part or
> faculty of it by this or that cause and for the sake of this or that [end]. . .
> . But the investigator of nature [*physikós*] and the one skilled in argu-
> ment and definition [*dialektikós*] would define each of them differ-
> ently, for example, [in answer to the question] what is anger: the one
> [would say] a desire for retaliation, or something of the sort; the other
> [would call it] an [increase in] heat [*i.e.*, temperature] and a boiling of
> the blood around the heart. The one [*i.e.*, the *physikós*] is giving us an

account of the matter; and the other [*i.e.*, the *dialektikós*] the form and the definition.[48]

It is not just that the thought-content of the emotion and its bodily symptoms *correspond*. The relationship is closer than that. The emotions are *lógoi énhyloi*, "enmattered forms," *i.e.*, forms *embedded* in matter. The matter in this instance is the bodily parts that experience motions or perturbations. The latter are a *language* of emotion.

The mind is constantly aware of its own body. It always has a sense of well- or ill-being of the bodily organs themselves. While we do not perceive the normal functioning of the liver, the pancreas, the kidneys, the spleen, etc., we do have a constant sense of gastro-intestinal comfort or discomfort; of whether or not we are breathing normally; whether we are too warm or cold; if our heartbeat is irregular; if our muscles and joints are comfortable or not; if our skin feels dry or itchy, if we are hungry or thirsty, and so on. As Aristotle says, "pleasure and pain follow upon every action and passive state."[49]

It is easy to see that changes in this sense of well- or ill-being can express emotions, and the ones that have the most pronounced bodily symptoms are fear and anger. Why, for example, do we tend to feel extreme fear in the abdomen? Probably it has something to do with loss of control of our bowels and bladder, one of the most basic things we learned as infants and an essential element of self-control. Fear or extreme uncertainty about ourselves tends to be expressed as abdominal discomfort or malfunction because the gastrointestinal tract performs a set of functions over which we have little control. Our role in digestion is very passive. Furthermore, we have little control over the need for food and drink itself. It is almost an addiction. We have to get our nutritional "fix" regularly. We just can't manage without it. If any substance that affects one's mood is a drug, then *food* is a drug, plain old ordinary food, with or without chemical additives. Once it gets into our bloodstream, it affects our mood in many different ways. And what a delicate thing digestion is! Too much of this, too little of that, something prepared very well, something poorly prepared – it all affects the way we feel. As Feuerbach said, *"Der Mensch ist was er isst"* (man is what he eats). In this light, it does not take much imagination to see why disturbances in the digestive system are so expressive of the emotion of fear.

On the other hand, describing anger, we commonly say things like "It makes my blood boil." The tension, the frustration, the desire to avenge oneself produce their own set of physical symptoms. The blood pressure rises, adrenalin flows, muscles become tense in readiness for action, the face becomes flushed, and so on. The physical symptoms reflect the intense desire to strike out at the source of the anger, a state of mind opposite from fear.

Looking quickly as some of the other emotions, we see that astonishment, dismay, sorrow, gaiety, disgust at something physically unpleasant also have their familiar physical symptoms – not to mention sexual desire. Even the less violent emotions (so to speak) such as hope, anxiety, affection, annoyance, contempt, etc. have measurable physical symptoms, as operators of lie detectors can attest. We humans think of ourselves as being less tied to our bodies than the other animals are. In a sense that is true because our minds are more fully developed than theirs, but in another sense, we are more tied to our bodies than they are because ours express a much wider range of emotions and desires than theirs.

It is not just specific emotions that are expressed with physical symptoms. We receive a large part of our identity in terms of the body, including our feelings of masculinity, femininity, strength, weakness, agility, clumsiness, beauty, ugliness, etc. Sexual desire is the complex expression of an emotion in terms of the body. Hence it should seem perfectly natural that our emotions should occur both as ideas and as bodily symptoms that are a kind of language expressing those ideas. It is worth our while to try to decipher the language, and not be content just to recognize it intuitively. I have tried to show in very broad outline how this can be done, and it can be done in much greater detail.

In moving the voluntary muscles, the mind *actively* identifies with its own body. In experiencing emotion, the mind *passively* identifies with the body. In both cases, the connection of mind and body is very close. In short, we are animals that have reason – or in Aristotle's definition, we are featherless, two-footed, *pólis*-dwelling animals possessing reason. On the one hand, the mind almost transcends its location in a physical body in a particular place and time. On the other hand, our animal emotions and appetites bring us back to earth. This combination has its good and its bad side. We must not blame our failings on the animals. "For just as man is the best of animals [when] perfected, so [when] separated from law and justice [he is the] worst of all."[50] So Aristotle comments at the beginning of the *Politics*. The other animals don't write poems or build spaceships, but they do not wage wars or commit genocide either. When allied with reason, our so-called "animal" desires are much greater than the corresponding desires of the other animals. We thereby add a dimension to eating and drinking, sex and violence that the latter lack. As Randall put it, "Man is the only animal who is constantly in heat." All this shows the closeness of the union in our natures between the rational and the animal.

Furthermore, this view of human nature avoids the confusion created by Freud and Hobbes and others who equate the evil and disorder in human nature with our animal side. Freud, for one, has an Augustinian view of human nature without the Augustinian theology. He blames the corruption in human nature on Darwinian evolution rather than the Devil, thereby giving the animals a bad rap. Aristotle, even though he does not believe in the corruption of the will by original sin, still provides a better framework than anybody else with which to comprehend human evil. It clearly is something peculiarly human, and is not to be blamed on the animal side of us. While Aristotle recognizes the imperfections in human behavior, he does not take a dogmatic position on the extent to which they can be removed. Here again, he shows his scientific frame of mind.

This completes my sketch of Aristotle's view of the relation of mind and soul, updated in order to show how well it accords with science. There is just one more point about which the reader may be curious, the question of the immortality of the soul. Plato, for his part, compares the soul to a boatman in a boat. Death is its separation from the body, and it survives the separation. Aristotle, on the other hand, doubts that the soul/mind survives the death of the organism.[51]

Here too, Aristotle's doubt about the immortality of the soul reflects his scientific spirit. There is no scientific evidence that the mind is able to exist apart from the body. The belief that it can is derived from faith rather than from science.

I. The Origin and Evolution of Life

I have traced Aristotle's view of the mind and the soul and outlined his theory of human nature. However, his encyclopedic interests did not stop there but ranged over the whole panoply of living beings. While many of the details he set forth were incorrect and sound primitive when compared with modern biology, he nevertheless can give us critical insight into the origin and evolution of life.

What was said earlier about the human mind and its relation to the human soul can be extrapolated to other forms of life. Soul/mind exists in all organisms. It was present in the earliest stages of evolution. In primitive life-forms, it was not in the nervous system, because one-celled organisms do not have any, but in the nucleus, which is analogous to the nervous system. In any case, some kind of unity existed. This would be true in eukaryotic organisms (one-celled organisms with a nucleus separated from the cytoplasm by a membrane), prokaryotic organisms (those lacking a clearly defined, separate nucleus), and pre-prokaryotic life forms. According to the latest estimates, it took close to three billion years for life to evolve to what we know today. The eukaryotic single-celled organism already represents a long process of evolution. Apparently much more time was needed to get from the origins to that stage than from there to complex multi-cellular organisms.

The foregoing account presupposes that the concept of *psyché* or soul accords with that of evolution. The problem is that in the conventional view, Aristotle is not an evolutionist. Each species has a clearly defined essence and is eternal. He doesn't actually say so, but it is inferred from other things he does say. As we shall see, this view of him is a holdover from scholasticism.

At this point, readers may balk. Even if they have gone along with the notion that Aristotle's view of soul and mind can be conjoined with modern science, it just may be too much of a stretch to suggest that he was a Darwinian. What is there in the texts to support this view? However, we must remember that he was a scientist, not a Platonizing medieval scholastic. No one who has immersed himself in Aristotle's writings can fail to recognize his willingness to change his mind in light of superior evidence. What is more, in this instance it is not clear that he actually has to change it, or at least not very much. It is far easier to make the transition from Aristotle's biology to Darwin than from his physics to Newton. He already has the *scala naturae*, the ladder of nature from the lowest creatures to the highest, and the way he describes it suggests an evolutionary development:

> Nature proceeds little by little from things lifeless to animal life in such a way that it is impossible to determine the exact line of demarcation, nor on which side thereof an intermediate form should lie. Thus, next after lifeless things in the upward scale comes the plant, and of plants one will differ from another as to its amount of apparent vitality; and, in a word, the whole genus of plants, whilst it is devoid of life as compared with an animal, is endowed with life as compared with other corporeal entities. Indeed, as we just remarked, there is observed in plants a continuous scale of ascent towards the animal . . .

> In regard to sensibility, some animals give no indication whatsoever of it, whilst others indicate it but indistinctly. . . . And so throughout the entire animal scale there is a graduated differentiation in amount of vitality and in capacity for motion.[52]

This sounds awfully Darwinian! On the other hand, let us not be hasty in making connections between Aristotle and Darwin. For one thing, a strict interpretation of the latter is that he was an unyielding materialist, and final causes cannot be admitted into his theory in any way, shape, or form. For another, the ladder of nature is not a Darwinian concept. Darwin did not believe in "higher" and "lower" life forms. That is an interpretation of him by people like Spencer and Huxley. For now, let us simply say that Aristotle's view sounds like a synthesis of natural selection, final causes, and the ladder of nature – if such a synthesis is possible.

Moreover, even if we are inclined to conclude that Aristotle truly was an evolutionist, two stumbling blocks remain. They are his notion that species have definable essences and the doctrine that actuality precedes potentiality. Let us consider the latter first. I will show a) that it is correct and b) that it is no barrier to evolution.

The terms "actuality" and "potentiality" may sound like mere verbiage, but they are not. The "actuality" of the organism is its fully developed state. The seed is *potentially* the mature organism because it contains not any old thing, but the genetic form of a specific organism. The fertilized egg of a flea doesn't grow into an elephant, and vice versa. The one egg is potentially an elephant, and the other potentially a flea.

Simply put, "actuality precedes potentiality" means that the chicken precedes the egg. But does it? The modern doctrine that "ontogeny recapitulates phylogeny" may help us find the answer. This doctrine or hypothesis holds that the developing vertebrate embryo runs through the stages of evolution. For example, it is suggested that the human fetus swims in a saline solution because our ancestors the fish lived in the sea. We also appear to have vestigial gill slits. Indeed, the process continues even after birth. Infants are born with a high larynx like that of the apes, which is incapable of forming the sounds of human speech. The larynx subsequently descends to the normal human position. Some biologists point out that the foregoing examples are speculative and question the doctrine. However, the biochemical uniformity of the various organisms on earth provides strong evidence for it.

Moreover, every single stage of evolution need not be repeated. One might simply say that ontogeny *telescopes* phylogeny, as the developing organism goes through a highly condensed version of evolution. In the case of the human embryo, that which took longest to evolve is squeezed into the shortest part of the embryo's development. The stages that took *less* time in evolution take up proportionately *more* time here. In these latter stages, the presence of the soul is more apparent.

For Aristotle the organism is a living entity precisely because it has the type of substantial unity called *psyché* or "soul." If the latter is present in the full-grown organism, it must also be in the seed. The seed's development seems so automatic that one might well say it is "programmed" to become the organism, and leave it at that. Nevertheless, the soul is in there pitching.

If "soul" or substantial unity is in the seed, then actuality precedes potentiality – because substantial unity *is* actuality. It is *héneka toû*, that for the sake of which the seed's development occurs, the "final cause." While the seed is only potentially the full-grown organism, it develops to fulfill the nature of the actuality it already contains.

Suppose the foregoing sounds plausible, but you still have difficulty envisioning the soul in the organism right from the beginning. However, as you observe the organism develop and the presence of the soul and the mind becomes more apparent, it is more obvious that the final cause is controlling the process. The fully developed human fetus resembles the adult human being a lot more than it does the fertilized egg it came from. Much more of evolution was ranged over in the nine months it took the fetus to develop from the fertilized egg than will be covered in the eighteen or twenty years required for it to become an adult. If we don't grasp the telescoping of evolution in the development of more complex organisms, we will fail to comprehend that millions of small transitions from one actuality to another are condensed and summarized therein. Because of the great evolutionary distance traversed in the development of the embryo and fetus, it is not obvious that the final cause was present all the time and thus that actuality preceded potentiality.

Evolution occurs by very small changes in actuality. Fish didn't develop all at once into amphibians, dinosaurs didn't evolve into birds with lightning speed, and it took the mammals more than 65 million years to produce *homo sapiens*. Evolution takes place through a slow accumulation of little changes. The individual variations are so small that it still is correct to say that actuality precedes potentiality. In short, this doctrine is no stumbling block to evolution. Put aside the narrow view of Aristotle that you have been taught and consider his own words as quoted above, for on this fundamental point he and Darwin seem to be in agreement.

However, we immediately encounter another problem. If species are constantly evolving, how can we say they have any fixed essence or definite nature? Biologists have observed enough variation among characteristics of related organisms that they often have difficulty drawing boundary lines between species. As the biologist Ernst Mayr notes: "Widespread species may have terminal populations that behave toward each other as distinct species even though they are connected by a chain of interbreeding populations."[53] There might be a population of frogs in North Dakota that can interbreed with frogs of ostensibly the same species in Missouri. The Missouri frogs in turn interbreed with a similar group in Texas, but the ones in Texas and those in North Dakota cannot. The ability of its members to interbreed is widely regarded as the most essential characteristic of a species, but apparently this is not so. Hence, as George Lakoff argues, "none of the defining characteristics of the biological concept *species* is necessary, and so the concept is not definable by necessary and sufficient conditions."[54]

If Lakoff simply means that no single characteristic absolutely defines a species, the statement is much weaker than it appears to be. But no, he argues that "species are not . . . classical categories defined by common essential properties. In fact, species in evolutionary biology are not classical categories at all."[55] In other words, there are *no* essential characteristics of species, a much more extreme position.

The Aristotelian concept of species is not invalidated by the fact that intermediate forms abound and it is often hard to draw lines between closely related populations. The judgment that a given group of organisms constitutes a distinct species is based on a number of factors involving both form and function. As Aristotle says, "It is impossible that a single differentia, either by itself or with its antecedents, shall express the whole essence of a species."[56] For example, his three defining formulas for man – *logikòn zôon, politikòn zôon*, and featherless biped – contain five characteristics. Where ambiguities arise, as in identifying the different species of hominid that preceded *homo sapiens*, the definitions of the species will resemble each other because they are based on smaller distinctions than are those between widely different species.

The definition of a species can be judged on its own merits regardless of what the species evolved from or may evolve into. A biological organism and the species to which it belongs are form embedded in matter, and matter is inherently changeable. This alone implies evolution. The species are not Platonic forms, eternal and unchanged. Since Aristotle denied the existence of the Platonic world of ideas, why would he want to shape the science of biology in its image? Indeed, on the basis of the foregoing arguments, we can safely conclude that Aristotle's concept of essence does not stand in the way of the evolution of species.

The most essential trait of all living creatures is that they are alive, that they are characterized by the substantial unity called the *psyché* or "soul." The kinds of "soul" – vegetative, animal, and rational – are all *powers* that can have indefinitely many gradations. Typically, when Aristotle categorizes groups of organisms, he does it by their powers. For example, some animals can do A and B, but not C. Some can do A and C, but not B. Others can do A, B, C, and D. This does not sound like someone looking to establish rigid boundaries. On the contrary, the sense we get is of nature shuffling the deck.[57]

Not only does Aristotle's biology accord with a theory of evolution, but it adds a dimension to Darwin's theory that the latter seems to lack. While the concept of natural selection is brilliant, we tend to be mesmerized by it, as if it were a magic wand waved over all living creatures, relieving them of the need to do anything to evolve besides letting natural selection take its course. However, there is more to evolution than just the interaction of genetic equipment with environmental conditions. As Aristotle says, even animals have a share of voluntary action or "free will."[58] They can feel pleasure and pain. Within their limits, they pursue their *phainómenon agathón*, their apparent good. The higher up the scale of intelligence we look, the more we see volition influencing evolution. Presumably, less volition was needed for the amphibians to evolve from fish than for certain mammals to go back into the ocean and become whales and porpoises. The best example of this interaction is provided by human evolution. Once our primate ancestors started using their brains by signaling, trying to stand upright, and working together in more highly organized groups, they had a dramatic effect on natural selection. The ones who could do these things best reproduced the most and survived, and the species evolved in the direction of these characteristics.

In the space of perhaps three million years, a group of primates with less than one-third the cranial capacity of humans evolved into *homo sapiens*. My research in linguistics suggests that the attempt to develop language, more than anything else, caused the evolutionary process that led to the human species. I spoke earlier (Section D, above) of human language as primarily a system of categories. When I saw how powerful the categories are and how much they explain about the acquisition and use of language, I realized that they also explain the origin of language and of the species itself. As we can see from the successful efforts in recent years to teach chimpanzees and other apes American Sign Language, these primates clearly have the capacity for a crude form of human language. I agree with those critics who say this is not the genuine article. The chimps do not form new words, and they do not pass their artificially imposed ability on to other chimps. However, at some point the primates did develop this ability on their own, and I am suggesting that the evolution of our species began with the development of a crude and rudimentary category system. The attempt to develop speech was what got our primate ancestors started on the way to becoming human. We share 98 percent of our genome with chimpanzees. It is the remaining 2 percent that makes all the difference. Presumably most of that 2 percent has to do with language. Aristotle's primary definition of man as the *logikòn zôon*, the animal with rational discourse, seems especially apt in light of the foregoing. This explanation, if correct, also shows the role intelligence and volition have played in evolution.[59]

It should be evident that Aristotle's views are not to be mistaken for the doctrine of Lamarck and Lysenko that characteristics acquired during the lifetime of an organism can influence heredity. There is no evidence that he thought the genome is influenced in this way. Even while lacking modern biochemistry and genetics, he clearly believed that anatomical and physiological traits are transmitted by heredity.

Despite all that has it been said, it still may be hard for some to accept the notion that Aristotle was a precursor of Darwin. Yet in all of Aristotle's thought, this is where he most closely anticipates a key area of modern science, so the idea ought not to be surprising. At the very least we can say that evolution is strongly implied in Aristotle's biology. How little he would have had to change his ideas to move explicitly in this direction! For example, he asserts that in reproduction the male supplies the genetic information, and the female is just the passive receptor. It would not have been an enormous step for him to imagine it coming from both sexes. After all, simple observation makes it obvious that a child inherits traits from both parents. The mixing of the genetic material causes variations that would lead one to think of eventual changes in species. It doesn't take a great leap of imagination to picture the relatively small changes in circumstance that could have enabled Aristotle to make the remaining inferences. If Alexander the Great had not died quite so young and Aristotle had had more time to travel around the Macedonian empire, he might have had his own little voyage of the *Beagle*.

Even if he might never have developed a theory as complete as that of Darwin, at least the possibility of it might have occurred to him. In Chapter 4, I criticized Randall for denying that Aristotle had a theory of language and mind. Here too we ought to approach the texts without the usual modern prejudices, for the latter do not stand up to scrutiny. Indeed, Darwin himself had a better opinion of Aristotle than most others in the modern period:

> From quotations which I had seen, I had a high notion of Aristotle's merits, but I had not the most remote notion what a wonderful man he was. Linnaeus and Cuvier have been my two gods, though in very different ways, but they were mere schoolboys to old Aristotle.[60]

We must not take a narrow and dogmatic view either of Aristotle or of Darwin or assume that either was unwilling to modify his views in any way. Rather than occupying irreconcilable positions, they have much common ground. If, ultimately, differences remain, these are the sharply focused kind discussed earlier. Here as elsewhere the possibility remains of reconciling Aristotle and modern science.

We must remember that the four causes are not four separate entities; the final cause does *not* operate independently of the other three. The organism has substantial unity or "soul," but the soul is limited by the fact that it is the form of a body. Thus, Aristotle says that all living beings try to share in the immortal and divine *insofar as they can*: They reproduce. They cannot survive individually, but only by reproducing an offspring like themselves.[61] The issue still remains whether or not the organism really is a substantial unity and thus has a *héneka toû* or "final cause," but at least we can approach this question without employing a parody of Aristotle's position and turning him into a straw man.

Aristotle's ideas comprise a scientific teleology, not a religious one. The universe is such that soul/mind exists in it. Since mind is the highest power of the soul, it is natural that as more complex life forms evolve, they will tend to have greater intelligence. But this says nothing about how far the process can go, and whether or not the more intelligent species will survive. Our intelligence and free will enable us both to adapt better than other creatures to changes in the environment and to destroy ourselves and it. We also are subject to the whims of nature. There could be cycles of evolution just as some cosmologists think there are cycles of expansion and contraction of the cosmos. The point, in answer to critics like Stephen Jay Gould, is not that "progress" to "higher" forms is inevitable, but that life on all levels is essentially soul/mind. This is true even of the bacteria, which in sheer quantity are the dominant life form. Life tries to survive and develop in any way it can. How far it succeeds is not the issue.

After the origin of species, it remains for us to consider the origin of life. Here too we find that Aristotle anticipates modern biology, and that in both the literal and the figurative senses of the word, he has something vital to add to the discussion.

We begin with his observation at the beginning of the passage from *History of Animals* quoted earlier: "Nature proceeds little by little from things lifeless to animal life in such a way that it is impossible to determine the exact line of demarcation, nor on which side thereof an intermediate form should lie."[62] Although this statement was uttered 2,400 years ago, it could easily be mistaken for something said in the twentieth century. If one showed it to all the scientists in the world without identifying the author, 99.99 percent of them would never guess its source, and a high percentage would be incredulous on being told the truth. Nevertheless, here again Aristotle anticipated modern science, but with a difference: His conception of the origin of life is based on the substantial unity of the organism or "the soul." Life comes into being when "soul" is present, even if it is hard to say exactly when that happens.

As before, we need to translate the word "soul" into the lingo of modern science, and making the connection between Aristotle and biochemistry is not as hard as it may seem. In recent years, a central problem for biochemists theorizing about the origin of life has been what type of macromolecule predominated, the two contenders being proteins and nucleic acids. The former are less complicated than the latter and would thus seem to be the building blocks out of which life arose. However, as Olomucki points out, they "are not informational macromolecules and therefore cannot multiply by themselves. So what could have been the mechanism by which their structure was memorized?"[63] This difficulty leaves nucleic acids as the alternative, but the problem with the latter is that they are too complicated to be formed spontaneously in the primeval molecular "soup."[64] Here is the solution to the dilemma that scientists have figured out, as described by Olomucki:

> Some recent papers, in particular those which earned Thomas R. Cech and Sidney Altman the Nobel Prize in Chemistry in 1989, actually demonstrated that informational and catalytic properties could really be combined in the same molecule, a polynucleotide. So we now have good reason to assume that the oldest polymers were the RNAs which in the beginning would have played the dual role of repositories of genetic memory and catalysts. Viewed from this perspective, the egg *is* the chicken.[65]

The primeval RNA that the scientists are presupposing, a more versatile type of molecule that precedes the more specialized types, sounds suspiciously like substantial being. Olomucki's conclusion, "the egg *is* the chicken," sounds awfully Aristotelian. It almost seems as if the scientists are stumbling onto Aristotelianism without realizing it. Perhaps some modern-day Molière could write a comedy patterned after *Le Médecin malgré lui* (*The Doctor in Spite of Himself*) called *Les Aristotéliens malgré eux* (*The Aristotelians in Spite of Themselves*).

All kidding aside, the issue remains whether or not the pristine combinations of molecules from which life arose really were substantial unities. If they were, they were a primitive form of mind because soul is essentially mind. At the other end of the scale of life we have conscious mind, but ultimately the two are the same. In other words, life arose when combinations of molecules began to function as substantial unities with a rudimentary version of the blank tablet. This was not conscious thought, but it was the primeval ancestor of conscious thought.

It is hard to draw a clear boundary between living and non-living matter, but we can imagine how life may have arisen. Actuality preceded potentiality as non-living forms evolved into living ones over many millions of years. The earliest stages of evolution seem to have taken much longer than the latest. Perhaps certain combinations of molecules at times behaved with substantial unity and at times did not. Slowly, very slowly, they took on full substantial unity. The spark of life may have sputtered on and off for eons before it became a steady and enduring flame.

It then took hundreds of millions of years or perhaps longer for primitive organisms to acquire the complex structure of eukaryotic one-celled organisms. Once this stage was reached, the pace of evolution quickened, as multicellular organisms developed, leading to the complex life forms of more recent ages.

Broadly speaking, all this is implicit in the writings of Aristotle, if we read them without prejudice and with imagination. Although lacking much of the knowledge science since has gained, he was a pioneer of genius, anticipating modern ideas in unsuspected ways. Indeed, the more we look at him as a scientist, the more amazing things we discover in his work.

J. First Philosophy and Natural Science

I hope I have satisfied the reader that Aristotle really does offer intelligible and plausible solutions to a number of key problems of modern thought. While part of his system requires correction from science, the part that remains intact can reform "philosophy" and heal the dualism in modern ideas.

Such changes would be truly revolutionary. How ironic if Aristotle, having been ignored or rejected for centuries, should return to solve the problems of the people who rejected him! This would parallel what he did in the fourth century B.C., when he found a middle way between Platonism and materialism. Here in the late twentieth century it is not Platonism at one of the extremes, but something vaguely resembling it, the modern-day discipline of "philosophy," a quasi-Kantian parody of Socrates. At the other extreme is a dogmatically materialist science.

But wait! What if the reader is not convinced that Aristotle had solved all the problems of "modern philosophy" before it ever came upon the scene? As I said at the beginning, I am not offering a package deal. One still can accept the criticism of twentieth-century "philosophy" as an ill-conceived discipline. Let us pause, therefore, to consider what will happen after "philosophy" dies, regardless of whether an Aristotelian revolution occurs. This will provide a better vantage point, neutral ground from which to decide how much of a paradigm change should actually take place.

Imagine that "philosophy" as an independent discipline no longer exists. We can be sure that, as Rorty says, "the great dead philosophers" will continue to be read. They will be part of the history of ideas, but it will not be enough to put them there and leave it at that. Something more definite will be needed to replace the paradigm within which they previously were studied. We will need to understand precisely their relationship to other disciplines.

As noted earlier, "the history of philosophy" is an interdisciplinary tradition. Different parts of it belong to different sciences. At the same time, its heart and core is "first philosophy" or "metaphysics." The latter is what gives "the history of philosophy" any claim it has to constitute a separate discipline. Now if metaphysics is closely related to those parts of the tradition that belong to the sciences, I really am asking, what is the relationship between metaphysics and science? This is what I now will consider, using the conceptual framework provided by Plato and Aristotle, the two greatest metaphysicians.

The word "metaphysics" does not come from Aristotle but is a later invention. He used the term *próte philosophía*, or "first philosophy," to designate the special branch of science that deals with the concepts underlying all the specific sciences and all of human knowledge and experience. Aristotle defined first philosophy as the science that studies "being *qua* being," in other words, the most universal science we have. It tries to sum up all our knowledge and state what is ultimately real.

The phrase "being *qua* being" sounds "metaphysical" in the pejorative sense of the term. It conjures up images of medieval scholastics and their reputed searching in pitch-dark rooms for metaphysical black cats that are not there. However, Aristotle was decidedly not a medieval scholastic. He was fully a scientist. In his conception of things, first philosophy is closely tied to natural science and strongly influenced by it. We must keep in mind, however, that Aristotle's view of natural science was broader than that which prevails today.

Plato didn't use the term "first philosophy," but he most certainly dealt with the subject, and we can use the term to draw a comparison. Plato's conception differs from that of Aristotle. The relationship is reversed. Instead of first philosophy being dependent on science, for Plato it is a *super-science* that *contains* the specific sciences. This is because the latter deal with the physical world, which, Plato believes, is an inferior imitation of the world of pure, abstract ideas. The sciences are to be studied only insofar as they help the mind and soul ascend to this ideal realm. The higher the mindgoes, the more it understands ideas in their abstract purity, and the more easily it comprehends science. Since mathematics is a realm of abstraction just below the realm of pure ideas, mathematics is superior to the physical sciences. It is to be studied not as a tool of the latter, but to help the mind attain the world of ideas. A comment made by Einstein about "seeing all of Euclid's geometry in the axioms" epitomizes the experience the mind has in making this ascent. It is a kind of intense vision that has some of the character of mysticism, except that it is a vision of *ideas*. Rational vision plays an even more important role in Plato than it does in Aristotle, and when we see its importance in Plato, we understand where Aristotle gets it from.

The pursuit of moral excellence is just as important as intellectual. In Plato's account the two are united in the person of Socrates. As Plato presents him in various dialogues, Socrates both describes and embodies the soul's ascent to a higher realm. Thus, first philosophy *qua* super-science deals both with the world of ideas and the method of reaching it. Platonism is not just a theory but a way of life.

One of the most important components of Plato's thought is the doctrine of innate ideas. Plato thinks that the physical objects we perceive with our senses only serve to make us aware of the abstract ideas already contained in the mind. The study of mathematics epitomizes this process. The objects that we see in the world around us are such crude imitations of the pure concepts of mathematics that we could not have discovered them through mere sense-perception. Hence, we must be rediscovering ideas that already were present in our minds. Plato calls this process "recollection," and it is recollection of a very special kind. We are remembering ideas that were in our minds, even if we weren't consciously thinking about them. As Socrates says in the dialogue *Meno*, "What others call 'learning,' I call 'recollection.'"

Aristotle was apparently a student of Plato early in his career and was much taken with Plato's thought. However, he came to disagree with Plato on a number of key issues. Above all, he rejected the theory of ideas and the doctrine of innate ideas. According to him, we do not "recollect" abstract concepts that already are present in our minds. We proceed by means of *epagogé* or *induction*. This means we derive abstract ideas from particular perceptions by generalizing. "All human beings by nature desire to know," he says, and so we start from what is more knowable to us, the world of the senses, and try to get to what is more knowable in itself, *i.e.*, universals, abstract ideas.[66] But there is no Platonic realm of pure ideas for us to reach. It appears that the highest we can attain is scientific knowledge of the universe we live in, although the pursuit of that knowledge imitates the divine. In *Metaphysics*, Book XII, Aristotle provides an account of God, the Unmoved Mover, the pure intelligence that is the ultimate source of all motion in the universe, and he speaks of the divine in key passages in *De Anima* and the *Nicomachean Ethics*. Apart from that, it is unclear what knowledge of it he thinks we can have.

Aristotle is an *empiricist*, someone who believes that all our knowledge comes from what we experience by means of our five senses together with ideas derived from sense-perceptions. Empiricists believe that there is nothing in the mind that was not previously in the senses. In other words, we have no innate ideas. As Aristotle says, the mind cannot think without a *phántasma*, a mental percept derived from one or more of the five senses.

However, the mind is a self-conscious unity that becomes aware of itself when it perceives or thinks. The mind itself is something like an innate idea. Thus, traces of Plato's *rationalism* and *idealism* are still apparent in Aristotle's thought, and he does not completely fit the conventional definition of an empiricist.

Aristotle rejected what he didn't like in Plato and did the same with the materialism of his day. He took what he liked in both and created a science, or a set of sciences. Many of his ideas, including teleology, the unity of mind, the relation of mind and body, and the relation of mind and soul, accord perfectly well with Plato.[67] Nevertheless, if the theory of ideas and the doctrine of innate ideas are incorrect, then first philosophy is not a super-science. It depends not on discovering a higher reality through pure thought, but on gaining scientific knowledge of the world we live in.

Maybe this is the best we can have. On the other hand, the possibility remains that in the end Plato will prove to be right. Perhaps at some point our knowledge will enable us to transcend this world and discover whatever caused or created it. In no way is Plato "out of the question." Nor is Plotinos, who in the third century A.D. revised Plato's ideas and created a theory known as Neoplatonism. Plotinos retained the notion that the physical world is only a pale reflection of a higher realm, which we apprehend through transcendent rational insight. While the idea that the mind directly apprehends a higher reality has some of the elements of mysticism, Plato and Plotinos are not mystics. They are rationalists, and their rationalism encompasses science, yet is not held down by a dogmatic materialism. Since we do not know the limits of our knowledge and our mental powers, we should avoid setting any arbitrary limits.

If ultimately Plato proved to be right, it would be relatively easy to revise Aristotle to restore the Platonism. We know this can be done because St. Thomas Aquinas partially did it. He showed that Aristotle's ideas can be reconciled with a Christian Platonism. Other scholastics went farther in this direction. St. Bonaventura and Duns Scotus, for example, were more Platonistic than St. Thomas. While many of the scholastics fashioned a

Platonized Aristotelianism in the service of Christian theology, others combined Platonism and Aristotelianism with an eye to the natural world. Modern science came into being as the result of a long medieval criticism of Aristotle's physics in light of Augustinian Platonism, with its emphasis on mathematics. Actually, the criticism of Aristotle's physics began in the ancient world, was continued by the Arab Aristotelians of the eleventh and twelfth centuries, and reached an advanced level during the latter part of the Middle Ages.[68]

At its best, as in the work of Nicolas Oresme, medieval science brilliantly anticipated modern science. At its worst, scholasticism combined Plato and Aristotle in grotesque fashion, trying to give scientific explanations by reifying Platonic abstractions. William of Ockham's nominalism was a reaction against this tendency and was a direct antecedent of Hobbes and the other British empiricists.

Since the sources of modern science in the Middle Ages are clear to behold, we are naturally led to ask, why didn't the mind-body dualism and the split between first philosophy and science occur then and there? The answer is that the medieval thinkers, whether they were Platonists or Aristotelians, well understood that first philosophy and science are closely related. There was no reason to take rigid positions in either area that would cause it to be split off from the other. However, when the Copernican theory and Galilean science appeared on the scene, the scholastics tried to preserve the medieval world-view and strongly resisted the changes. Science in turn overreacted to scholasticism, taking dogmatic positions of its own. A polarization of views occurred. No Aristotle or St. Thomas was on hand to reconcile the conflicting sides. The result was the dualism of "modern philosophy." Meanwhile, science made amazing progress and was able to function more or less independently of first philosophy.

To a man, the writers from Descartes through Kant were all trying to come to terms with science. Hence, their view of the relation of first philosophy and science was more Aristotelian than Platonic. We noted in Chapter 5 the extent to which they all were wrestling with Aristotelian issues. Those who believed in innate ideas were more Platonic than the others, but none of them conceived of first philosophy as a super-science.

Later in the modern period Hegel and Marx made notable attempts to create a first philosophy that truly would be a super-science. Hegel described the attainment of it by means of a historical dialectic: Individuals and societies go through different stages of consciousness before the realization of the Absolute Idea. Marx kept the Hegelian dialectic, but transformed Hegel's idealism into materialism. In our own time, we have seen the upheaval inspired by the commitment to the super-science of dialectical materialism.

Plato, Plotinos, Hegel, and Marx had many interesting and brilliant ideas, but none of them succeeded in establishing the truth of their respective systems as such. If any of their metaphysical systems is a valid super-science, we ought to be able to prove that natural science is derivable from it. Hegel, for example, tried to do exactly that, to show the dialectical character of natural science based upon his metaphysical theory, but this is widely regarded as the most unsatisfactory part of his thought. He had better luck with the social sciences, but not enough to provide conclusive support for his overall theory. This is not to say that the effort to establish first philosophy as a super-science never will succeed, but up to this point, a convincing case has not been made, nor does it seem likely that in the foreseeable future it will be.

Meanwhile modern science has been so successful in advancing knowledge that it has almost convinced itself and others that it is independent of first philosophy, or at least of Platonism and Aristotelianism. Indeed, many scientists and their adherents have tried to turn science itself into a first philosophy. If everything in the world is reducible to matter, then everything can be explained in terms of physical and chemical processes and first philosophy becomes more or less identical with natural science. However, the materialist reduction, despite the predictions of its adherents, has never taken place. What did happen was that *matter* became an ever more formidable concept as it was extended over more and more areas of nature. But this was matter as science understood it. Even though science was totally dependent on mathematics (*i.e.*, mathematical *form*), it behaved as if mathematics was just a tool in the hands of the physicists. The mathematical concepts were not given the same metaphysical status as the material world they were used to describe. Where mathematical form, mind, and values might fit into the modern world-view was left to the "philosophers" as science forged ahead, learning more and more about the nature and operations of matter. As Randall observed, the scientists found Lady Philosophy invaluable in private, though they were apt to cut her dead in public. They were content to define matter loosely and downplay the importance of form *in principle* while finding it indispensable *in practice*.

While this arrangement allowed great advances to occur, it caused an array of intellectual and cultural problems. The "modern philosophers" of the seventeenth and eighteenth centuries were unable to solve these problems, and their successors have had no better luck. We still have no consensus about which first philosophy accords with natural science. Instead, we have the false discipline of "philosophy," which makes a virtue out of its own confusion. This is a highly unsatisfactory situation. It may be an exaggeration to say that science is a headless horseman, but surely it lacks sufficient direction. It is weakest precisely where "philosophy" has failed to guide it: in understanding human nature and the relationship between the natural and the human worlds. In the confused growth of knowledge that has resulted, our educational and research system has become a leviathan.

One of the first things to realize in trying to escape from this predicament is how artificial is the separation between first philosophy and natural science. We need to go back to a more classical and a more medieval view of things. Indeed, if we retrace our steps to discover what went wrong, we see that the separation began in the Middle Ages. Dualism did not emerge full-grown from the head of Descartes. It resulted from the bifurcation of medieval thought into a) scholasticism and b) what eventually became modern science. Scholasticism was too metaphysical. It made a bad combination of metaphysics and natural science, and resisted modern science when it came on the scene. The latter in turn overreacted to scholasticism, and dualism resulted. However much dualism may have reflected the *Zeitgeist* of the modern period, it is unnecessary, and we can free ourselves from it.

The effort to resolve this difficulty brings to mind a conversation that once occurred between John Dewey and a German professor of philosophy. The latter observed that if we are not careful about the way we formulate our ideas in metaphysics, "metaphysics will have no more certainty than physics." Dewey was astounded at this comment. "No more certainty than physics!" he exclaimed, "No more certainty than physics!" He couldn't believe his ears. After all, what branch of human knowledge has greater certainty than physics?

They both had a point. We want our science to be sound, both conceptually and empirically. The question remains whether the truths of mathematics and metaphysics are sounder than those of physics and how solid the foundations of our knowledge really are. Nevertheless, it seems to me that Dewey got the better of the exchange, and Dewey's position on this issue is Aristotelian. In answer to the question raised at the beginning of this section, we can say with confidence that unless and until someone succeeds in creating a superscience of metaphysics or first philosophy, the Aristotelian view of its relation to natural science is correct.

This view includes Aristotle's statement of the relation of matter and form, which is sounder than the materialist version put forth by modern science. Science's version is confused, self-contradictory, circular, and question-begging. The scientists and their friends are alternately arrogant and defensive in maintaining it. It presupposes that science can explain all natural phenomena by reducing them to some combination of material processes. Form becomes irrelevant, even though mathematics, physics, chemistry, biology and their allied disciplines are all totally dependent on it. This is an unsatisfactory state of affairs. Despite all of science's wonderful achievements, it still is science without metaphysics, a truncated, dualistic science.

Whether or not Aristotle's own first philosophy turns out to be correct, at least he provides us with the best terminology and conceptual framework to understand the relationship between first philosophy and natural science. From his vantage point, we can look at our whole intellectual tradition, see the overlap between "philosophy" and "science," and have the best chance of evaluating properly the claims of the various first philosophical theories.

If materialism should win out and we should prove to be nothing more than "organic robots," in Dennett's phrase, then the first philosophy that would express this reality would be that of Hobbes or Spinoza. In any event, the issue would be decided. We would not have the confused situation that has persisted through most of the modern period, where a conceptual dualism – in essence, the "mind-body dualism" – has created an academic dualism, a split in the way knowledge is conceived and pursued.

On the other hand, what if the issue were not resolved and the dualism of the modern period persisted? If the most sophisticated versions of opposed positions tend to converge, and everything boils down to a residue of critical differences, are the differences that we have been considering decidable? Instead of Aristotle's view that the soul and mind are substantial unities existing in nature, couldn't the answer be a neo-Kantian/Humean one? That is, the soul and mind are regulative principles in Kant's lingo or fictions (*i.e.*, hypotheses) in Hume's. If as regulative principles they can do everything that Aristotle's real substantial unities can do, what's the difference?

But is this likely to happen? Could we really have parallel explanations of the phenomena of mind and soul without any way of choosing between them, however exhaustively we worked out the details?

Such a situation, if it actually occurred, would be reminiscent of the Ptolemaic-Copernican controversy that raged for a century before it finally was laid to rest. Both theories explained the phenomena. In fact, until Kepler showed that the orbits of the planets are elliptical and not circular, the Ptolemaic theory predicted the positions of the planets more accurately than the Copernican. I submit, however, that based on the type of evidence I have presented in this essay, no such protracted debate will occur. An investigation of the details will soon favor one view over the other.

At least it should be apparent that Aristotle's hylomorphism is an intelligible and plausible alternative to modern dualism. Even if readers are uncertain whether Aristotle's view of the mind and the soul is correct, I trust I have shown that he represents a real alternative to the current paradigm. How lackluster the latter appears in light of the possibilities that the new synthesis offers! Although the "philosophers" continually dress up the old pseudo-problems in new form, the pretense is wearing thin. The threadbare material of the new garments barely conceals the decrepit body within. By misconstruing their own activities, they have created a verbose, obscure, pretentious, self-serving parody of a discipline. Until they acknowledge this, let them stay where I left them at the end of Chapter 3, in the eighth circle of Dante's Inferno, up to their chins in their own *cacca*.

If at least they recognize the falsity of the paradigm of "philosophy," they can gain admission to Purgatorio, *i.e.*, the partitioning of "philosophy" among other disciplines that I envisioned. But if they want to get to Paradiso, they need to latch onto the ideas of Aristotle, *il maestro di color che sanno*, the master of those that know, as Dante described him. Only Aristotle can get them there. The scope of Aristotle's ideas, their richness, their detail, and their scientific character outclass nearly everyone else in the tradition, including all the writers between Descartes and Kant. While St. Thomas and Hegel were, like Aristotle, encyclopedic in their interests, Thomas owes so much to Aristotle that he hardly is a counter-example. Furthermore, Thomas's version of Aristotle's ideas is, I fear, not as good as the original, nor does he have a natural science as good as modern science with which to combine them. As for Hegel, he had his own hobbyhorses to ride. His ideas were imaginative and often brilliant, but they were vague and tied to a speculative metaphysics that is hard to understand, let alone confirm.

Plato is the sole exception, and his relationship to Aristotle is even closer than it is conventionally understood to be. Consider the following:

> "It is impossible not to be impressed, in reading Aristotle, by how much of a Platonist he is and how much of a non-Platonist he is, and by how closely these polar traits are fused."[69]

I must take issue with this comment by another of my teachers, Justus Buchler. The polar opposite of Plato is not Aristotle, but the materialists. Aristotle is closer to Plato than he is to them. Plato posed problems, as in *Meno*, *Protagoras*, *Parmenides*, *Theaetetus*, and *The Republic*, to which Aristotle found answers.[70] Aristotle toned down – so to speak – Plato's ideas and turned them into science. Yet at many a climactic point in his writings, he sounds like a Platonist.[71] The transcendent impulse that motivates his science can hardly be missed. Plato for his part was not against science. He simply had other priorities. While not actually a scientist, he provided in his writings a treasure house of scientific ideas, of which Aristotle took full advantage. Aristotle got so many ideas from Plato that his triumph in large measure would also be Plato's. Moreover, the possibility remains that Aristotle's pursuit of scientific knowledge might ultimately lead back to Plato.

While acknowledging Aristotle's debt to Plato, I do not want to overstate it. Having just presented his ideas on a wide range of topics, I will now try to say what it is that gives them their particular power. First of all, Aristotle is the supreme empiricist. He is wide-ranging and thorough. He captures the details of common-sense experience and states them with precision. Yet while firmly grounded in everyday experience, he raises common sense to the level of genius, uniting it with the most brilliant concepts, which he fashions from a wide variety of sources. This perhaps is his supreme ability – to take ideas from other people, chew them over, digest them, and end up with what he needs to build up his system. We see him doing this in many of his treatises. The first of the three books of the *De Anima* is devoted to analyzing the problems his predecessors had in understanding and defining soul and mind. The solutions follow in the next two books. A similar analysis occupies the first book of the *Metaphysics*. In other works as well we see him wrestling with the ideas of his predecessors and contemporaries. He has an uncanny ability to identify the soundest ideas of thinkers from opposite ends of the spectrum and synthesize them. Hylomorphism is the most dramatic example. It is a happy medium between Platonism and materialism. I remarked above that Aristotle "tones down" Platonism. He does the same with materialism, or maybe one should say, he "tones it *up*," restoring form to its proper place where the materialists have omitted it. In any case, again and again Aristotle scrutinizes the ideas of a wide variety of thinkers and removes their more extreme and questionable features, while holding fast to what is most solid in them. St. Augustine and Kant also digested and synthesized ideas from many sources, and like Aristotle, they have been highly influential. However, in my judgment Aristotle did it better than anybody else. His amazing ability to express himself with precision comes, at least in part, from the process of honing his ideas against those of many others.

Aristotle did this with the thinkers of his own time, and one can extrapolate the procedure to those who came after him, as I have done in this essay. We saw, for example, that a concept of the unconscious is implicit in Aristotle's writings. It deals with the same issues as Freud's does, but is less speculative and less extreme. Similarly, Aristotle's concept of moral reasoning and ethical principle covers much of the same ground as Kant, but is less rigid and grounded more solidly in experience. Because of the world-view from which he was starting, Kant could not find a place for mind, values, and teleology in the natural world, so he simply put them in another realm outside of nature. Except for that, his discussion of them has much in common with Aristotle's. That two of the soundest thinkers in the tradition are in accord on many points is no small matter. In the area of psycholinguistics, Aristotle and Chomsky have much in common, but Aristotle is less dogmatic than Chomsky and deals with a wider range of topics and problems.

To some, Aristotle's toning down of others' ideas makes him dull and mundane. He has been called "the morning after," whereas Plato is "the night before." However, Aristotle appears dull only to the most superficial reader. Even while criticizing the excesses of other thinkers, he speaks carefully to the issues they raise, and he is seldom, if ever dogmatic. As I pointed out in comparing him with the "modern philosophers," the interplay of ideas is ongoing. Aristotle said a lot, but he did not say everything. Within the framework he erected, there is plenty of room for his own ideas and those of the others in the tradition imaginatively to interact. Recognizing his dominance of "the history of philosophy" does not consign the others to oblivion, but actually shows them in a better light. It enables us to get more out of them than we otherwise could do. Thus, Aristotle revives and enhances the whole tradition.

All this is in stark contrast to the skeptical, disunified conception of philosophy offered by Rorty and his colleagues. It is philosophy brought back to life and together with science forming a seamless whole. To bring about this desirable state of affairs, it is not just the "philosophers" who need to change their thinking and grasp all that Aristotle can do, but the scientists as well. At the dawn of the modern period, they corrected Aristotle's mistakes. Now it is his turn to help them escape the limits they needlessly have set to their own work. Putting the soul, mind, and values back into nature does not mean what they think it does. It does not open the door to pseudo-science or turn science into the handmaiden of theology. On the contrary, when in the twelfth and thirteenth centuries Aristotle's ideas burst over Europe like a bombshell, they were widely regarded as atheistic. While Aristotle believed in the reality of minds and souls, he doubted they survive the death of the body. St. Thomas showed that Aristotle's ideas can be reconciled with Christian belief, but in and of themselves they are no more religious in the Judaeo-Christian sense than are the ideas of Spinoza or Einstein.

The best of medieval scholasticism subjected Aristotle's physics to a mathematical criticism inspired by Augustinian Platonism. This led eventually to modern science. The worst of medieval scholasticism combined Platonic and Aristotelian ideas and produced a monstrosity. It turned secondary qualities like hotness and coldness into physical forces. No wonder modern science resisted this. But this was not true Aristotelianism. In the genuine article the qualitative analysis stays where it belongs.

St. Thomas Aquinas synthesized Aristotle with thirteenth-century science, but that was only a preliminary attempt compared to what can be done with the science of today. How amazing that a man writing nearly 2,400 years ago developed his ideas in a wide range of disciplines, and in many of those fields was ahead of where we are now! What is more, though he worked out his most brilliant ideas in the absence of modern science, when we make a serious effort to connect them with it, wonder of wonders – they fit! Given the fact that the modern world has been unaware of the harmony between these seemingly disparate ideas, we ought to give the new paradigm a try instead of clinging to the conventional, dogmatic conclusions about mind and body and about first philosophy and natural science.

As for the differences between Aristotle and modern science, they boil down to a few key issues, among them the existence or non-existence of final causes and of the soul, the unity of mind, and the mind's ability to move the body. The resolution of these issues will determine which paradigm wins out. Ultimately, the question will be resolved, if it can be, by theory combined with observation and/or experiment. We should keep in mind how modern science itself got established. There wasn't much proof of the Copernican theory, and some of the objections to it that were raised were reasonable ones. The new theory triumphed for a variety of good reasons – its simplicity, elegance, and explanatory power – but it took time.[72]

If indeed Aristotle's ideas win out, the sciences and the humanities will be brought together in a new interdisciplinary scheme of things. The neo-Aristotelian first philosophy will be shared by everybody, and there will be no need for separate "philosophy" departments. Reductionism, dualism, and skepticism will be swept away as if by a tidal wave. It will be a paradigm shift of Copernican, Darwinian, or Einsteinian proportions.

How wonderful it would be if the scientists could throw off their blinders and see that final causes, the soul, and the mind have a natural place in science. Then they could truly say, "This Aristotle was one of us." Indeed, Aristotle together with Plato would rank alongside Newton and Einstein.

Aristotle supplies just what modern science lacks. The account I have given of his ideas only scratches the surface. Imagine how powerful the combination would be. It would provide the human race with something it never has had: a knowledge of matter allied with an understanding of mind and human nature. We could expect to see a series of revolutionary discoveries. An understanding of the mind-body relationship together with an understanding of language and mind should lead us to a detailed knowledge of mind and brain. The human sciences would catch up with the physical ones. What might this not do to relieve the evil and suffering in the world? Such a state of affairs is hard for us to conceive because we are so used to dualism, to knowing much about the workings of nature and little about ourselves. But with the bizarre imbalance in our knowledge gone and with artificial barriers between disciplines removed, the prospect of great progress would lie before us.

To be sure, none of this guarantees that the human race will find happiness or even keep from destroying itself. The synthesis of Aristotle and modern science will not be the solution to all human problems, but it will provide humanity with opportunities it never has had before. Again and again since modern science came upon the scene, people have been predicting the advent of an earthly paradise. Yet somehow, the heavenly city of the Enlightenment philosophers and other modern visionaries has failed to arrive. There is no guarantee that overcoming the imbalance in modern thought will bring it about, but if moral and metaphysical philosophy can truly work together with natural philosophy, who knows what might not happen?

We do not know how much a unified science may accomplish, and it certainly does not preclude a religious solution to our problems. While Aristotelianism is not religious in the Judaeo-Christian sense, it is more supportive of religion than is materialism. Just as it does not exclude the possibility of the ultimate triumph of Platonism, it does not rule out sources of insight through faith. We do not, after all, know the limits of science. We should keep in mind Newton's saying that we are like children playing on the shores of the ocean of knowledge. Newton, in fact, was a religious man, but his religious writings are far less well known than his scientific ones. One surmises that he would have agreed with St. Thomas Aquinas that between true faith and true reason there can be no conflict.

Newton seems to have had a sense of the proper relationship between science and religion. Would that others would follow his example. As pointed out in Chapter 7, science must recognize its limitations and guard against turning itself into a religion.

We must all strive to keep strongly held beliefs from getting the better of us. The reader will have noted that at times I speak of Aristotle with an enthusiasm approaching religious fervor. Indeed, a student once suggested that I found The First Church of Aristotle Scientist. On the other hand, given the fanaticism with which the materialists cling to their belief in matter, this might not be a bad idea. I can imagine myself preaching the good news about substantial being, form, the soul, the mind, and the mind's power to move the body to an audience of scientific unbelievers. I picture myself being greeted at first with smiles and guffaws. Then when the audience perceives that my criticism is serious, the laughter gives way to boos, hisses, and heckling. The reproaches come at me from all sides, yet I persist, arguing strenuously and loud and long. Finally, my enthusiasm prevails. One scientist and then another jumps up and shouts, "I see it! I see it!" and steps forward to sign a pledge card for Aristotle.

While it may be possible to win over a small number of the scientists by rational argument, it might take something as emotional as this to get through to them. I fear that the vast majority cannot bring themselves to consider the possibility that Aristotle was right. The sky might fall, but final causes cannot exist, there can be no souls in nature, and the mind cannot act upon the body.

Nevertheless, I predict that sooner or later the union of Aristotle and modern science will occur, and what a wrenching experience it will be for the materialists! The trauma they will undergo will itself be an event to be memorialized in the history of science. Picture visitors passing among the exhibits in a museum of natural history. The placard in front of one case reads, "This is a chunk of the meteorite that landed in Siberia in 1908 and left a crater half a mile wide." Above the display is a photograph of an immense hole in the ground with trees flattened as far as the eye can see. Then, moving on to the next case they spy a tablet saying, "This is a piece of the brick the scientists shat when they finally realized that Aristotle was right about final causes, the mind, and the soul and was ahead of them in many areas of science." The visitors can decide for themselves which was the greater event in natural history.

However the paradigm change might happen, it is clear that being right is not enough. Even the most intelligent people do not readily relinquish their most deeply held beliefs. If rational arguments do not work, one does not quite know what to try. In the next chapter, I will consider what to do about this dilemma.

Notes

1. Noam Chomsky, *Reflections on Language* (New York: Pantheon Books 1975), pp. 5–6.

2. Martin Olomucki, *The Chemistry of Life*, trans. by Isabel A. Leonard from *La Chimie du Vivant* (New York: McGraw-Hill, 1993), pp. 126–27.

3. *Metaphysics* VII, xi, 1037a5–7.

4. *De Anima* II, i, 412a28–412b1.

5. *Ibid.*, 412 b 29-413a2.

6. See *Metaphysics* X, i, 1052a35–36, 1052a23–26, 1054a13; IV, ii, 1003b26–35; *De Anima* II, i, 412a20–29.

7. The argument for the unity of mind is in ch. ii, 426b8 ff.; the blank tablet and the formal identity of the mind with its objects in ch. iv; the mind as a form of forms in ch. viii. *Epagogé* is presented in *Posterior Analytics* II, xix, the final chapter of the treatise.

8. *De Anima* III, ii, 426b20–21.

9. *Ibid.*, 430a1–2.

10. Literally, "It has no actual existence until it thinks." *De Anima* III, iv, 429a23–24.

11. *De Anima* III, iv, 429b31.

12. *De Anima* III, iv, 429b6–8.

13. *Ibid.*, III, viii, 432a1–3.

14. *Posterior Analytics* II, xix, 99b34–100b4.

15. See *Nicomachean Ethics*, VII, iii, a discussion of moral weakness, where Aristotle explains seemingly irrational behavior by attributing it to a dreamlike condition. The two treatises, *On Dreams* and *On Prophecy in Sleep* are among the *Parva Naturalia*, a series of short essays on psychology and biology.

16. *Nicomachean Ethics* III, v, 1114a30–1114b13.

17. *De Anima* III, viii, 432a5.

18. *De Anima* III, xi, 434a6–10.

19. Mozart, "A Letter." In Brewster Ghiselin, ed., *The Creative Process: A Symposium* (New York: The New American Library, Mentor Books, 1952), p. 43.

20. See Dennett, *op. cit.*, ch. 8, "How Words Do Things with Us." Skinner's book on the subject is entitled *Verbal Behavior* (New York: Appleton-Century-Crofts, 1957).

21. Japanese syntax (word order) tends to be the opposite of English syntax. Take, for example, the Japanese expression *teeboru no ue no handobooku*, which translated into fluent English means "the handbook on top of the table." However, translated more literally, it would be "the table's top's handbook," which is gibberish in English. (The Japanese particle *no* is similar to the English possessive *'s'*, but has a much wider use.) Note the difference in conception here: the English phrase works downward, from the handbook to the top to the table, whereas the Japanese thought process is upward, from the table to its top to the handbook.

22. Aristotle's ten categories are "substance" or substantial being, quantity, quality, relation, place, time, position or posture, state or condition, action, undergoing or passion. According to Aristotle, these are the ten ways anything can be said to be.

23. *Nicomachean Ethics* VI, ii. 1139a35.

24. *De Anima* III, x, in particular 433a32–33.

25. *Nicomachean Ethics* VI, ii, 1139b5–6.

26. *Metaphysics* I, i, 980a22.

27. See *Metaphysics* XII, chapters vi–vii, for his discussion of the Unmoved

Mover, his conception of the divine. See also chapter ix. Relevant too is the discussion of the *bíos theoretikós*, the contemplative or speculative life in *Nicomachean Ethics* X, vii and viii. See especially X, vii, 1177b27–ll78a8.

28. *De Anima* III, x, 433b12–13.

29. *Nicomachean Ethics* IX, ix, 1170a16–1170b1.

30. *De Anima* III, iv, 429a22–24.

31. *Nicomachean Ethics* X, iv, 1174b23–24 and 1174b33–35.

32. Descartes and others use the argument from "phantom pain" or the claims of amputees that they still feel their lost limbs to support the theory that the mind is located solely in the brain. Presumably, these are hallucinations and disappear in the course of time.

33. Aristotle, *De Motu Animalium* 701b24–28.

34. *De Anima* II, i, 413a2–3.

35. *Metaphysics* VII, xi, 1036b28–33.

36. Aristotle's concept of habit emerges from his discussion of moral virtue in Books II–IV of the *Nicomachean Ethics*. From the many examples of virtue and vice that he brings up, it is plain that the mental state is the critical factor in governing behavior.

37. *Nicomachean Ethics* II, i, 1103a33–34.

38. See *De Motu Animalium* 701a25 ff.

39. *Nicomachean Ethics* VII, iii, 1147b3–5.

40. *Nicomachean Ethics* I, xiii, 1103a4–11. The term "virtue" in contemporary English has a largely moral connotation, but it originally meant excellence of all kinds. The word "virtuoso" preserves some of the earlier meaning. The Greek *areté*, which we translate as "virtue," has this broader meaning, so it is quite natural for Aristotle to distinguish between moral and intellectual *areté*.

41. *Metaphysics* I, i, 980a22–26.

42. *Nicomachean Ethics* III, v, 1114a30–1114b13. See p. 158.

43. See *Nicomachean Ethics*, I, vii, in particular 1098a8–11, "and we say the function of an individual of a certain class and of a *good* individual of this class is the same (like a harper and a good harper, and indeed this is absolutely the case with everything) . . ."

44. *Politics* I, i, 1253a2–18.

45. In an undergraduate senior seminar Randall told us, "This is widely regarded as the best definition of Romanticism that has ever been given."

46. Arthur C. Guyton, *Basic Human Neurophysiology*, 3rd ed. (Philadelphia: Saunders, 1981), p. 222.

47. *The Collected Poems of A. E. Housman* (New York: Henry Holt, 1940), *More Poems*, XIII.

48. *De Anima* I, i, 403a17–403b3.

49. *Nicomachean Ethics* II, iii, 1104b15.

50. Aristotle, *Politics* I, i, 1253a32–34.

51. See *Metaphysics* VII, xi, especially 1036b26–33.

52. History of Animals VIII, i, 588b4–23, tr. D'Arcy Wentworth Thompson in *The Basic Works of Aristotle*, ed. Richard McKeon (New York: Random House, 1941). p. 635.

53. Ernst Mayr, "Species Concepts and Their Applications" in Elliot Sober, ed., *Conceptual Issues in Evolutionary Biology* (Cambridge, Mass.: MIT Press, 1984), cited in George Lakoff, *Women, Fire, and Dangerous Things: What Categories Reveal about the Mind* (Chicago and London: Univ. of Chicago Press, 1987), p. 190.

54. Lakoff, *op. cit.,* p. 191.

55. Lakoff, *op. cit.*, p. 187.

56. *Parts of Animals* I, ch. 3, 643b29–31, tr. William Ogle in McKeon, *op. cit.*, p. 654.

57. This view is apparent not only in the passage from the *History of Animals* quoted earlier in this section, but also throughout the *De Anima*. It also is stated in the passage from the concluding chapter of the *Posterior Analytics* quoted earlier in this essay and at the beginning of *Metaphysics* I, i.

58. *Nicomachean Ethics* III, ii, 1111b8–9.

59. The role of categories is discussed in more detail in *The Categorical-Mnemonic Method of Language Learning* and *New Linguistics Report,* two unpublished manuscripts written by the author.

60. Charles Darwin to William Ogle, on the publication of the latter's translation of Aristotle's *The Parts of Animals*, 1882. *Life and Letters of Charles Darwin*, ed. Francis Darwin (New York, 1896), II, 427. Quoted in Randall, *Aristotle*, p. 219.

61. *De Anima* II, iv, 415a27–415b8.

62. *History of Animals* VIII, i, 588b4–6.

63. Martin Olomucki, *op. cit.,* p. 56.

64. *Ibid.,* pp. 57–58.

65. *Ibid.,* pp. 59–60.

66. See *Posterior Analytics* I, ii, 71b35–72a6: "Things are 'prior' and 'more knowable' in two senses; heck, the same thing isn't prior by nature and prior in relation to us, nor more knowable [in itself] and more *knowable* to us. And I mean by 'prior and more knowable to us' the things that are nearer to sense-perception, and by '*absolutely* prior and more knowable' the things that are farther from the senses. The most universal concepts are farthest, and the particulars are nearest; and these are opposite to each other."

67. Teleology can be found in Plato's *Republic*, particularly at the end of Book I. The argument for the unity of mind occurs in Plato's dialogue *Theaetetus,* 184–86. Most likely, that is where Aristotle discovered it.

68. For an excellent summary of this development, see *The Principle of Inertia in the Middle Ages* (Boulder: Colorado Associated University Press, 1976) by the physicist Allan Franklin. See also Randall, *The Career of Philosophy*, Vol. I, ch. 10, "The Medieval Roots of Galilean Science."

69. Justus Buchler, *Nature and Judgment* (New York: Grosset & Dunlap, 1966), p. 93.

70. Aristotle answered the doctrine of recollection in the *Meno* with the concept of *epagogé*; he explained the problem posed in the *Protagoras* of whether one can know the good and yet not do it by his analysis of *akrasía*; he answered the paradoxes of the *Parmenides* with the laws of identity and non- contradiction; the problems raised in the *Theaetetus* were seminal for his psychology; and Aristotle's *Politics* responds to the problems raised and the positions taken in Plato's *Republic*.

71. For example, in *Nicomachean Ethics* X, vii, where he compares the highest life man can live, the life of the mind, to the divine; also in that work, the account of the vision that guides us, III, v, and the discussion of moral weakness, VII, i–iii; in the *Metaphysics*, not only the account of the Unmoved Mover in Book XII, but that of substantial being as form at the end of Book VII; in *De Anima* II, iv, where all living things are represented as imitating the immortal and divine; and in *De Anima* III, ii, and III *passim*, where the concept of the unity of mind seems clearly to be built upon the same idea in Plato's *Theaetetus*.

72. See Thomas Kuhn, *The Copernican Revolution* (New York: Random House, 1957).

9
Putting Mind Back into the Minds of the Scientists

In the preceding chapter, I showed that it ought to be possible for us to discover a connection between mind and body that preserves the integrity of mind and does away with the primitive concept of it that has reigned during the modern period. The subject of that discussion could be called the "metaproblem": showing that a plausible alternative exists to dualism, reductionism, and skepticism, the choices currently available. It would have been easier if we did not have to bother with the metaproblem and could get right to the problem itself, but because the old ways of thinking are so firmly fixed in our minds, it was necessary to dislodge them sufficiently to see that an alternative to them really exists. The problem then remains of working out the details of the new solution and showing that it is correct.

It turns out, however, that before you even can get to the metaproblem, an additional difficulty arises, namely, persuading the scientists and their friends merely to *consider the possibility* that a reasonable alternative exists. The cardinals who refused to look through Galileo's telescope are a famous instance of this attitude. An even more extreme form of it is epitomized by the comment of the materialist Donald Davidson: "Plato is not even wrong; he is out of the question." While Aristotle modified Plato's views, presumably to a materialist he too is "out of the question." What a convenient way of getting rid of your opponent's position: just refuse to admit that he has one! I call the task of overcoming this extreme form of closed-mindedness "the metametaproblem."

To be sure, a few scientists have been more open-minded than the others about the connection between Aristotle and modern science, as evidenced by the comments made in 1974 by a Nobel Prize winner:

> That Aristotle anticipated the concepts of modern genetics was the thesis of Dr. Max Delbruck, . . another of the Nobel laureates. Although Aristotle had no access to the knowledge later gained with micro-

scopes, he believed that male semen contains the blueprint for every part of the body. . . . This "form factor" furnished by the male, like the DNA controls growth without itself being altered in the process, according to Aristotle. If the Nobel Prize were conferred posthumously, Dr. Delbruck said, Aristotle should get one.[1]

Delbruck was not alone. As noted earlier, Chomsky also entertained the possibility, however briefly, of looking to Aristotle for an answer to the questions he was raising. There are others as well. It is encouraging that at least a few of the scientists are open to this possibility.

More typically, however, one can expect stubborn resistance and ridicule. I recall experiencing the latter during an interdisciplinary seminar in graduate school. I was trying to explain Aristotle's concept of the *psyché* or "soul" as the substantial unity of the organism when I was disconcerted to see two graduate students in psychology tittering with glee. I tried to ignore them, hoping they would stop, but when they persisted, I asked them what was so funny. One of them replied, "What do you mean by 'the soul'? A creature with wings and a harp?" I tried to convince them that that was not at all what I meant, but in vain. Evidently, they had been so strongly conditioned to react negatively to the word "soul" that no amount of reasoning could dissuade them.

Doubtless those two students would think *I* am the one refusing to look through Galileo's telescope, but it is they who are the dogmatic ones. Dogmatism is not just stubbornness in the face of obvious facts, but also the refusal to consider reasonable alternatives when there are problems with existing theories. The notion that Aristotle understood language, soul, and mind better than modern science does sounds as silly as the Copernican theory did to most people in the year 1600. Despite the complexity of Ptolemaic astronomy, the alternative seemed impossible. "Imagine the earth traveling at enormous speeds around the sun," they would object. "Why aren't we all flying off into space?" This was before Galileo had worked out the law of gravitational acceleration and Newton the concept of momentum, so the question made sense. In other words, Galileo had to convince people that the heliocentric theory was a viable alternative to the geocentric theory even when a number of critical questions about the former still lay unanswered. That was Galileo's metaproblem. His metametaproblem was getting them to listen at all.

Similarly, Darwin had to persuade people that the theory of evolution was correct before Mendel's explanation of genetic inheritance became known. Although he had worked out a solution to the problem of how species evolve, he still had a metaproblem and a metametaproblem. What is more, we can well understand why the last-named may be the most frustrating of all to deal with: People's most cherished beliefs as well as their egos and their reputations are on the line.

Great advances in science require great leaps of imagination, and with each such advance new difficulties arise. Further leaps are needed to get beyond the problems caused by the earlier ones. Modern science provided a wonderful understanding of matter, but strange mental gyrations occurred in order to preserve traditional views about mind. We have become so accustomed to these difficulties that we fail to see how unnecessary they are and how inadequate the attempts to deal with them have been. Yet even highly educated and intelligent minds cannot break out of the familiar patterns. How can we help them to see their own irrationality?

Earlier, I quoted Alfred North Whitehead's inspired comment that the history of philosophy is little more than a series of extended footnotes to Plato and Aristotle. That could be called Whitehead's Wonderful Wisecrack #1. Germane to the present discussion is Whitehead's Wonderful Wisecrack #2: People who spend their lives with the purpose of proving that life is purposeless constitute an interesting subject of study. We could draw a corollary from this: People who brilliantly use their minds in order to reduce mind to matter constitute an equally interesting subject of study. Then Corollary #2 to W.W.W. #2 might be: People who regard the brain as the most complex object in the universe, but are indifferent to or contemptuous of the mind, are similarly worthy of our attention. Or Corollary #3: Those who ingeniously use their intelligence to reveal a universe in which intelligence has no place, etc., etc.

To persuade scientists in the late twentieth century to take Aristotle seriously – for that is what the metametaproblem just described boils down to – one has to find some ingenious way to work upon their psyches.

There has to be a way to break down their resistance, to make them look at themselves from a new perspective. Comedy is often a very good way to accomplish this purpose, because in comedy, as Bergson and others have reminded us, we are able to look down upon ourselves from an Olympian standpoint and laugh at our petty concerns and pompous folly. Perhaps one could write a satire, like Jonathan Swift's *The Battle of the Books*, in which Swift portrays the ancient and modern writers as warriors battling over possession of Mount Parnassus, the home of the Muses, and the surrounding territory. The record of their strife is contained in what he calls "Books of Controversy," which he describes in the following way:

> In these books is wonderfully instilled and preserved the spirit of each warrior, while he is still alive; and after his death his soul transmigrates there to inform them. This at least is the more common opinion; but I believe it is with libraries as with other cemeteries, where some philosophers affirm that a certain spirit, which they call the *brutum hominis*, hovers over the monument till the body is corrupted and turns to dust or worms, but then vanishes or dissolves. So, we may say, a restless spirit haunts over every book.[2]

In Swift's account, the ancient and the modern authors, after much quarreling on the shelves of the library, divide themselves into opposed armies. The modern army has a contingent of bowmen led by Descartes, Gassendi, and Hobbes. As for the ancients,

> The army of the ancients was much fewer in number; Homer led the horse, and Pindar the light-horse; Euclid was chief engineer; Plato and Aristotle commanded the bowmen; Herodotus and Livy the foot; Hippocrates the dragoons. The allies, led by Vossius and Temple, brought up the rear.

A battle ensues, in the course of which

> ... Aristotle, observing Bacon, advanced with a furious mien, drew his bow to the head, and let fly his arrow, which missed the valiant Modern, and went hizzing over his head. But Descartes it hit; the steel point quickly found a defect in his head-piece; it pierced the leather and the pasteboard, and went in the right eye. The torture of the pain whirled the valiant bowman round, till death, like a star of superior influence, drew him into his own vortex.[3]

One could certainly do worse than imitate Jonathan Swift. However, in this battle the ancients win. While I want them to do well, I am not trying to attack modern science, but to show that it and Aristotle complement each other. Centuries ago, the scientists exposed Aristotle's weaknesses. Now it is only fitting that he return the favor and compensate for their failings.

What I am seeking is along the lines of the example I used before, Woody Allen's motion picture *Sleeper*, with its theme of progress in some respects and regress in others. If only one could expand on that theme.

Maybe one could get more ideas from Allen, who like Swift, has a flair for satire and the mock-philosophic. For example, in one of Allen's short stories, entitled "Mr. Big," a female philosophy major at Vassar, needing help on a term paper for a Western religion class, hires a private detective to help her find God. The detective, possibly influenced by her outstanding physical attributes, takes the case. In the course of his investigation, he consults a rabbi, a bank robber, and the Pope, who happens to be visiting New York. It turns out that the philosophy major at Vassar is really a physics professor at Bryn Mawr, and she killed God. When the detective, whose name is Kaiser Lupowitz and who by this time has gone to bed with her, discovers her misdeeds, he confronts her, jabbering about the great philosophers. Finally, he shoots her, and, like Socrates in the dialogue *Phaedo*, philosophizing almost until the moment of death, he bids her farewell, but unlike Socrates, it is someone else who is dying, and he babbles pseudo-existentialist gibberish before killing her.

Here I look to Woody Allen and Jonathan Swift as earlier I looked to Dante and Rabelais – what is required to rouse the scientists and the philosophers from their dogmatic slumbers? Comedy, satire, poetry? It cannot be done with rational argument alone. There has to be a hook, a way of appealing somehow to their imagination, to their deepest insight and their most profound intuition.

In the midst of my reflections, I reach for one of my editions of Aristotle's *Nicomachean Ethics*. By chance, I open it to the page containing the very passage I am seeking, the one on the vision of the good it almost seems one must be born with:

> But suppose someone says, "Everybody strives for what seems good to them, and they do not have power over their own imagination, but [depending on] what sort of person each one is, so his goal [in life] appears to him. If therefore each person is responsible for his own character, he will in a sense be responsible for his imagination; if not, no one will be responsible for doing evil things, but will do these things through ignorance of the [proper] end, thinking he will obtain the greatest good through them. However, the end he aims at [in life] is not of his own choosing, but he must be born having, as it were, vision, whereby he judges well and will choose what is truly good; he is well-endowed by nature who is well-endowed in this. For the greatest and noblest thing, that one cannot obtain or learn from another, but is something one has by nature, such a thing he will have; and to be well and nobly endowed by nature in this respect is to be well endowed in the full and true sense of the word.[4]

Our truest nature is a kind of vision that comes to us. We don't know where it comes from, but it constitutes our heart of hearts, our deepest self – something that made Aristotle Aristotle, and makes me me, and Woody Allen Woody Allen.

Aha! It comes to me. "Woody Allen" – that's his *professional* name. In the back of my memory I seem to recall his given name, but I can't quite remember it. I reach again to my bookshelf for a reference volume, *The Cambridge Fact Finder*. Here it is. Woody Allen's real name is Allen Stuart Konigsberg, born in 1935 in Brooklyn, New York.

Konigsberg – that is an Anglicization or Americanization of Königsberg. This means Woody Allen's ancestors came from the city of Königsberg, the home town of guess who – Immanuel Kant.

Königsberg – now called Kaliningrad since the Russians took it over after World War II – is a port on the Baltic Sea, and it wasn't a very big town in the eighteenth century – 25,000, maybe 50,000 people. Why, Woody Allen's ancestors might have rubbed shoulders with Professor Kant – for example, when Kant took his famous afternoon walks through town and was so punctual that the housewives used to set their clocks by him.

So that's where Woody Allen gets his philosophic nature – it runs in the family. We can imagine one of his ancestors spotting Kant on one of his afternoon walks and after sidling up to him, saying very respectfully, *"Entschuldigen Sie mich, Herr Professor Kant, darf ich Ihnen eine kleine Frage stellen?"* (Excuse me, Professor Kant, may I ask you a little question?) We can picture Kant, himself a man of humble origins, kindly assenting, and then as he discovers the philosophic bent of his companion, he invites Herr Königsberg to accompany him regularly on his post-meridional stroll.

Many people had the name Immanuel in those days, so it might well be that that was Mr. Königsberg's first name. If Woody Allen's ancestor was named Immanuel Königsberg, and came from Königsberg, and like his descendant was philosophically inclined, what could be more natural than that sooner or later he should meet up with the other philosopher from Königsberg named Immanuel, Immanuel Kant? So there they were, Immanuel Königsberg and Immanuel Kant, whiling away their afternoons walking through the streets of a seaport town, philosophizing like Socrates and his pupils in the agora of Athens, or like Aristotle the "peripatetic" (*i.e.,* the one who walks around) lecturing to his pupils in the Lyceum, or Zeno the Stoic in like fashion walking up and back along the Stoa (*i.e.,* the portico) of Attalus.

What's that? Do I hear expressions of doubt issuing forth from your lips, dear reader? Put them to rest, please. This interpretation is as plausible as a lot of what goes on in "the history of philosophy." For one thing, it tells us something about Woody Allen. Think, moreover, of Moses Mendelssohn (1729–1786), the embodiment of Enlightenment rationalism and the model for the hero of Lessing's play *Nathan der Weise* (Nathan the Wise). If he was a contemporary of Kant's, why not Immanuel Königsberg?

And if that doesn't satisfy you, here's another key piece of evidence: Woody Allen and his co-producer Marshall Brickner have created many of their movies walking along the streets of Manhattan, up Madison Avenue and down Lexington Avenue, up Lexington and down Madison (for some reason, they eschewed Park Avenue). For years they could be seen, oblivious of the roar of traffic, talking and gesticulating as they walked along. Many critics have commented on this unique method of composition, but now we recognize its true meaning. It is an atavism, the recurrence of an ancestral trait.

Okay, now we have it. Woody Allen makes a movie in which he plays both himself and his putative ancestor, Immanuel Königsberg. In this film, instead of going forward in time as he does in *Sleeper*, he climbs into his capsule and goes backward. He meets up with his ancestor, and they confer with Kant. Then on their way through the seventeenth century, they talk to Descartes and to the Port-Royal logicians, who give Allen a personal message for Chomsky. They move through the sixteenth century and trade ideas with Rabelais about the excremental tradition in satirical humanism, then on to the thirteenth century, where Dante and Virgil give them a quick tour of the Inferno, along the way pointing out the philosophers up to their chins in *cacca*. Finally, they arrive in ancient Greece, where they start off with a visit to the oracle at Delphi. Then it's on to see Alexander the Great and Diogenes the Cynic, whom they interview after their famous encounter.* Naturally, a good neurotic like Woody Allen would not miss a chance to compare Oedipal notes with Sophocles, with whom he has a long, heart-to-

---

* The story goes that Alexander, having heard of Diogenes' fame as a philosopher, went to see him in order to reward him for his merit. He came upon him taking a sunbath. "Tell me what you want," Alexander said to him, and Diogenes replied, "Stop blocking my light." Whereupon Alexander said, "If I were not Alexander, I would be Diogenes."

heart talk. Nor would he pass up the opportunity to exchange ideas about comedy with Aristophanes.

At last, the pair meet up with Socrates, Plato, and Aristotle, who react to modern ideas along the lines I was describing earlier. One can imagine his encounter with Aristotle. "Mr. Aristotle, I'm terribly sorry to have to tell you this, but 2,400 years from now there's going to be a man named Robert Greene putting awful language into your mouth. He has you using all sorts of bad words like 'F – -' and 'S – -.' What do you have to say about that?"

It's a replay of *Sleeper*, only we have gone backward in order to look forward instead of forward in order to look backward. The ancients are impressed by the progress made by the moderns in understanding and harnessing matter, but are not really surprised by it. They are not so much surprised as disappointed at the regress in the understanding of man and the alienation of man from nature. What surprises them is that this could occur in the midst of so much progress. It is the dualism, the Frankensteinian Platonism, and the skepticism that throw them for a loss. But if it perplexes the philosophers, it does not seem strange to the tragedians, as Aeschylus, Sophocles, and Euripides walk up and join the conversation.

And so Woody Allen and Immanuel Königsberg spend days and weeks sojourning in Greece, talking to the artists and the thinkers, the historians, the generals, and the statesmen, until finally they clamber back into their time capsule and return to their respective places in the modern age.

What advice or what message do the ancients give them to bring back that might persuade the modern materialists to question their own dogmas? Could satire combined with science fiction make the ancients come alive again? There is no telling whence might come the breath of inspiration, or the Newtonian apple dropping on their heads that would cause the flash of insight, the intellectual spark to let them see clearly what a handful of them now see through a glass, darkly. Earlier I compared materialism to a religion, and what we are talking about now is something akin to a religious conversion. One thinks of the different forms of conversion described by William James in *The Varieties of Religious Experience*, or St. Augustine's eloquent description of his own conversion, part of which I quoted earlier. The mind struggles for a long time with an idea to which it is strongly attracted, but still resists as hard as it can. In some individuals consciously and in others unconsciously, it desires intensely to yield, yet it refuses to do so until it satisfies itself that it is not betraying its deepest beliefs, but discovering its true self.

It is difficult, if not impossible, to say how this might happen. But combatting the scientists' anti-historicism along with the philosophers' skepticism would be an excellent start. Just as "philosophy" must be understood as part of science, "science," whatever else it is, must be seen as a historical phenomenon. How can scientists, who believe so strongly in biological evolution, deny so vehemently the historical conditioning of their own ideas? We do not need to construct time machines to let them rove back into the past so that they can rediscover the true nature of their own minds. They can project *themselves* backward and forward in time, if only they will do it. In ways we do not even suspect, we have the ability to transcend our limitations in time.

> It avails not, time nor place – distance avails not,
> I am with you, you men and women of a generation, or ever so
>   many generations hence . . .

Those are the words of Woody Allen's fellow Brooklynite Walt Whitman, but they could as easily have come from the mouth of Socrates, as reported in Plato's dialogue *Phaedo*:

> We shall eagerly do these things as you say, said Crito. But in what way do we bury you?
> However you like, he said, if indeed you catch me and I don't elude you.
> He laughed softly as he spoke, and turning to us he said, I can't persuade Crito that I am this Socrates who is talking to you now and marshaling every one of the arguments. He thinks I am the one whom he will shortly see dead, and he asks how he should bury me! . . . While he said to the judges at my trial that truly I would stay, you must pledge to him that quite surely I will not stay when I die, but depart and be gone. . . . But you must cheer up and say it is my body you are burying, and you can bury it however you please, and most of all as you think is lawful and proper.[5]

Whether it be Socrates, Plato, or Aristotle on the shores of the Aegean or Walt Whitman crossing Brooklyn Ferry, it is the same timelessness or transcendence of time:

> Others will enter the gates of the ferry and cross from shore to shore,
> Others will watch the run of the flood-tide,

Others will see the shipping of Manhattan north and west, and the
    heights of Brooklyn to the south and east,
Others will see the islands large and small;
Fifty years hence, others will see them as they cross, the sun half an
    hour high,
A hundred years hence, or ever so many hundred years hence, others
    will see them,
Will enjoy the sunset, the pouring-in of the flood-tide, the falling
    back to sea of the ebb-tide.

Just as you feel when you look on the river and sky, so I felt . . .

I too many and many a time cross'd the river of old . . .

What is it then between us?
What is the count of the scores or hundreds of years between us?

Whatever it is, it avails not – distance avails not, and place avails
    not,
I too lived, Brooklyn of ample hills was mine,
I too walk'd the streets of Manhattan Island, and bathed in the waters
    around it . . .
I too had been struck from the float forever held in solution . . .

Closer yet I approach you,
What thought you have of me now, I had as much of you – I laid in
    my stores in advance,
I consider'd long and seriously of you before you were born.
Who was to know what should come home to me?
Who knows but I am enjoying this?
Who knows, for all the distance, but I am as good as looking at
    you now, for all you cannot see me?

What gods can exceed those that clasp me by the hand, and with
    voices I love call me promptly and loudly by my nighest name as
    I approach?
What is more subtle than this which ties me to the woman or man
    that looks in my face?
Which fuses me into you now, and pours my meaning into you?

We understand then do we not?
What I promis'd without mentioning, have you not accepted?

What the study could not teach – what the preaching could not
    accomplish is accomplish'd, is it not?

Flow on, river! flow with the flood-tide, and ebb with the ebb-tide!
Frolic on, crested and scallop-edg'd waves!
Gorgeous clouds of the sunset! drench with your splendor me, or the
    men and women generations after me!
Cross from shore to shore, countless crowds of passengers!
Stand up, tall masts of Mannahatta! Stand up, beautiful hills of
    Brooklyn!
Throb, baffled and curious brain! throw out questions and answers!
Suspend here and everywhere, eternal float of solution!

You have waited, you always wait, you dumb, beautiful ministers,
We receive you with free sense at last, and are insatiate
    henceforward,
Not you any more shall be able to foil us, or withhold yourselves
    from us,
We use you, and do not cast you aside – we plant you permanently
    within us,
We fathom you not – we love you – there is perfection in you also,
You furnish your parts toward eternity,
Great or small, you furnish your parts toward the soul.

Notes

1. Walter Sullivan, "Of Aristotle, Atoms and a Retiring Sage," *The New York Times*, 12 Oct. 1974, sec. 1, p. 1 *et seq.*

2. Jonathan Swift, *A Full and True Account of the Battel Fought last Friday, Between the Antient and the Modern Books In St. James's Library.*

3. Ibid. After the word "vortex" Swift notes, "Alluding to his absurd system."

4. Nicomachean Ethics III, v, 1114a31–1114b12.

5. Phaedo 115c–116a.

10
The New University

Let us be optimistic that sooner or later reason and good sense will prevail, and the primitive notions of mind and human nature that now reign in science will be replaced by something much better. Without trying to predict exactly when and how this will happen, we can imagine how it might occur.

Once "philosophy" has been abolished and its component parts transferred to other disciplines, as envisioned at the end of Part I, the events occur that were sketched in Chapters 5 and 6: the unity and coherence of "the history of philosophy" are seen more clearly in a new interdisciplinary environment, and it becomes plain to all that no boundary exists between "philosophy" and "science." Even before a consensus emerges that Aristotle's views, as outlined in Chapter 8, are correct, we see the problems of "modern philosophy" fading away. Then the synthesis of Aristotle and modern science actually is achieved, and the various disciplines begin to work together in greater harmony than ever before.

On the other hand, perhaps I am being too optimistic and am rushing things. This all may not happen as rapidly as I imagine it. Even if "philosophy," the sick man of Academe, finally succumbs, or administrators put it out of its misery and redistribute its usable parts among the appropriate disciplines, the changes might not be very great. The "history of philosophy," while now part of the history of ideas or the history of science, might still be studied and taught in the same uncertain, skeptical, weakly coherent way as before when it was located in "philosophy" departments. The epistemologists, while finding it harder and harder to ply their trade, might yet find niches for themselves in the interstices of psychology and cognitive science. Only the logicians would prosper because they already were independent and their weak ties with "philosophy" were easy to sever.

Still, it is hard to believe that once "philosophy" disappears, the change will amount to little more than a game of musical chairs, an administrative reshuffling imposed from above for the narrowest of reasons: to eliminate faculty positions, to reduce clerical expenses, and so on. Let us imagine the change being made out of conviction, from genuine intellectual motives. The skeptical rationale that constituted "philosophy" is gone, even if it hovers for a while above the remains of the former discipline like an unholy spirit. Now the "philosophers" have to make something of their new situation. Will they regard themselves merely as exiles dreaming only of returning to their former home, or will they at last start to see themselves in their broad and true identity? Let us hope they will realize that the territory they were trying so desperately to stake out for themselves was not their real home, and that, having rejoined the rest of Academe, they are where they belong.

A new process of questioning begins as they see "the history of philosophy" in a new light. As they grasp more and more firmly its unity and coherence and its connection with other disciplines, they find they have a much better framework for general education than previously existed. Thus, all students benefit, and "the history of philosophy," or whatever it now is called, attracts far more students than it ever did in the old paradigm.

Indeed, we need to find a new name for "the history of philosophy." As the reader will recall from Chapter 2, that was the name given to a broad and loosely defined tradition that did not fit onto the procrustean bed of skeptical epistemology. Having dispensed with the latter, we should also identify the tradition more clearly. Thus we will see how interdisciplinary it is and what a wide range of writers is included in it. To my mind, "the mainstream of Western ideas" fulfills this function. Another and more familiar name for the same thing is the great books or the great ideas of Western civilization. Whichever of these expressions one prefers, they both name a coherent tradition that ranges over many fields.

At first blush, "the mainstream of ideas" may sound vaguer and more ambiguous than what it replaces, but I think it is exactly the overarching term we need. Schools of thought like the Platonic tradition and the Aristotelian tradition can still be clearly identified within it. These two can even be regarded as one because they are so closely related. Both make the concept of *form* central. We also can speak of the materialist tradition, which makes the concept of *matter* central and includes modern science. Thus, we avoid setting up false disciplinary boundaries and making an artificial distinction between "philosophy" and "science." No violence is done to other identifiable schools of thought like the Stoics and the Epicureans. These fall more or less in the materialist tradition. As for Descartes and his successors, they could still be called "the modern philosophers," so long as it was clear that this is just a term of convenience. If we choose an alternative, we should avoid other pitfalls. While their main focus is psychology, to speak of them as "psychologists" would cause people to confuse them with experimental psychologists, so we might simply call them "epistemologists." This name would not preserve the disciplinary fences around them, but merely emphasize that their main interest is theory, not observation and experiment.

Similarly, within "the mainstream of ideas" we can move more freely between "philosophy" and "literature" than is possible using the conventional terms. Many great works of literature express scientific or philosophical ideas, and many famous authors were both artists and thinkers. Plato, for example, was both a "philosopher"* and a great literary artist. Lucretius was both an epic poet and a major figure in "the history of philosophy." Nor can Dante, Pascal, Goethe, and many others be squeezed into a narrow compass. The great authors of Western civilization range far and wide without regard to disciplinary boundaries, and they have a great deal to say to each other. If we do not erect barriers between "philosophy" and "literature," we will get the full benefit of this dialogue. While certain members of the tradition such as the "modern philosophers" are very sharply focused on particular issues, we can see them more clearly from a broad perspective than from a narrow one. This is not a paradox, but simply what results when we overcome the excessive specialization of the twentieth century. The Western tradition has both coherence and richness, and we can experience both qualities to the fullest. "The mainstream of ideas" is the best term I can think of to signify both the breadth and the coherence of the tradition.

During the twentieth century the natural connection between the mainstream of Western ideas and all the specialized areas of knowledge has been severed in the name of a narrow conception of science and scholarship. If the connection is restored, many disciplines will flow back together. If Aristotle's ideas truly can be joined with those of modern science, the unity of the tradition will be clearer still.

I predict that this will happen. The neo-Aristotelian "metaphysics" or first philosophy or primary science that will result will be shared by everybody. There will be no need for "philosophy departments" to develop and teach it, for it will not be esoteric. Its connections with all fields will be apparent, and everyone will understand it. It will be a part of general education

* *I.e.,* "thinker," "man of ideas," "scientist."

and will be taught by people from all disciplines. A model for this type of instruction already exists. In the past generation, as English composition has expanded to try to fill the chasm in general education, a genre of composition course has arisen called "writing across the curriculum," in which instructors from many disciplines teach composition classes oriented toward their respective disciplines. In like fashion, we will see "Aristotle across the curriculum," although it may not be called by that name. Whatever the name, students will be given a framework encompassing all disciplines, and one of its chief architects will be Aristotle. It will not be dogmatic. As anyone familiar with the writings of Aristotle knows, he never forces a conclusion. He is very willing to settle for something less than certainty when that is all the facts will warrant. Thus, there will be no need to give simple-minded, dogmatic answers to controversies that might be raging within and among different fields. Perhaps the home base for this type of presentation would be the history of ideas, *i.e.*, history departments, or perhaps it would be an independent program run by all the disciplines in common. The latter seems to me the better approach.

It is exhilarating to contemplate all these changes. Yet as stated in the Introduction, this is not a package deal. The excessive separation of disciplines should be ended whether or not Aristotle is synthesized with modern science. In any case, once the scholarly activities that formerly constituted "philosophy" have found a home in other disciplines, the broadening of "the history of philosophy" that I have just described *is* likely to take place. This will be a momentous development all by itself because it will bring home to people how artificial many of the disciplinary boundaries are. As the realization sinks in, the academic reform will not stop with "philosophy." If one ill-conceived discipline can be transformed, questions will be raised about others. The time not only is ripe for such questions, but even rotten. Whether the former "philosophers" lead the charge or somebody else does it, it will occur. "Philosophy" is far from being the only ill-conceived discipline. There are the "linguists" who don't speak many languages, the "psychologists" who don't believe in mind, the "English teachers" who hate grammar, the professors of education who babble endlessly about method and have little to say about content, and so on – the whole academic Ship of Fools.

Continuing to peer into the future, we can picture the former "philosophers" as members of other disciplines. Not only are they engaged in self-criticism, but they also are asking questions about the new environment in which they find themselves. And why should they not do this? Even before "philosophy" gave up the ghost, we knew how artificial the boundaries between disciplines were. But we didn't think much could be done to remove them. Oh, there was a lot of talk about being "interdisciplinary," but the attempts to follow through were rarely more than superficial. Now, however, the false paradigm of one discipline has vanished into thin air, and we see the beginnings of an interest in having the other disciplines take a serious, critical look at one another. We are not sure whether it will start with the former "philosophers" themselves, those self-proclaimed heirs of Socrates, but it is an idea whose time is long overdue, so that once it appears, it will quickly catch on.

This development coincides with another widespread phenomenon that has been occurring in our society, namely downsizing. It is high time the academic world went through this process. What happened in steel, automobiles, machine tools, electronics, communications, and many other businesses and industries is bound to occur in Academe. While a mild retrenchment has been going on in higher education since the mid-1970s, its main effect is that administrators have saved money by using part-time instructors while increasing their own numbers and pay. The real downsizing has yet to occur.

This is so despite the fact that for many years, dire assessments of our educational system have been appearing regularly. Studies by foundations, by the government, and by the universities themselves are continually telling us about the unsatisfactory state of affairs from kindergarten through graduate school. We have grown used to the periodic lamentation, the institutional handwringing, and the solemn promises to bring about reform that never amount to anything. It is easy enough to see why nothing much is done. The administrators, bureaucrats, and foundation heads who sponsor and conduct the studies have a vested interest in the *status quo*. Yes, they would like to change things, but not too much, for if the problems really were solved, we wouldn't need so many administrators, bureaucrats, and foundation heads.

But there is another reason why the criticism is ineffective, and that is because it comes from outside rather than from the people most directly involved. This point is brought home by a current example of external criticism, namely the effort being made in the United States to control medical costs. Insurance companies, health maintenance organizations, and federal and state governments are looking over the shoulders of physicians, badgering them to economize. After several years of this activity, costs are still out of control, so that the criticism is largely ineffective. Moreover, many doctors have suggested that should the insurance companies and the others have their way, the quality of care will be threatened. They may be right. Reform clearly is needed, but it ought to be done by the doctors themselves. The question is, which ones would be best suited to do it? A few statistics may give us some clues. Between 1971 and 1995, the number of physicians in the United States more than doubled, from 334,000 to 720,300, but the number of "family physicians," as general practitioners now are called, increased only from 50,000 to 59,900.[1] It is generally agreed that there are too many specialists and not enough family doctors. Could this have something to do with the runaway costs? Again, we have often been told that many unnecessary procedures are performed. The foregoing statistics seem to explain why. Thus, the people who appear to be best qualified to lead the criticism and begin the reform are the family doctors. They can be the gadflies in the effort to reduce the excessive specialization and to stimulate the specialists to criticize themselves. To be sure, outside agencies and the public will play a role as well.

The problems of the doctors remind me of an anecdote about lawyers I recently heard, dealing with a man who chances to meet an acquaintance, an attorney practicing in a small, remote town. The man asks how he is doing, and the acquaintance replies, "Oh, I think I'm going to have to go somewhere else. I'm the only lawyer in town, but there isn't enough business here for me to make a living." He bemoans his situation a while longer, and then they part.

Six months later, they encounter each other again, and the man inquires where his friend is located. It turns out he is still in the same town. "But how could you stay there if things are so bad?" "Well, business is a lot better now." Incredulous, the man asks, "What happened?" His friend replies, "Another lawyer came to town."

It is not only the number of physicians that has increased dramatically in recent years. In 1960, there were 285,933 lawyers in the United States, whereas in 1991 the number was 805,972.[2] Even more widespread agreement exists than in the case of medical specialists that there are too many attorneys. Whatever is done to remedy the situation, the lawyers themselves will have to play a central role in the restructuring if it is to be done properly.

Skepticism about many professions is widespread and growing. Given the variety and extent of its problems, more and more attention will be turned to education. However, most of the proposals for reform put forth in recent years are for superficial changes. Something more substantial needs to be done, and we do not want the reform and the downsizing of Academe to be performed by Congress or by the state or federal departments of education or by foundations or even by university administrators. The deeper criticism that is needed can come only from the academics themselves.

However, as we saw in the case of "philosophy," it is not simply a matter of each discipline criticizing itself. If things were as simple as that, reform might have occurred long ago. Instead we have to decide who among the academics is best qualified to criticize whom. A few pages back I mentioned several disciplines about which questions can be raised. Take psychology, for example. As a psychology professor at the University of Colorado admitted in 1972 during an interdisciplinary seminar in which I participated, "What we do isn't science." That is an opinion shared by many people outside the field. When you consider the volumes and volumes of material the psychologists have produced, a substantial body of knowledge should have resulted, and it is nothing of the sort. This alone is enough to raise doubt about what the psychologists are doing. Nevertheless, some of it does have value, and it is critical to separate the wheat from the chaff, the gold from the dross, the truth from the baloney. Is it 50 percent baloney, or 60 percent, or 70 percent, or 80 percent, or 90 percent? We need to know. We can hardly ask the American Psychological Association to answer a question like this. It should be done by persons who are knowledgeable but detached. Peering into the future again, we see the former "philosophers" in a unique position to lead the search for an answer, not only because they have just gone through a transformation themselves, but because "psychology" and "philosophy" are so closely related. In fact, "psychology" is just as ill-conceived and self-contradictory as "philosophy" was. The two never should have split apart. The "philosophers" disdained to be part of empirical science, and the "psychologists," with their "behaviorism," exhibited intense hostility to the concept of mind. Now that the philosophers have mended their ways, it is the psychologists' turn to be criticized.

The case is similar with English, as well as education, linguistics, and the social sciences. Indeed, all of Academe needs to be scrutinized, and now we have the formula for doing it: Since it is unrealistic to expect the individual disciplines to criticize themselves, they will criticize each other, and they will go about it in a serious and thorough way. Faculty will team-teach interdisciplinary courses. More than that, they will study each others' reading lists for Ph.D. comprehensive examinations, as if they were going back to school again. In order to have time for these new activities, they will need to be released from other obligations. Normally, professors are expected to do research in their field and publish the results. However, this too is research, albeit a new form.

The mention of scholarly research brings us to the next stage in the process of reform, stemming the tide of academic publication. For years, publication has been the main path to advancement in Academe. The expression "publish or perish" has been a cliché for generations. Even before the enormous expansion of colleges and universities after World War II, everyone knew that the way to get ahead in Academe was not by being a good teacher, but by publishing a lot. Quality was important, but quantity was what really counted. Consequently, the shelves of university libraries are bulging with journals and books that nobody reads – or hardly anybody. It is high time somebody other than specialists started reading the books and journals hardly anybody reads to find out if there is anything of value in them.

This is another way members of different fields will evaluate each other, by plowing through the enormous quantity of publications. Some of the excesses are well known: the dubious experiments in psychology, the flights of fancy of literary criticism (or "lit crit"), the vaporous methodology of the educationists, the jargon of the social scientists. All this is common knowledge, but hitherto no one has been in a position to do anything about it. Now all disciplines will be examined, and with an approach most likely to provide the right combination of expertise and detachment.

The natural sciences will suffer this scrutiny better than the social sciences and the humanities. The same ills are present in both, but are easier to deal with in the natural sciences because the latter are so well founded, both in theory and in practice. They also are well integrated with each other. Their main problem is the one discussed in earlier chapters, namely, overcoming the dogmatic materialism that is limiting their progress outside the realm of matter.

In addition to obscure research, another form of academic publication serves the same purposes of career advancement and ego-tripping. This genre could be called "reinventing the wheel" or "old wine in new bottles." Once professors make a name for themselves, they find it hard to resist the temptation to pontificate on a variety of subjects where they have little that is new, interesting, or important to say. Because they are well known, libraries, colleagues, and students are likely to buy what they write – enough at least to pay the costs of publication. Sometimes their books even make money. In any case, there are a lot of publishers around, and they like their roster of authors to include some famous names. Thus, it is easy for established authors to get published.

Yet another practice to be scrutinized is that of putting out new editions of textbooks with minor changes and with a few chapters rearranged so that students cannot use secondhand copies of previous editions.

Once the interdisciplinary criticism gets started, it will become a serious undertaking. Piles of books and articles will have to be gone through in order to discover what is good and separate it from what is not. I suspect that the mountain of material will turn out to be mostly mediocre rather than truly bad.

Speaking of distinguishing the bad from the merely mediocre reminds me of some Harvard students I read about who used to go down to New York every spring break trying to discover the ten worst movies in town. They would split up in order to cover all the theaters in New York City, and would watch a movie only long enough to determine if it was bad enough to be in the running. Most of the films were not all that bad. Hence, as *The New York Times* reported, students could be seen rushing out of theaters all over town.

Think of applying this approach to academic research! Imagine one group of professors trying to find the ten most worthless experiments in psychology, or the hundred or the thousand. Another group would seek out the silliest books and articles of deconstructionist and other literary criticism, yet another the most vacuous examples of educational methodology, and so on with the rest of the disciplines. Word of this project would get around, and help would get come from other interested parties, like the thousands of surplus Ph.D.'s the system has produced. Many are unable to find a position in higher education, while others help fill the army of part-timers that keep Academe going. In 1970, 474,000 people were teaching in colleges and universities, 22 percent of whom were part-time. In 1994, there were 838,000 college and university teachers, of whom 35–40 percent were part-time. In 1997, the number of college and university teachers was estimated at 915,000, and no figures were given for part-timers![3] The university system is a vast sweatshop, and many of the exploited would be interested in a project that might help reform it. Members of the public who are interested in reforming the system would also be caught up with the idea. Even if it proves impractical to track down every single article in every obscure journal and read every page of every obscure book, the word will get around, and professors will think twice before rushing into print with half-baked ideas.

The goal is not to eliminate publication. The aim of this criticism is to identify what is valuable and get rid of what is superfluous. Many a publication has a germ of validity that is expanded for all it is worth in order to advance the career of its author. The new guiding principle that will replace "publish or perish" has a passing resemblance to Einstein's theory of general relativity. Like the slowing of the clocks and the shrinking of the measuring rods as one approaches the speed of light, ideas would undergo a similar effect in the minds of their authors as they approached the threshold of publication. Instead of expanding prematurely, research and writing projects would shrink to a size appropriate to their actual degree of intellectual development. Books would turn into monographs, monographs into articles, articles into lectures and colloquia, lectures into lecture notes. Thus, underdeveloped ideas would not see the light of day before their time. The environment also would benefit, since a lot of trees and energy would be saved, and there would be less pollution.

In order to make this shrinking effect occur, somebody has to plow through all the material first, or at least a great deal of it. Let no doubt arise that this is a worthwhile activity, particularly when we compare it to other areas of scientific research. Think of all the time, energy, and expense devoted to exploring the solar system. Space ships have flown all the way to Jupiter and Saturn. They have sent probes deep below the surface of those planets, discovering layers of hydrogen and helium thousands of miles thick, and strata of other materials as well. If it is worth all that trouble to find out the composition of distant planets, it certainly is worth trying to discover the fecal content of a number of academic disciplines, especially when the future of the educational system is at stake. We know it is not a thousand miles thick like the hydrogen and helium on Jupiter and Saturn. If we took all the phony baloney in the books and journals hardly anybody reads and laid it end to end, would it reach from New York to San Francisco? Would it cover the state of Texas? Would it stretch around the world? It is worth finding out.

There will need to be a journal to publish this information, a journal to end all journals, appropriately entitled *Academic Bullshit* and containing the details of many bad publications. Moreover, this is too good an idea to stand alone. Academic prolixity and complexity has its twin brother in government, so there will need to be a similar journal called *Government Bullshit*. The idea will spread, and copycat publications will appear, such as *Medical and Legal Rip-offs*, *Journalistic Distortions*, etc. The idea of informed, yet independent criticism is one that will take hold.

Once under way, the criticism will be hard to stop or to confine. It will cause the kind of rethinking of disciplines that I did of "philosophy" in this essay. Take English, for example. As Peter Elbow has asked in a well-known book, what is "English"? By virtue of teaching freshman composition to all undergraduates, English departments are usually the largest on campus, but the heart of "English" is English literature, which is so voluminous that earning a Ph.D. in it requires tackling an enormous reading list. Thus, the study of English literature tends to crowd out the study of other literature that bears on it, such as Greek, Latin, French, German, Italian, etc. – preferably read in the original languages. Furthermore, a literature professor should have a proper background in history, including history of ideas, and know something about the sciences. After all, many of the writers in English literature did have this kind of broad background. Milton, for example, knew a lot about science; Frost and Eliot knew Greek and Latin. Many English writers studied Latin literature – in Latin, of course – and many were familiar with French or Italian authors in their native languages. Since the first professorships in English literature were set up only about 150 years ago and the latter came to dominate the discipline only in this century, making "English" less insular than it now is would not be as radical a change as it might seem. To borrow a phrase, what do they know of English who only English know? Like "philosophy," "English" turns out to have been defined arbitrarily. English literature can still be studied, but in more of a balance with related fields.

Similarly, the psychologists might now be more willing to rethink their discipline. Apropos of this possibility, I recall a conversation I had in the mid-1970s with Walter Kintsch, a psychology professor at the University of Colorado and researcher in memory. I was trying to persuade him of the brilliance of Aristotle's psychology. He made a comment in rebuttal that ostensibly was about Aristotle but really was a paraphrase of Locke, and I pointed this out to him. He immediately grasped the distinction and for a few moments we seemed to be sharing an understanding of how helpful to modern psychology Aristotle could be. Alas, the moment passed. Fled was that vision, as Keats would say. Returning to the reality of modern psychology, he observed that it would take too much time and trouble to study the texts so that one could master them and really get something out of them. I mumbled something to the effect that it would be worth the trouble, but I could have saved my breath. Now, however, under changed conditions, the psychologists might be more receptive to the idea.

"Linguistics" provides another striking example of narrowness. While the systematic study of language goes back to the ancient Greeks and Romans, in the late nineteenth and early twentieth centuries its scope was limited so as to make it more scientific than it previously was. In one respect, the "linguists" (as they call themselves) succeeded: They did excellent work in phonology, the analysis of the sounds of language. But there is much more to language than phonology – for example, meaning. Any fool can tell you that the systematic study of meaning, that is, of vocabulary, is an inherent part of the study of language. However, they didn't know how to deal with it; therefore, it wasn't part of "linguistics." This brings to mind the couplet composed by Oxford students about one of their professors:

> I am the master of this college,
> And what I know not, is not knowledge.

The other good thing the "linguists" did was to compile data on languages all over the world, many of which are threatened with extinction. But how much can they do with these data when they lack an adequate understanding of any aspect of language except phonology? Even their knowledge of grammar is diffuse and unsystematic.

Interestingly enough, a man of genius, Noam Chomsky, came along in the late 1950s and did just the kind of criticism of linguistics that I am advocating. However, for all of Chomsky's brilliant efforts to broaden the field and make connections with philosophy and psychology, he suffered from the same flaw that afflicts the others, and so his revolution fizzled.

The criticism of linguistics will focus on its narrowness. Just as the "psychologists" during this century have been largely "behaviorists," and the "philosophers" skeptical epistemologists, so the "linguists" are primarily phonologists. Their attempts to advance beyond phonology have not gotten very far, and will not do so until they broaden their thinking. Grammar cannot be understood without meaning; both grammar and meaning can be understood by means of a system of categories; and the best set of categories comes from – you guessed it – Aristotle.

I have given examples of what might happen in the fields with which I am most familiar, and we can expect the criticism of other disciplines to proceed in similar fashion. The failings of the educational system are manifest to practically everybody, and a great deal of sentiment exists for reform, but the people running the system have been able to keep public discontent dammed up. We are constantly told how complicated the problems are and how difficult they are to solve. However, we first must understand what the true cause-effect relationship is. Our complex and expensive educational institutions function far less efficiently than they should, and there is a great deal of confusion about what to do. The institutional complexity stems from the educational inefficiency which in turn is caused by the intellectual confusion, and it is the last-named that is paramount. Gad, that was an obscure and stuffy sentence! Why not say it in plain English? And here it is: We could do something about the administrative dogshit and the educational horseshit if it weren't for all the bullshit coming from the professors. The problem is intellectual before it is practical. It is that we have no clear and adequate rationale for change, just a lot of blather. If the ideas were right, the right practical arrangements would follow – maybe. But if good ideas are lacking, it doesn't much matter what the practical arrangements are. They will not remedy the essential flaw.

In particular, the ideas that need to be changed are the paradigms or fundamental ideas that control the disciplines. The contorted rationalizations, self-serving justifications, and general resistance to change that the reformers will encounter are easy to imagine. It will be hard for them not to be led astray by all the red herrings thrown across their path. They will need a motto to express their purpose, a slogan worthy to be ranked with "In God We Trust" and "*E pluribus unum*," namely, "*Ne permittas eis te cacare*" ("Don't let 'em bullshit you"). Yet we can be confident that once a good idea takes hold, it will not die, but will inspire more and more people. And so, looking further into the future, we see the process continuing. By this time, many different people are involved: the former "philosophers," professors in other disciplines, redundant Ph.D.'s, part-time faculty, and finally members of the public. And why shouldn't the public join in? After all, university libraries are open to them. They too can get into the stacks and read the journals nobody reads.

In no way, shape, or form should the criticism that results be likened to McCarthyism. It is not censorship. No one is blacklisted. Moreover, times are far different from the McCarthy era, when Academe was a bastion of free speech withstanding attack from the rest of society, or from the '60s, when the counterculture, the civil rights movement, and the anti-war protests all found a home in the universities. Now it is the universities who are trying to control speech, the universities that are ill and clogged with fat. For years they have freely examined all the other institutions in society. If everything else is open to criticism, why should they be sacrosanct? It is their turn to be scrutinized.

All the while this is happening, departmental boundaries are becoming less and less significant. Scholars are going back and forth across them ever more freely. At length, we see something we never expected to see, the barriers between disciplines actually disappearing. They seemed solid enough to last for centuries, but they have turned out not to be so. Like the Berlin Wall, we thought they would never come down, but here they are, coming down around us. At first, only a few were hacking away at them. Soon they were joined by others. Now many people are hard at work knocking down the academic walls. Unlike the one in Berlin, these walls are more mental than physical, and they are not in one single location, so we can imagine the same scene occurring on campuses far and wide. Classes are still being conducted, and other normal activities are going on, but with the barriers between disciplines reduced to rubble, many a spontaneous interchange is occurring. The former philosophers are having a lively conversation with the psychologists and the professors of literature. Anthropologists, sociologists, linguistics professors, musicologists, art historians, political scientists, economists, historians, psychologists, cognitive scientists, biologists, physicists, chemists, mathematicians, astronomers, and geologists are also moving freely about holding impromptu discussions. Faculty from professional schools and administrators also join in as members of the public buttonhole professors, waving copies of articles and books, questioning this or that position or complaining about the length and obscurity of their work. A motley crew of professors, legislators, and members of the public rush into the education schools, berating the faculty about the vagueness of their prescriptions and lamenting the state of the education system. The scene is reminiscent of the idealism of the 1960s and '70s. However, while animated, it is civil, unlike the riots in 1968 at Berkeley, or at Columbia, where students took over buildings and camped in the President's office, smoked his cigars and drank his bourbon (or whatever it was he drank), and later battled the police. By contrast, this is a joyous occasion and whatever apprehension people feel about the immediate future is drowned in the enthusiasm of the moment. A revolution has occurred, and just as in Berlin when the wall came down, it is being celebrated with a street festival. People share the exhilaration of the moment, recognizing the promise intellectual liberation holds for all of society.

Yet both revolutions and parties have their mornings after. The aftermath of this revolution is that much academic activity has been found to be superfluous and ineffective, and many faculty members are uncertain about their future. Even if they can save their jobs, what they do will be changed, perhaps radically. It will doubtless be painful for them, but consider how many industries have gone through this experience in recent years, as jobs have been modified or eliminated in defense, electronics, steel, coal, machine tools, automobiles, communications, textiles and clothing, the retail industry, management, and finance – the list is long. Why should Academe be immune?

In the past, when legislators and members of the public demanded change, one of the chief complaints was that professors do too much questionable research and don't teach enough: make them teach more courses and the public will get its money's worth out of them.

While that view was partly correct, the realization finally takes hold that the real problem is deeper. By and large, the professors are narrowly trained and the students poorly prepared. Merely having the former teach more classes still leaves the blind leading the blind, or rather the tunnel-visioned leading the nearsighted.

The professors must broaden their training, and they also have to deal with the immediate threat to their jobs by replacing the research that has been lost. Lo and behold, they think of a way to do both. When they began their critique of each other's disciplines, they quickly saw how stimulating it was to get deeply involved in other fields. What is stopping them from continuing this involvement and even giving it freer rein? This does not necessarily mean that physics professors will teach Shakespeare and English professors physics, although in a few cases it might. The more common occurrence will be faculty venturing into related fields, like the former philosophers going into literature and literature professors studying the writers in the Platonic/Aristotelian and the materialist traditions (*i.e.*, philosophy and science); or the former philosophers, the social scientists, and the psychologists entering each other's domains more widely and deeply than they ever did before.

This sounds like professors going back to school, becoming graduate students and even undergraduates again. After finishing their Ph.D.'s, they thought those days were behind them. But bringing them back, after a fashion, is something to be desired, a way of recharging their batteries, of staying young in heart and mind, if not in body. Moreover, the threat of unemployment or less desirable employment spurs them on to add to their academic skills. At the same time, institutions are being transformed, fields are being redefined, and much experimentation is occurring. The academic scheme of things is becoming less complicated than before and less expensive to operate, with smaller administrations, less bureaucracy, and lower clerical costs. The departmental structure that came into existence near the end of the nineteenth century is becoming less important and even disappearing. The organization of universities is returning to something like what it was before the specialized disciplines arose. Once again, the primary organization of faculties is in larger groupings, such as divisions of the humanities, the social sciences, and the natural sciences. Under this system in the past there was real faculty governance, and now we begin to see it again.

Some object that it is impossible to return to those less complicated days because universities have become Leviathans, giant research corporations in all but name. Not only do departments zealously defend their turf, but the leading professors are like sports and entertainment stars. While they do not command the same salaries as the latter, their needs and whims affect salary and budget decisions for everybody. Many move around from school to school like free agents in sports, looking for the best deal they can get. Under these conditions, it is argued, top-heavy administrations are needed both to raise funds and to resolve disagreements among departments and faculty members that at heart are financial. However, the best way to change things is to strengthen the rest of Academe, which in the course of the twentieth century has grown too weak to do anything about them.

In rethinking their professional identities, the professors cannot help but investigate how their respective disciplines came into being. They have to go only a short way into the past. Once they retrace that little distance, they find themselves back in the period when science still was called philosophy, when the different specialties were harder to distinguish from each other, and people moved freely among them. In short, they rejoin the mainstream of Western ideas.

Perhaps it is hard to imagine them all studying the great books and even learning to read them in the original languages. But in order to rethink the specialized disciplines, they have to return to their sources. When asked why he robbed banks, Willie Sutton replied "Because that's where the money is." Similarly, the great books are worth studying because that's where the ideas are, including the ones that shape disciplines.

It might seem that by downplaying specialization in favor of general education or liberal education, we would be turning professionals into amateurs. But because the specialties flow from the mainstream of ideas, there need be no conflict between the two. The true amateur is far from being a dilettante, and the true professional understands the limitations of specialized knowledge. The study of the great books is anything but amateurish and is a lifelong pursuit. For example, I have taught Plato's *Republic* approximately thirty times, and it never grows stale. There is always something more of value to be discovered in it. After teaching it a few times, I realized that it is as up-to-date as today's newspaper – actually, it is way ahead of today's newspaper. Similarly, in the course of this essay I have given the reader an idea of the fertility of Aristotle.

Thus, with much less pressure to publish than before, the professors-turned-students can be more critical of their own former activities. The exact details are hard to predict, but a balance will be achieved between the study of the great books and research in specialized disciplines. Although the ratio will be varied to suit individual needs and inclinations, it will be a much better one than exists today.

Some changes will be needed in the way priorities are set. Suppose, for example, an English professor of today were offered time off from regular duties and were given the choice of learning to read Homer in Greek versus doing literary studies of lesser modern poets. Is there any doubt what most would choose?

Yet to my mind this isn't even a choice. When I first learned to read Homer in the original, the experience was like that described by John Keats in his poem *On First Looking into Chapman's Homer*:

> Then felt I like some watcher of the skies
> When a new planet swims into his ken;
> Or like stout Cortez when with eagle eyes
> He star'd at the Pacific – and all his men
> Look'd at each other with a wild surmise –
> Silent, upon a peak in Darien.

Keats was all excited about a translation! Had he been able to read the original, he could have called the poem *On First Looking into Homer's Homer*! Not only was this a whole new world to me, but learning the Homeric prosody made Latin epic poetry, which imitates the Greek, accessible. I also was able to read the Greek dramatists with much greater facility, as well as other Latin poets.

In the modern world we usually read poetry silently, but classical poetry was meant to be recited. Because it is highly structured in rhythm, meter, and inflection, it is relatively easy to memorize. It is part of an oral tradition of literature. The authors in that tradition are worth studying *in the original languages*. For us, with all our technology getting in the way of the direct experience of art, it is a whole new experience. Classical culture was different from modern culture, and yet it is the source of our civilization. A person cannot claim to be liberally educated without being intimately familiar with it.

Of course I am not suggesting that only the great books be studied and the others neglected. It is a question of correcting an imbalance, an imbalance against the great books rather than in their favor. Even if everybody is not immediately persuaded of their value, as long as some are studying them seriously and letting them guide research into contemporary problems, they will prove their worth once again, as they have done many times before.

My insistence on reading them as much as possible in the original languages may sound frightening to some, and unnecessary. Why should English speakers in particular bother to learn other languages when the whole world is learning English? However, anybody who has become proficient in a foreign language understands its value. An unmistakable sign of the depth of the problems in our academic system is the decline of foreign-language study.[4] Both faculty and students need to improve their foreign-language skills. How can the faculty ask the students to do what they don't do themselves?

The reasons for including foreign languages in a liberal arts curriculum are not what most people think, so I will state them. Preparation for tourism is the least important. Preparation for international trade or diplomacy is a more serious purpose, but it affects a relatively small number of people. Above all, we should study foreign languages a) to read texts in the original languages, b) to improve our skills in our own language, and c) to repeat the most important educational experience of our lives, the one none of us remembers, learning our native tongue. I do not mean that we can literally repeat that primal experience, but we can recapture its essence. Language more than any other human creation reflects the nature of the human mind, and in revealing our thought processes it can be the key to all other disciplines. But to teach it in a way that makes this plain, we would have to go beyond the narrowness of contemporary linguistics.

The conventional methods of learning a foreign language are a far cry from fulfilling the goals just described. Furthermore, they are very inefficient, a fact that makes language study doubly unattractive to most students and to the public. While in one area, conversation, the audio-lingual method developed during the twentieth century is a significant advance, the rest of language learning, including all other essential areas, remains in a primitive state.

By combining ideas from different disciplines, we can remedy the ills of language pedagogy. Just as I worked past the problems of "modern philosophy" by combining it with a broader view of Aristotle, I have perfected a method of accelerated language learning by fusing Aristotle and twentieth-century linguistics. As a result, language study can a) become vastly more efficient, and b) reveal much about the thought processes by which all languages were created. Along with philosophy, it can go from the periphery to the very center of education.

I suspect many readers will agree that teaching methods have not caught up with mass education and that dramatic improvements are possible in all areas. My research in language learning suggests that the way to better teaching lies in escaping narrow specialization, combining disciplines, and getting back into the mainstream of Western ideas.

Far from being watered down in the new scheme of things, professionalism is enhanced. A deeper amateurism triumphs over a narrow professionalism, and in so doing broadens and enhances it. For example, a few pages back I was saying how wonderful Greek and Latin poetry is and that studying it leads to a deeper understanding of modern culture. But why confine oneself to Europe? Wouldn't it be great to read Chinese and Japanese poetry, or to learn Sanskrit and read Hindu literature? Nor should we omit reading the Bible in the original languages. There is so much worth studying that the choices are never-ending. You need to be ready constantly to re-think your priorities because you never know what you are going to discover next, and it is not always apparent that you have made the right choice. To a casual observer the fairly substantial effort I have made to acquire a modest knowledge of Japanese might seem a waste of time. Nevertheless, it has been of the highest value. Japanese is so different from the European languages I have studied that I have learned things about the nature of language that I never would have learned had I confined myself to them; this knowledge has improved my skills so that I have made greater progress in European languages than if I had stuck to them alone; in the future, I probably will become fluent in Japanese, and another new world will open up to me; finally, since the Japanese writing system consists of Chinese characters, the accelerated method I figured out for learning them has made Chinese accessible as well. This is all the result of an "amateurish" study of Japanese.

Much of this essay is about a false professionalism being subsumed into a true amateurism. In the death and life of philosophy, a pseudo-profession, a false conception of philosophy dies, and the real philosophy comes back to life. As Goethe said, *Stirb' und werde*, die and become.

Between true amateurism and true professionalism no conflict exists, but narrow professionalism is inferior to true amateurism. The latter is more strenuous and demanding than the former because there is always something more you can do. You are always thinking of broader horizons. In this manner, you come closer to using your full capacities than in any other way.

The colleges and universities that emerge from all the changes I have sketched resemble the Renaissance or ancient Greece more than the twentieth-century Leviathans we know. The new scheme of things is based on the ideal of liberal arts education, whose traditional home is the undergraduate college. Indeed, it looks as if I have expanded the undergraduate college to encompass the whole university. The faculty have turned into undergraduates again, as they re-take many of the liberal arts courses they had in college. On the other hand, how many of them actually had a genuine liberal arts education? How many scientists had a proper background in the humanities, and how many humanists a comparable background in science? How many studied Greek and Latin, or even became proficient in a modern language? I envision them pursuing the liberal education most of them never got, rather than re-doing the smattering of general education courses going by that name in the twentieth century. What we have today is pre-professional education, and most American colleges ought to be forbidden by the Federal Trade Commission to call themselves "liberal arts colleges" on the ground that it is deceptive advertising. Most of them are really pre-professional academies. Although they pay lip service to the ideal of liberal education, they make only a half-hearted attempt to provide it.

It is not just the lack of liberal education that ails the undergraduate colleges. Standards are not very high and getting steadily lower. After College

Board scores had been declining for years, early in the 1990s the College Boards were "dumbed down," an act that concealed the extent of the decline. Meanwhile, the preparation of entering students has been growing gradually worse, and more and more of the undergraduate curriculum in more and more colleges is devoted to remedial work, whether or not it is called by that name. The extent to which colleges are in the remedial education business is a scandal that administrations do their best not to publicize.[5] Moreover, course sequences like freshman composition, that are not classified as remedial, are work that should have been done in high school. English departments all over the country are bloated with composition teachers, many of them part-timers, trying to fulfill this basic educational need. Yet even after going through the composition sequence, most students can't write; English composition is truly one of the most egregious examples of the failure of the educational system, particularly in light of what students have to pay to go to college, and English is only part of the story. Students are weak in geography, history, math, science, foreign languages. In short, a large percentage of America's 3,700 two- and four-year colleges are glorified high schools, and in some cases, "glorified" is too strong a word. The best preparatory and high schools in the country undoubtedly are superior to the majority of undergraduate colleges – at least where their curricula overlap, in the first two years of college. Now there would be an interesting study to make – one comparing these two groups of institutions! Its results would rock the educational establishment to its foundations.

Still, for all the failure of our educational system to live up to the ideal of liberal education, that ideal retains its splendor and the undergraduate college is its home. It is not just that the students are at the right point between youthfulness and maturity, what the Greeks called the *akmé* or the *hóra*, the prime of life. They also are at the proper stage intellectually before the commitment to a profession and a career. This is the right time to imbue them with the ideal of amateurism within which their professionalism can flower. If the colleges provided the genuine article and the other reforms I have been describing were enacted, that ideal would permeate the system. There is a saying, "It doesn't matter where you did your undergraduate work. It's where you got your graduate degree that counts." If one's undergraduate training was merely pre-professional, that statement is likely to be true. But if one receives a liberal education, it isn't true at all.

If liberal education is so important, then I ought to state what it is, and I shall do so. My description or definition may not prove to be very different from what many others have said. However, with the rest of this essay as background, the reader may be able to get a reasonably precise idea of what a liberal education is. Thus, we may hope to avoid the vagueness and the banality that often characterize discussions of this subject.

Liberal education is correctly associated with the ancient Greeks and with the Renaissance scholars, artists, and scientists who revived interest in the ancients. The individuals that spring to mind as embodying this ideal are many-sided people like Leonardo da Vinci and Michelangelo Buonarroti. Plato and Aristotle fit the model, as do many others one could cite. Well-roundedness and a breadth of interests and talents are rightly regarded as essential qualities of a liberally educated person.

The common conception is correct but somewhat vague. What, for example, does "well-roundedness" mean? What combination of interests and abilities will satisfy this criterion? I will try to offer a more precise definition than usually is given.

Since no one person can master all of human knowledge, individuals must specialize in one or more areas in order to be of any value to themselves or to society. It is equally important to understand how the different branches of knowledge are related to each other, particularly how the areas one knows are related to those one does not. This harks back to what was said earlier about amateurism and professionalism. The true amateur understands what real devotion to a subject entails, and the true professional understands the limits of his or her professionalism. Even when you think you have mastered a specialty and have little more to learn about it, there are always new horizons. Although you cannot know everything, you can imagine the perspective you would have if you did. From that perspective, you would spot connections between familiar areas and others, often widely separated from the ones you know. To discover some of these connections you must be willing to venture into different disciplines, to seek new experiences and broaden your horizons. Of course you will not have the time or the energy to follow out every lead, but still you will find inspiration and fresh ideas for the activities you are able to pursue. For finite minds like ours, it is the next best thing to knowing everything.

No formula exists to tell individuals exactly how to find the right balance between being a specialist and a generalist, or being an amateur or a professional in any given area. Still, the principle just stated is clear enough, and it can be applied to specific situations. In this essay, for example, I have applied it to the narrowness and excessive specialization in twentieth-century academic life. The overspecialization is widely recognized, but despite all the talk about being interdisciplinary, people are unable or unwilling to do much about it. The solution presented in this essay comes from the greatest writers of the West, whose ideas can help us find the right balance.

Another key element of liberal education is understanding the relationship of knowledge and action and avoiding the extremes of action without thought and thought that is unable to act. Again one thinks of the motto of the Jesuits, "In action, contemplation." That saying describes the goal to be reached. A liberal education guides one in reaching it. The great books provide examples in history and literature of unique and difficult choices people have had to make as well as models for behavior. Even more than that, they teach the power of ideas. One need not become a Platonist and believe that the world of ideas is more real than the physical world. But one cannot be well-educated without comprehending the effect of ideas throughout human history, for good and for ill, and without personally experiencing their power. Randall, for example, in the passages quoted at the beginning of this essay, recognizes the influence of ideas in history, but then he disparages them. Boethius' view of Dame Philosophia is much better. Her head at times touches the heavens.

The liberally educated person, then, recognizes the influence of ideas, and at least to some degree is imbued with them. What prevents him or her from going to the other extreme, that is, retreating into the world of ideas in order to escape from an unpleasant reality? This is another question to which no simple answer can be given. For some individuals, the world of ideas is the right place. Others have no recourse because the reality they face is so hostile and unpleasant. On the whole, however, the great books lead one to a balance between thought and action. Their authors well knew how much can be achieved when good ideas are put into effect and how much harm can be done when bad ones are. Moreover, if your heart and soul are filled with the power of an idea, you don't want to keep it a secret. You want to spread the word and let others know about it.

At the same time, idealism must be balanced with realism, and there is no simple formula for doing it. The great books are filled with the ambiguities of choice, and thus provide an antidote to themselves. For example, I have found St. Augustine's *Confessions* a hard book to teach because students tend to read it as if St. Augustine were preaching to them, when he isn't doing that at all. Once they realize that the *Confessions* is not a handbook or a catechism, but a unique self-analysis, they are on the way to recogniz-

ing its greatness. It may even be better not to tell the students. Let them figure it out for themselves.

If thought does not exist in a vacuum, but is connected with action, and
if the person imbued with ideas wishes to share them, then the liberally educated person will seek to benefit society. The ways in which this happens
vary widely with the circumstances. In classical Greece and Renaissance It-
aly, the participation of the individual in the life of the city-state was ideal-
ized. But the relation of the individual and society may not always be so
clear. If the society is hostile or evil, the individual will be alienated from it
or even be forced to flee. Examples are plentiful, from Socrates to Dante to
Solzhenitsyn, of how the creative individual benefits his society even while
being at odds with it. In any event, the society to which the liberally educated person belongs is that of all rational beings, in principle the whole human race and any other rational beings who may exist.

The liberally educated person also seeks to understand the place of
mankind in the natural world. In and of itself, this quest does not lead to any
specific religious belief. That comes from elsewhere in one's experience.
However, it leads one to explore the human impulse to believe in and practice religion in its many forms. It also prompts one to view human arts and
activities against the backdrop of the natural world. We cannot all be Platos
and Aristotles, Michelangelos and Leonardos, but we can achieve a balance
between our knowledge of art and science.

To sum up, then: a liberal education helps one understand how the different areas of knowledge are related to one another, and to what extent one
should be an amateur and to what extent a professional. It helps one understand the relationship between knowledge and action, between the individual and society, and between mankind and the natural world. In short, it
liberates one to pursue knowledge broadly and deeply and thereby to
achieve the richest and fullest experience human beings can attain.

The ideal of liberal education can and must guide us in an age of science
and technology, of business and bureaucracy. If, as it rethinks the depart-
mentalization that came into being a century ago, Academe pursues this
ideal, it will solve many of its current problems.

That is exactly what we are imagining will happen, as we return once
again to the future, where the new university is taking shape. The quantity
of publication is diminishing as professors are judged not so much on what
they have published as on how much they know. In general, they are teaching more, but in a variety of subjects, so that they also are studying much

more. Having earned one Ph.D., they might appear to be trying for a second or a third. However, what they are doing might better be described as strenuous amateurism.

Now that they are so interdisciplinary, the question arises what it is they are professors of. For example, "philosophy" broke up into history of ideas, logic, psychology, etc. In Chapter 2, I compared it to a stock split. Does this mean that every former "philosopher" is now a professor of three or more disciplines? The idea sounds silly. Furthermore, what are they calling themselves?

While there are some joint appointments, in general we see departments losing ground, if they are not simply abolished. Professors are first of all members of divisions or faculties, like the humanities, social sciences, natural sciences. They may still call themselves "sociologists," "psychologists," "historians," etc., but the Berlin walls of the mind have come down, and these terms lack the exclusivity they previously had. A former "philosopher" might say, "I work in the history of ideas, or what is broadly called 'philosophy.'"

If you are a faculty member, not only is it less clear than before what it is you are a professor of, but you are also as much a student as a professor. Hence, titles and gradations of rank are losing their meaning. Furthermore, more than 90 percent of the students in higher education are undergraduates, and the vast majority of the faculty are occupied in teaching them.[6] If most of the colleges are glorified high schools, then most of the faculty are glorified high school teachers. What is the point of calling them "professors" anymore? Since most of them are not researchers, the title of "professor" should be saved for the minority who really are. It should not be beyond human ingenuity to figure out a suitable title for the others. In any case, there are now fewer little professors with big egos, if only because fewer people are called "professor."

As academic ranks are simplified, the same thing happens with salaries. The minute distinctions upon which salary increases were based disappear, and a more uniform pay scale with fewer invidious distinctions is introduced. Thus, one more bone of contention is removed.

Reform follows reform. One of the most beneficial consequences of all the changes that are occurring is a dramatic raising of standards throughout the educational system. It started at the top, and it is working its way down. First more was required of the senior professors, and then of the junior professors. If they must do more, they expect the same of their students. If more is expected of the graduate students and the undergraduates, then the high school students must do more to get into college. And so it goes down the line, through the high schools, the junior high schools, and the elementary schools.

One might think that with distinctions of rank disappearing, the widespread problems of discipline and the lack of respect for authority would worsen. In fact, the opposite occurs. Not only do the teachers pass on to the students the greater demands being made on themselves, but, feeling better prepared, they have more self-confidence. They refuse to put up with nonsense from the students, and they insist that the administrators back them up. As noted earlier, the real problem is an intellectual one. If the instructors have a proper understanding of what they are doing, they will exert the necessary pressure on administrators, students, and the public to get it done. It is precisely because they lacked this self-confidence and because the system prevented them from developing it that they were so put upon.

Similarly with the students, when more is required of them, they become more aware of their own deficiencies. There is nothing more humbling than feeling ill-prepared and foolish. And so tougher standards cause a miraculous transformation, from graduate school down through elementary school.

The logical consequence of higher standards is another major reform. The cheapening of degrees on all levels ceases. It is harder to get them, and they mean more once attained. The Ph.D. is no longer a mere stepping stone in one's relentless careerism, and the master's and bachelor's degrees also regain much of their lost aura. Indeed, so does a high school diploma! If a problem arises about distinguishing the new and more valuable degrees from the old ones, universities can take a lead from governments practicing currency reform. When, for example, the French government deflated the franc, the currency was called "the new franc." Thus, we would have "new Ph.D.'s," "new M.A.'s," and so on.

With degrees harder to get, not quite so many will be seeking them. It is scandalous that the graduate schools are still humming when for two decades there has been an increasing surplus of higher degrees. If administrators and department chairs respond that nobody is twisting people's arms and forcing them into graduate school, they sound like the tobacco companies. Nobody is forcing people to smoke either. Perhaps all graduate application forms and letters of admission should be required to contain the following message: *GOVERNMENT WARNING: The following course of study may be dangerous to your financial health.*

The list of reforms already is long, and there are more to come. So far we have gotten rid of inflated publications, inflated ranks, inflated degrees. There is one more form of academic inflation to be dealt with, namely, the inflation of grades. The procedure just described for degrees holds as well for grade point averages, that might be lower than the old ones, but indicative of greater achievement. Stricter standards put the quietus on not one, but two familiar features of higher education that we might not associate with each other, but in fact are closely related. I refer to teaching evaluations and grade inflation, both of which came into being during the time of the protests against the Viet Nam War, the civil rights demonstrations, and the counterculture. Grades began to be inflated when faculty members felt morally obligated to help students keep their military deferments by grading less strictly than they had previously done. Meanwhile, another demand of the protesters, student evaluation of teaching performance, was seized upon by crafty administrators as a weapon against the faculty. They were useful to the former in the situation that developed in the 1970s after the lush times of the 1960s. When the enormous expansion of the educational system after World War II peaked in the late 1960s, and a contraction began to occur, there soon were thousands of surplus M.A.'s and Ph.D.'s on the job market. With continuing budgetary pressures, administrators and department heads found a convenient way to economize. They hired the excess graduates as part-time teachers at a great saving in salaries and benefits. The practice grew so prevalent that by the mid-1990s, 35–40 percent of faculty in higher education were part-time instructors.[7] Needless to say, during this period the number and pay of administrators rose dramatically. After all, they were needed to compete for the grants that were getting smaller and scarcer, to conform to the regulations and requirements that were increasing in number and complexity, and to keep tabs on the army of cheap laborers. In this situation, teaching evaluations became a critical weapon in the hands of the administrators to keep the peons in line. Social scientists were put to work designing the evaluations to give them an air of validity, but not to investigate the effects of the universities turning into sweatshops. Anyone who has worked in a sweatshop knows that the proprietors practice what in psychology is called "transference." They try to rid themselves of any guilt they might feel for being exploiters by making the exploited feel guilty. They dare not do it directly, but the implied message is, "It's your own fault you're a part-timer. If you had worked harder or been more cooperative or just been a better person, you might have a full-time job. So be grateful for the pittance we give you and don't you dare complain." Teaching evaluations are a powerful weapon in this campaign of innuendo. Their pseudo-scientific facade thinly masks questions that are inherently demeaning and that carry a presumption of guilt. Anonymity allows disgruntled students to vent their spleen and so the administration is in the position of sponsoring hate mail. Furthermore, there are no standards for evaluating the results, which are interpreted in any way administrators desire to support whatever hiring and firing decisions they wish to make. In short, rather than raising the level of education, evaluations lower it. They encourage conformity and mediocrity in teaching, and they exert strong upward pressure on grades. It is hard for instructors to be strict with students on whose good will their continued employment depends. Only tenured professors are free from this pressure, and they are in the minority on nearly all faculties.

As standards rise, all this changes. Grade inflation ceases and student evaluations become superfluous. As both students and teachers become better prepared, they value knowledge less for the purpose of advancing their careers and more for its own sake. The significance of grades diminishes. They do not disappear because they do have some value, but they cease to play a central role in judging a student's progress. Similarly, when professors continue to have the experience of being students, and when both they and the students are more deeply committed to the pursuit of knowledge for its own sake, teaching evaluations, at least in the form in which they currently are given, become an absurdity. They are superfluous for the same reason that grades diminish in importance. Any serious lapse on the part either of students or of professors would not escape notice.

All these reforms make it possible at last to do something about the education schools, those bullshit factories, which have retained their role in the system even though they have been severely criticized for decades. With professors in all disciplines more actively involved in teaching than ever before and a thorough curriculum reform having occurred, the importance of the education schools is diminished. It may be possible to eliminate them, or at least to curtail them. Teacher training can now be done as a part of regular graduate education.

In the midst of everything else, let us not overlook college athletics. While a return to the Hellenic ideal of education will naturally include athletics, what we see today is much the same distortion of that ideal as in the rest of Academe: an overemphasis on professionalism to the detriment of true amateurism, and the turning of an educational activity into a business. Actually, the complaint is not so much that big-time college athletics is a business and a profession rather than an amateur activity, but that there is so much hypocrisy and corruption attendant on it. Some of the hypocrisy is merely the right hand not knowing what the left hand doeth. The public wants contradictory things from the educational system and has never resolved the contradictions.

Without question athletic ability is something colleges should foster along with intellectual ability. Yet even those athletes who are good students find it hard to be both at the same time. Hence, athletes should be given the option of taking a lighter schedule of courses during their four years of eligibility, and then finishing their degrees afterward. Under this arrangement, those who are less able students might never finish their degrees, but that is what happens anyway. An alternative would be to get rid of big-time athletics altogether. Whatever the solution, the main thing is to end the hypocrisy. If that is done, individual schools will be better able to decide what is right for them.

It is not just athletics that are hard to squeeze into a four-year undergraduate curriculum. Liberal arts can hardly be studied in that time span, and it also is becoming increasingly difficult to provide a proper background for science majors. Since we are rethinking everything else, it comes as no surprise to discover that undergraduate education must be rethought too. There is nothing sacred about the four-year college. It began in colonial times, and now needs to be expanded. The question is how will it be done and for whom.

While all students will benefit from the rise in standards, the expansion of undergraduate education will not be for everybody. It will be primarily for the future scholars and scientists, the doctors, lawyers, and engineers, and other high-level professionals, perhaps 20 percent of the 14 million undergraduates. The expansion would occur in both directions: into high school and beyond the four years of traditional college education. That is the only way students could take all the courses they need.

Students will have ample opportunity to exercise all their options. We need not go all the way to the old British system, where they had to make life choices at the age of eleven. In America we don't have that problem, but we have our own unique form of torture, the frenzy of getting into college and earning a degree. Preparing for college is a little like running for president. People start years in advance, putting aside money, meeting qualifications, studying for the College Boards, figuring out finances, considering options, etc. Then when they finally get to college, it is a rat race. They are thinking about grades, worried about finding a job when they graduate or anxious about getting into graduate school, concerned about the debt they are piling up. What is more, they have direct experience of the failings of the system. They know as well as anybody that they are receiving an inferior product at an inflated price. Earning a college degree is one of the ingredients of the American Dream, but it has turned into the American Nightmare.

An excellent way to reduce the hassle would be for the better students to start taking college-level courses in high school. This type of program already exists, and it should be greatly expanded so that it is normal procedure for college-bound students to take some college courses there. Thus, they would show their prospective alma maters what they could do and thereby eliminate much of the arduousness of college admissions. The importance of the College Boards, for example, would be lessened. The students would simultaneously be adding some of the extra time needed in the undergraduate curriculum. And so we would kill several birds with one stone.

The expansion in the other direction would probably not be more than a year beyond the traditional four. The details would vary with individual students and could be worked out in consultation with their prospective graduate or professional schools. The overall effect would be to reduce further the distinctions between different branches of education – one more example of barriers coming down.

As noted above, we also would be less dependent on other bureaucratic ways of measuring progress such as the College Boards. It is too much to hope that these could be dispensed with, but at least they would play a smaller role than they do today. With a more unified curriculum and generally higher standards, students' performance in high school would be a more reliable indicator of their college potential than at present. Those who slipped through the cracks and got into colleges for which they were ill-prepared would not remain there long. Moreover, the high schools from which they came would have a strong incentive to maintain their reputations by representing their students' abilities and accomplishments as accurately as possible.

I am nearing the end of my list of reforms. Having spoken about various kinds of academic inflation, I do not wish to omit financial inflation. As a result of all the foregoing changes, costs will go down. It is easy to see why: emphasizing the great books is more economical than the present cafeteria-style education; bureaucracy will be reduced; wasteful specialization and dubious research will be eliminated. If many colleges today are glorified high schools, and high schools improve, then maybe we won't need 3,700 colleges. Amazing, isn't it, what simplifying the curriculum and raising standards will lead to.

While some of the problems I have been describing in this essay are not obvious and needed to be fleshed out, many of them have been well-known for years, including most of those mentioned in this chapter. One could draw a comparison with the Chinese parable of the Emperor's clothes, but in this case, the Emperor is not alone in lacking clothing. Academe is a veritable nudist colony. The question is, when will the public wake up and do something about it?

What a long way we have come! It may seem incredible that merely getting rid of "philosophy" will precipitate all these reforms. Yet if the head moves the body, and not the other way round, why should the same principle not hold for institutions? Despite the excessive specialization that exists today, the different parts of the educational system affect one another. A revolution at the top will indeed cause miraculous changes throughout.

On the other hand, I have got so deeply absorbed in imagining all the reforms that I may have deluded myself into believing that such sweeping changes could actually occur. When one is swept up in a vision of an ideal world, it is easy to lose one's ability to distinguish between fantasy and reality.

Still, it depends on what reality you are talking about. We have grown so inured to the bizarre conditions under which our educational system operates that we accept them as normal. Nobody bats an eye when thousands of children have to pass through metal detectors before they are allowed into school. If we passively accept so obvious a symptom of the ills that beset the system, it is no surprise that we do nothing about the more subtle problems. To us, these conditions constitute reality. In truth, it is hard to know which is worse, the problems themselves or the mental paralysis with which the public greets them. Perhaps my attempt to find a solution is quixotic, but if that is so, think of Don Quixote. He is crazy, or deluded, but the people around him are so sordid that his ideal world looks more real than theirs.

The revolution I have sketched may be a fantasy, but the need for liberal education has been recognized in the twentieth century. A number of attempts have been made to provide it, and we might briefly consider them. In most instances, the results have been disappointing. When, early in the century, Harvard, along with other universities, stopped requiring its undergraduates to know Latin and Greek, something adequate had to be found to replace them. Around the time of World War I, Columbia University drew up a list of great books and made them the center of its general education curriculum. Subsequently, the University of Chicago under Robert Hutchins, as well as the University of Virginia, did the same thing. However, these schools and their imitators have found it hard to do the great books properly and still meet the need of their students to fulfill pre-professional requirements. Given the limitations placed on their general education programs, it was an impossible task to begin with. Thus, in 1937, St. John's College of Annapolis, Maryland, decided to take a radical approach. It drew up a list of great books that simply became its undergraduate curriculum, both in the humanities and in the sciences. The entire college was set up around this program, and the conventional academic bureaucracy was eliminated. Hence, there are no departments; nor are there any "professors," since all the instructors are called "tutors." To remove any vestige of narrow departmental thinking, each one teaches nearly the whole curriculum. The tutors have little time to write for publication, since preparing themselves in so many subjects is a rigorous undertaking. The students also study the whole curriculum, which includes instruction in classical Greek and French as well as mathematics. Since the great books take precedence over pre-professional requirements, in order to fulfill the latter, students often must lengthen their undergraduate studies beyond four years. Conventional letter grades are given because most go on to graduate or professional schools and some transfer to other colleges. However, grades do not play a central role within the curriculum. Because the college is small and students participate actively in the courses, their progress is continually observed. They are told their grades only on request.

It may seem as if I am describing the Renaissance or ancient Greece rather than something existing in our own day, and it sounds too good to be true. However, St. John's has been offering this curriculum for nearly sixty years, so at least we know it is not a figment of someone's imagination. Although it added a branch campus in Santa Fe, New Mexico, it has maintained the purity of its program by remaining small.

If this approach is so good, why doesn't the rest of American education imitate it? The reader can find all the reasons in the foregoing narrative. An educational revolution would be required. Even if that revolution should actually occur, we would not expect universities to imitate everything about the St. John's program. I have tried to show what it would take to achieve such a program on a massive scale and to give a very broad outline of what it would be like in that setting. This is the educational system that would follow from the death and life of philosophy.

The question of what would be required to offer liberal education on a large scale brings up a question that is often raised and that I have saved for the last. The trend in our time has been to make education available to as large a number of people as possible. Will very many of them meet the demands of an education worthy of the name of liberal? It seems plain that not many will. Is not liberal education, therefore, by its very nature elitist?

If we pause to reflect, we recognize that "elitist" is a much-abused word, as is the word "democratic." In the strictest sense, every profession is an elite, and the higher its standards, the more of an elite it is. However, in the name of democracy, general educational standards have been weakened sufficiently to pose a threat to professional standards themselves. The latter are further jeopardized by a narrow professionalism. Both of these developments lead to elitism in its most pernicious form because it hides behind a façade of democracy. An elite is acceptable only if everyone has a fair chance to join it.

Liberal education has always been for the few because, traditionally, only a few were educated. It remains to be seen how many people it actually can reach. Mass education is still so new that we have not explored its possibilities. I mentioned earlier my own successful effort to find a faster way to learn languages. To me at least it is clear that much more efficient methods of learning can be found than the prevailing ones. In the meantime, the ills of Academe, on all levels, can be remedied by a healthy dose of liberal education.

To be sure, the elite of Athens, Rome, and Florence were liberally educated, not to mention the leaders of the British Empire, who were classically trained in the public (*i.e.*, private) schools. That would suggest this type of schooling is only or primarily for the few. But on the other hand, where are the most radically democratic ideas to be found? Why, in the great books, of course! Where else would you expect to find them? They are there, along with the opposing view. The question remains open just how democratic society can become, and the great books do not prejudge it. Furthermore, the idea that high culture is snobbish, effete, and useless also vanishes when we realize how much it has in common with the best of popular culture, which also is produced by, so to speak, an elite. While the latter lacks the brilliance of high art, it has the same genuineness of expression and universality of theme. High art always has been nourished by popular culture, from Homer (if not before) to the present day. Mozart, for example, made use of Austrian folk tunes, and Beethoven wrote arrangements for Scottish and Irish songs. This same connection is to be found in politics and social affairs, where the extremes somehow attract each other. One thinks of the famous party at Leonard Bernstein's apartment in the late 1960s, when the Black Panthers rubbed elbows with the rich and powerful. Similarly, St. John's College, with its classes run largely by students, downplaying of grades, and lack of departments and rank, seems exactly the kind of institution demanded by the radicals of the 1960s and '70s. Yet it is next door to the U.S. Naval Academy and down the street from the Maryland State Capitol, teaching the curriculum on which many of the world's elites have been nurtured.

"Elitism," then, is a false issue. The choice is not between education for the few versus mass education. A full liberal education clearly is not for everybody, not for all 14 million undergraduates in America today. Determining its nature and just whom it is for have been a problem throughout the twentieth century, as the number of students increased enormously. It remains to be seen what percentage of undergraduates can benefit from liberal education, and the answer depends on a wide range of issues and circumstances, including those discussed in this essay.

The issue is not elitism versus egalitarianism, but something in between those two, a failing more characteristic of the middle class. To say this is not to denigrate the middle-class virtues of thrift and hard work or bourgeois morality in general. What I have been criticizing is a bourgeois mentality taken to extremes, a bureaucratic *Weltanschauung* and a narrow-minded professionalism, seen both in its constipated and its diarrheic manifestations. The purpose is not to destroy professionalism, but to save it from itself. It is true that when you are flying around at 40,000 feet, you may not be comforted if the captain suddenly announces over the intercom, "This airplane was designed and built and is being flown by amateurs." Nor if you are observing open-heart surgery being performed on a loved one will you be reassured to hear the surgeon look up from his work and say, "We're all amateurs here!" Still, the highest level of professionalism is amateurism raised to the highest level. No professional training can anticipate all the difficulties and dangers that may arise when the training is pushed to its limits or even beyond. Think of Apollo 13. The time may never come when amateurism and professionalism are so much in harmony that the captain will say over the intercom, "We're having a spot of engine trouble. Is there a philosopher on board?" Yet even while discovering ever more scientific wonders, we can grasp how little we actually know, as did Newton when he compared human beings to children playing on the shores of the ocean of knowledge. Or to put it in the words of Alexander Pope:

> A *little Learning* is a dang'rous Thing;
> Drink deep, or taste not the *Pierian Spring*:
> There *shallow Draughts* intoxicate the Brain,
> And drinking *largely* sobers us again.
> Fir'd at first Sight with what the *Muse* imparts,
> In *fearless* Youth we tempt the Heights of Arts,
> While from the bounded *Level* of our Mind,
> *Short views* we take, nor see the *Lengths behind,*
> But *more advanc'd*, behold with strange Surprize
> New, distant Scenes of *endless* Science rise!
> So pleas'd at first, the towring *Alps* we try,
> Mount o'er the Vales, and seem to tread the Sky;
> Th' Eternal Snows appear already past,
> And the first *Clouds* and *Mountains* seem the last:
> But *those attain'd*, we tremble to survey
> The growing Labours of the lengthen'd Way,
> Th'*increasing* Prospect tires our wandring Eyes,
> Hills peep o'er Hills, and *Alps* on *Alps* arise!

Seeing the world in this way, the scientists may once again be glad to call themselves philosophers.

Notes

1. U.S. Bureau of the Census, *The Statistical Abstract of the United States 1995*, and *The Statistical Abstract of the United States 1997*. In 1971 approximately 315,000 physicians were professionally active. In 1995 646,000 were professionally active.

2. *Ibid.*

3. *Ibid.* The 1995 *Statistical Abstract* estimates the percentage of part-timers at 35 percent, but the 1997 edition puts the number at 40 percent. It is interesting that no figures for part-timers are given for 1997.

4. The number of people studying languages is low, and just how low becomes even clearer as soon as one realizes what the figures represent. In 1990 in the United States, out of approximately 14,000,000 college and university students, 1,184,100 were enrolled in foreign language courses. The typical language requirement, in those colleges that have one, is four semesters or the equivalent. With that amount of study, the students do not learn very much, and few of them go farther than four semesters. In 1971, 5,271 foreign language M.A.'s were awarded in the United States. In 1992, the number was 2,926. In 1971, 988 Ph.D.'s were granted in foreign languages; in 1992, 850. Thus, the number of people in the United States with advanced training in foreign languages is small and getting smaller. While there are millions of non-native speakers of English and non-English speakers in the U.S., these numbers reflect immigration, not language study. (The foregoing figures were taken from *The Statistical Abstract of the United States, 1995.*)

5. Karen W. Arenson, "Classes Are Full At Catch-Up U," *The New York Times* (May 31, 1998). "The News of the Week in Review." In 1995, remedial classes were offered at 78 percent of colleges in the United States. 96 percent of public community colleges offer them. The Ivy League schools claim they have no remedial courses, but they have peer tutors and writing centers.

6. In 1970, the total enrollment in higher education in the United States was 8,581,000. In 1995, it was 14,210,000, of whom 12,171,000 were undergraduates, 1,736,000 were graduate students, and 303,000 were first-time professional students. There were 833,000 faculty, and 2,259,000 degrees were awarded. (U.S. Bureau of the Census, *The Statistical Abstract of the United States 1996.*)

7. *The Statistical Abstract of the United States 1995, 1997.*

Appendix
Aristotle's Argument for the Unity of Mind

The following article grew out of a paper read at a workshop on Aristotle's metaphysics and epistemology held at Florida State University, Tallahassee, January 3–8, 1983. The author attended the conference with support from the National Endowment for the Humanities.

Of the perennial issues in philosophy, the question of the unity of mind has received greater attention among modern writers than it did among the ancients. Indeed, the emphasis placed on this question by Descartes and Kant can help us to appreciate how essential it was in the thought of Aristotle. This article will explicate the argument or proof of the unity of mind which appears unobtrusively in *De Anima* III, ii, and has tended to be overlooked or misconstrued in light of other concerns. I will show that this argument also helps us to understand Aristotle's concept of the soul, and will conclude by comparing his views on this issue with those of Descartes and Kant.

Aristotle's researches on plants and animals are outmoded and are not taken very seriously by modern biologists. However, his theory of the soul and his psychology deserve a much different status. The *De Anima* and the *Parva Naturalia*, together with various passages scattered throughout the *Nicomachean Ethics* and other treatises, constitute a kind of "metabiology" and "metapsychology," bearing with great force upon the concerns of present-day epistemology, psychology, and biology. Unfortunately, these writings are not given their due today, and even within the Aristotelian tradition, they have not received the same degree of attention as have his metaphysics, physics, logic, ethics, politics, rhetoric, and poetics. In the Middle Ages, despite the influence of St. Thomas Aquinas, the main interest was not in Aristotle's psychology and biology. If it had been, a truly scientific Aristotelianism might have emerged, and the course of modern science would have been different. In the modern period, interest in psychology did become paramount, but this occurred in the context of a materialistic science. An atomistic physics and chemistry was dominant, and biology was not in the forefront of science. Hence, the disfavor into which Aristotle had fallen was reinforced by disinterest.

Descartes and Kant were, to use the terminology of Thomas S. Kuhn, the paradigm-makers of the modern period. They created the framework of investigation in which modern philosophy developed. Their dualistic conception of reality survives in one form or another unto the present day, despite numerous attempts to bypass or replace it. Within their theories, the concept of mental unity plays a central role. However, their arguments for it are weaker than that of Aristotle.

Aristotle was not the first to give such an argument or proof, for he was anticipated by Plato in the dialogue *Theaetetus* (184–86). It seems beyond doubt that Aristotle was familiar with this passage, and presumably he built upon it.[1] Of the several places where he discusses the unity of perception or of mind, the most important is *De Anima* III, ii (426b8–30). Further comments occur in chapters iv, v, and vii of *De Anima* III.[2] In the final chapter of *De Sensu*, the unity of perception is asseverated; although he is talking there about perception, he seems to be alluding to his earlier remarks on the subject.[3]

In light of the passages in *De Sensu* and with a superficial reading of *De Anima* III, ii, one might be led to the conclusion that all Aristotle is talking about is the common sensorium or *sensus communis*, the "master sense-organ" in which the perceptions of the individual senses are received and conjoined.[4] In *De Sensu* clearly he is speaking of the unity of perception; this seems perfectly natural, since the treatise is a continuation of the discussion of the senses in *De Anima*. But something more than that is going on in *De Anima* III, ii. To see what Aristotle really is saying, let us look at the passage:

> Each sense then is of its underlying sense-object, existing in the sense organ insofar as it is a sense-organ, and distinguishes the differences of the sense-object; *e.g.*, vision [distinguishes] white and black and taste sweet and bitter; and similarly in regard to the other senses. But since we also distinguish white and sweet, and each of the objects perceived with respect to each other, by what sense do we perceive that they differ? It must be by some sense; for they are objects of sense. . . . Nor indeed is it possible to judge by separate [senses] that sweet is different from white, but both must be manifest to some one [sense]. So for goodness sake, if on the one hand *you* perceived one thing and I another, it would be clear that they were different from each other. But on

the other hand, it must be one thing that says they're different [*deî dè tò hèn légein hóti héteron*]; my heavens, sweet *is* different from white. The same [thing] therefore asserts this, and consequently, as it asserts [*légei*], so it thinks [*nóei*] and perceives [*aisthánetai*]. So then on the one hand that it's impossible to pass judgment on separate [objects] by separate [senses] is apparent; nor, on the other hand, at separate times, [as follows] from that. Gosh, just as the same [thing] says that good and evil are different, so also when it says the one or the other are different, the "time when" is not incidental (I mean [as it is when] for example, I *now* say they are different, not however that they *now* are different). But thus it speaks: both now, and also that [the difference is] now; it's at the same time then. Consequently, [that which judges is] undivided and [does so] in undivided time [*i.e.*, without an interval].[5]

Aristotle selects perceptions of two senses that cannot be interchanged: the tongue cannot see and the eye cannot taste, so there is no way the sense-organs themselves can distinguish each other's perceptions. He remarks that "it must evidently be by some sense [that we perceive the difference]; for they are objects of sense." Naturally he is talking about the common sensorium here, but it is immediately clear that he is talking about the mind as well: "It is necessary for one thing to say that they are different. . . . The same thing then, says it (*légei*); hence, as it speaks (*légei*), so it thinks (*nóei*) and perceives (*aisthánetai*)." Moreover, as he goes on to say, the perception must be simultaneous. The two sense-images are distinguished in one conscious act, by one organ, which is what – the common sensorium? The mind?

Quite likely he means both, for it seems clear from the text that he is describing the total act: the composite perception that is required, the mental intuition, and the utterance. After all, the common sensorium cannot issue statements. We are able to do that because we have grasped the distinction with our minds, which in turn are dependent on our perceptions. This interrelationship between discourse, thinking, and perception is also stated in another treatise, in a passage which rather pointedly refers to the *De Anima*:

On the one hand, therefore, the things that are spoken are symbols or signs of affections of the soul, and the things written are the symbols of the things spoken. And just as writing is not the same for all mankind, neither is speech the same. However, those things of which the latter are primarily signs, the mental affections [*pathémata tês psychês*] are the same for the whole of mankind, and those things of which these are likenesses [*homoiómata*], the objects, are the same. These matters, however, were discussed in the treatise on the soul . . .[6]

In *De Anima* III, ii there are two further references to both *aísthesis* and *noûs* (427a1 and 9–10), which also suggest he is not talking about the common sensorium alone. In *De Anima* III, vii, he expands upon his earlier account of unity, asking rhetorically, "Good grief, what difference [whether we] ask how [the soul] distinguishes things which are not of the same class, or contraries like white and black?"[7]

In other words, the argument for unity applies to any two (or more) perceptions or thoughts. Indeed, this is suggested in the original passage cited by the line "we . . . compare all objects perceived with each other . . ." (426b13–14) Finally, in a discussion of indivisible and combined concepts, he observes that "The thing that unifies, this is in every case the mind."[8]

It is true that at the conclusion of Book III, chapter ii, Aristotle says: "So then regarding the principle by which we call a living creature sentient [*tò zôon aisthétikon*], let it be defined in this way."[9] Why, one might ask, if the proof of unity is meant to be all-embracing, does he say only *aisthétikon*? Why not *aisthétikon kaì noétikon* (perceptual and mental)? Perhaps the fact that the proof is so inclusive itself provides the answer, encompassing both the senses and the mind. The inclusiveness is understood, so he does not need to repeat himself. Then too, in the next chapter Aristotle launches immediately into a discussion of *mental* activities. If all he were talking about in *this* chapter were the unity of *perception*, there would be no proper transition between the chapters, just the abrupt assumption of the new topic. On the other hand, if the first two chapters of Book III are viewed as providing a smooth transition between the discussion of the senses in Book II and the treatment of the mind that follows, then a proof of unity that applies across the board seems logical.

Furthermore, are we to assume that the mind is *not* a unity, whereas the common sensorium is? That would be absurd. On the contrary, Aristotle says forthrightly in the passages cited above that the mind *is* a unity. Yet he gives no separate proof for the unity of the mind. If we still insist that the argument in *De Anima* III, ii, has to do only with the common sensorium, we find ourselves saying that Aristotle gives a powerful proof for the unity of the common sensorium and none for the unity of mind. But the passage itself clearly contradicts this view. Finally, he speaks (in the passage just quoted) of "the principle in virtue of which we call a living creature sentient." What principle could he mean? It must be unity, a general condition of perception, thought, and discourse. We shall see in the discussion of Kant the consequences of a weaker argument that does not apply to all three.

Exactly how are the perceptions of the common sensorium organized or transformed into the thoughts of the mind? Aristotle does not provide an adequate *physical* model of the relationship between the two. It is probably just as well, for his primitive physiology, in which the common sensorium is located in the heart and the functions of the nervous and the circulatory systems are confused, would be of little help here.[10] Perhaps Aristotle realized how little he actually knew about the workings of the body and wisely did not tie his powerful psychology to a questionable physiology. If so, this may explain why in *De Anima* III, ii, he refers to the common sensorium without mentioning its bodily location.

Putting physiology aside, we quickly realize the subtlety of the relationship that must hold between the common sensorium and the mind. The line "As it speaks, so it thinks and perceives" does not tell us whether they constitute two separate entities or how they might be connected. Nor is this point clarified elsewhere. But in a number of places Aristotle gives us some hints:

> So the soul is just like the hand; shit, man, the hand is a tool of tools [*órganon orgánon*], and the mind is a form of forms [*eîdos eidôn*], and sense-perception is the form of perceived objects [*eîdos aisthetôn*].[11]

It sounds like doubletalk, but he is referring to levels of abstraction. In perception, the *eîdos* of the *aisthetón*, the sensory form of the objects perceived by the senses, has been *abstracted* from them. The mind, the *eîdos* of the *eidôn,* is the next level of abstraction. It is like a blank tablet[12] and needs mental images in order to think:

> But since nothing *is* anything separate besides [sensible] magnitudes, as it seems [*i.e.*, nothing exists independently except the objects of the senses], the objects of thought – both the so-called abstractions [of mathematics] and all states of sensible objects – exist *in the sensible forms*. And for this reason, without exercising sense-perception no one could ever learn or understand anything, but whenever one thinks abstractly, one must at the same time be contemplating some mental image [*phántasma*]; doggone it, mental images are just like perceived objects except that they're without matter.[13]

The mind "thinks the forms in mental images,"[14] using them as symbols of abstractions:

> It is impossible to think without a mental picture, for it happens to be the same mental state in thinking as in drawing a geometrical figure;

for there although we make no use of the fact that the magnitude of a triangle is a finite magnitude, yet we draw it as having a finite magnitude. In the same way the man who is thinking, even if he is not thinking of a finite magnitude, puts before his eyes a finite magnitude, but he does not think of it insofar as it is finite. And even if the nature of the object is quantitative, but indeterminate, he puts before himself a finite magnitude, but he thinks of it only insofar as it is quantitative.[15]

The greater abstractness of the mind also is made clear by its relative *apátheia*, impassivity or insensitivity:

But that the impassivity of the sensory and thinking parts [of the *psyché*] is not similar is obvious with regard to the sense organs and sensation. For the sense cannot perceive as a result of the excessively perceivable, *e.g.*, sound after loud sounds, or see or smell after strong colors and scents; but the mind whenever it thinks about something very intelligible is not less able to think of subtleties, but even more able; for the sensory [part of the soul does] not [exist] without the body, whereas the mind is separable.[16]

The foregoing passages, while not overlooking the differences between thinking and perception, show how dependent thinking is on images derived from the senses. Much of Book III of the *De Anima* deals with the mind's operations upon these images. Rational soul clearly is a further development of sentient soul. Hence, the anatomical structure and physiological processes that permit abstract thought must be a development or expansion of the common sensorium. For example, imagination (*phantasía*) is derived from perception (*aísthesis*);[17] there are two kinds of imagination, the sensory imagination (*aisthetikè phantasía*) and the deliberative or calculative (*bouleutikè phantasía*). Of these Aristotle remarks: "Sensory imagination . . . is found in all animals, but deliberative imagination only in the animals that reason."[18] This implies a continuum, not only when one thinks of it in evolutionary terms, but in terms of the variety of species Aristotle knew.

After seeing how close the connection is in Aristotle between sense-perception and thinking, should we conclude that the common sensorium and the mind are two separate entities or that the unity of the mind encompasses the unity of the common sensorium? Does the mind operate *in* or *on* the common sensorium, or is the common sensorium located *in* the mind? It is hard to say, but at least we can see why Aristotle would try to prove the unity of perception, thought, and discourse all at once.

* * * * *

The argument for the unity of mind helps us to understand not only Aristotle's concept of mind but his concept of life and soul as well. This is because thinking is the highest function of life:

> Living is defined in animals by the power of sense-perception, and in human beings by the [the power of] sense-perception and thought. But a power is referred back to its [corresponding] activity, and the main thing is the activity. It really seems that living in the fullest sense is perceiving with the senses or thinking.[19]

Thinking is the way we can best imitate the divine,[20] which is something all creatures strive to do:

> For the most natural of activities among living creatures . . . [is] making another like itself, an animal an animal, and a plant a plant, in order that they may share in the immortal and divine insofar as they can; for every creature strives for that, and for the sake of that does everything it does by nature. But "for the sake of" has two senses: for the sake of what and for the sake of whom [*i.e.*, the purpose or goal, and the being or creature (who benefits from achieving the goal)]. Since, then, they cannot share in the immortal and divine by continuous existence, because no perishable thing can endure numerically one and the same, insofar as each one can it shares in this, some more and some less; it itself does not endure, but something like itself, not one in number, but one in kind.[21]

All living beings – plants, animals, man – imitate a supreme being whose nature is thinking. Since mind, the organ of thought, is the highest part of the soul, and the argument for unity is essential for understanding mind, perhaps it can tell us something about the nature of soul.

Let us first consider what Aristotle says in the *Metaphysics* about being and unity. In X, i, he distinguishes four kinds of unity: "the naturally continuous, the whole, the individual, and the universal."[22] He asserts that the higher kind of unity is

... [that which] has a certain shape or form, particularly that which is such by nature and not by constraint (like things [joined] by glue or nails or by being tied together), but which has in itself the cause of its being continuous.[23]

He adds that "in a sense unity means the same as being."[24] In another passage he states this equivalence even more strongly:

[F]or indeed "one man" and "man" and "being man" and "man" are the same thing, and the duplication in the phrase "one man and being one man" does not signify anything different . . . and similarly in regard to "one," so it's obvious the additional term in these [phrases] means the same thing, and unity is nothing distinct from being; and further the substantial being of each thing is one not accidentally, but similarly is the very thing that *is* something [*i.e.*, from its very nature something that *is*] – so exactly as many kinds of unity as there are, just so many kinds are there of being.[25]

Add to this the conclusion of Book Zeta that substance or substantial being is form (1041b7–9), together with the statements defining soul in *De Anima*:

So the soul must be substantial being in the sense of the form of a natural body that potentially has life. But substantial being is *actuality*. [The soul] then [is] the *actuality* of such [a body]. But "actuality" has two senses, [analogous to] the possession of knowledge and the exercise of it. . . . Therefore the soul is the first actuality of a natural body possessing life . . .[26]

We can collate these passages into a chain of reasoning: Being is unity; substance (substantial being) is form; the soul is the form, *i.e.*, the first actuality of a living body; hence, the soul is a unity, the unity of the living organism.

Further, to be alive in the fullest sense is to think; all living beings imitate the divine, whose nature is pure thought, in whatever way they can; the mind is a unity and is the highest part of the soul; hence, the unity that constitutes the soul resembles or imitates that which constitutes mind. If life in the fullest sense is thinking, perhaps life in any sense is something like thinking. In that case not only would it be true that "the actuality of mind is life" (*Metaphysics*, 1072b27), but the converse would also be true: life is, in some sense, the actuality of mind. The argument for the unity of mind may apply to the unity of soul as well.

This means that the way the soul functions is something like the way the mind does – as a kind of judging unity. The unity need not be conscious. It is a unity of function that resembles thought. This is really not hard to comprehend, even on the lowest levels of life. An amoeba and a paramecium can scarcely have consciousness, but they do have reactivity, which seems to be unified behavior. Closer to the bottom of the scale, when we ask whether viruses are living or non-living, we are really asking whether any substantial unity, however inchoate or rudimentary, can be discerned in their behavior. All along the *scala naturae* we might follow this method of analyzing living behavior. In any event, it appears that from Aristotle's argument for the unity of mind there follows an argument for the unity of activity of any biological organism, no matter how simple. Indeed, given the importance of biology in Aristotle's thought, soul is the paradigm case of unity, apart from the Unmoved Mover itself.

At this point the question may be raised, if *noûs* (mind) goes all the way down the scale of life, why do we need to call it *psyché* (soul) at all? Although they are closely related, they are not equivalent. To function in a manner like thinking is still not quite the same as thinking. If we did eschew the use of *psyché*, we would have to use *noûs* in both a broader and a narrower sense. It is enough to know that for Aristotle *psyché* resembles and imitates *noûs*, thereby imitating the divine.

* * * * *

Because of the importance of the concept of mental unity in modern philosophy and in order to shed more light on Aristotle's argument, I shall briefly compare his views on this topic with those of Descartes, Hume, and Kant. I shall try to show the weaknesses of their positions, as compared with his.

Within their dualistic framework, they both make the unity of mind central. Descartes, for example, states:

> To begin this examination, I first take notice here that there is a great difference between the mind and the body, in that the body, from its nature, is always divisible and the mind is completely indivisible. For in reality, when I consider the mind – that is, when I consider myself in so far as I am only a thinking being – I cannot distinguish any parts, but I recognize and conceive very clearly that I am a thing which is absolutely unitary and entire ... it is one and the same thing which as a complete unity wills, perceives, and understands, and so forth.[27]

He forcefully asserts the unity of the mind but without any proof. He simply appeals to intuition, combining his appeal with a radical separation of mind and body. The intuition may be very sound, but it can be denied, which is precisely what Hume does:

> There are some philosophers who imagine that we are every moment intimately conscious of what we call our *self*; that we feel its existence and its continuance in existence; and are certain, beyond the evidence of a demonstration, both of its perfect identity and simplicity. The strongest sensation, the most violent passion, say they, instead of distracting us from this view, only fix it the more intensely.... To attempt a further proof of this were to weaken its evidence; since no proof can be derived of any fact of which we are so intimately conscious; nor is there anything of which we can be certain if we doubt of this.
>
> Unluckily all these positive assertions are contrary to that very experience which is pleaded for them; nor have we any idea of *self*, after the manner it is here explained. For, from what impression could this idea be derived? . . . It must be some one impression that gives rise to every real idea. But self or person is not any one impression. . . . [T]here is no impression constant and invariable. . . . [C]onsequently there is no such idea.[28]

Descartes is vulnerable to this sort of criticism. Hume denies the Cartesian view of mental unity on the grounds that he simply has no such idea. This leaves the issue to be fought on the basis of my intuition versus your intuition.

More definitive for the modern period were the views of Immanuel Kant, whose discussion of the unity of mind is closer to Aristotle's view than is Descartes'. However, the concept of unity with which Kant answers Hume is a priori and non-natural:

> Therefore a transcendental ground of the unity of consciousness must be found in the synthesis of the manifold of all our intuitions, and consequently also of the concepts of objects in general, and so of all objects of experience, without which it would be impossible to think any object for our intuitions . . .
>
> . . . . This pure original unchangeable consciousness I shall name transcendental apperception. . . . The numerical unity of this apperception lies *a priori* as the ground of all concepts.[29]

The nature of thinking is defined as follows:

> The sum of the matter is this: the business of the senses is to intuit,

that of the understanding is to think. But thinking is uniting representations in one consciousness. This union originates either merely relative to the subject and is accidental and subjective, or takes place absolutely and is necessary or objective. The union of representations in one consciousness is judgment. Thinking, therefore, is the same as judging, or referring representations to judgments in general. . . . The logical functions of all judgments are but various modes of uniting representations in consciousness. . . . Experience consists in the synthetical connection of phenomena (perceptions) in consciousness, so far as this is necessary.[30]

It is clear from these passages how strongly Kant is committed to the notion of mental unity. Unfortunately, within the Newtonian world-picture, he can't find any way of making the empirical unity substantial. Like Descartes, Kant thinks the body is a machine, and that animals are machines. Percepts and mental images are bodily objects or rather products, and thus are part of the machine's functioning. They are part of a deterministic chain of causes. Any unity they may have is "accidental and subjective."[31] In Aristotelian terminology, it is unity "by constraint," rather than natural unity. The living creature is therefore not a natural unity in Aristotle's sense, for it does not contain within itself a principle of motion and change, *i.e.*, the soul.[32]

Kant recognizes the need for unity every bit as much as Aristotle does. Statements or propositions have to be logical unities; thinking is an act of unifying; but he cannot find any natural unity in perception. His mechanistic conception of nature precludes him from discovering the biologically based argument that Aristotle is able to make.

One might conclude that this boils down to a conflict between two theories about nature, but that would be failing to see that Aristotle's argument is itself strong evidence against mechanism. To be sure, modern science had good reason to adopt a mechanistic view of the world. But to conclude that because mechanistic explanations work well when we are dealing with atoms and molecules, they must also apply to living creatures, is to beg the question. They may or they may not. If it can be shown that the unity of the mind is not "accidental," then the mind is not a mechanism. If the argument applies also to soul, *i.e.*, to the whole organism, then the body is not a machine either.

In this way Aristotle provides us with ammunition against the mechanistic view of nature that has prevailed since the mid-seventeenth century. I submit that Aristotle's argument for the unity of mind (and by implication the soul) is the strongest argument we have against both mechanism and dualism. Aristotle, as we saw, argues for the unity of discourse, thought, and perception all at once, not so much for the sake of economy as that they are so closely related to one another. Examining the views of Descartes and Kant on this subject, we see what happens when one of the three, perception, is omitted.

Merely by comparing the perceptions of two senses, Aristotle is able to establish the active role of the mind. That mental activity is more obvious in combining a subject and a predicate into a proposition, or in the thought that underlies the proposition, but in perception as well a unity is required if we are to give an intelligible account of it. Without the underlying unity of perception, the activity of the mind becomes difficult or impossible to explain on naturalistic grounds. In that eventuality one must have recourse to dualism in order to save the unity of mind.

It is hard to be sure of the exact nature of Aristotle's argument that only a unity can distinguish between two different percepts. Is it logical, psychological, metaphysical? However, Aristotle does not make a clearcut distinction between science and philosophy. He himself was the embodiment of the philosopher-scientist, of which there have been many other notable examples in the history of Western thought. The question whether Aristotle was right may be decided by scientists completely unaware of whose theory they are testing. For if they can produce a counter-example, that may be enough to decide the issue.

As strong, then, as Aristotle's argument is, we cannot be certain whether it really is conclusive. A great deal depends on its explanatory power versus that of the opposing theory. The issue of a mechanistic explanation of life and mind versus a truly biological one is likely to be fought out on the battlefields of molecular biology and artificial intelligence for years to come. Are we in fact *ousíai* (substantial beings) with *psychaí* (souls), or are we merely complex, conscious machines? Many researchers think they soon will be able to crack the secret of living matter and prove there is no essential difference between life and non-living matter. The most enthusiastic adherents of artificial intelligence believe that computer programs will eventually duplicate the judgment that is an essential characteristic of sentient organisms. If these people succeed in what they are doing, they will be contradicting the statement *deî dè tò hèn légein óti héteron*. A machine, an artificial product, will be able to make a judgment. On the other hand, if they are unable to do this, Aristotle's philosophy, after centuries of obscurity, may return to the forefront of science.

Notes

1. Not only should we assume that Aristotle was familiar with all the works of Plato available to us, but the arguments for the unity of mind that occur in the *Theaetetus* and the *De Anima* are very similar. This similarity includes the perceptions discussed: "hot, hard, light, and sweet" in *Theaetetus* (185e6) and "sweet and white" in Aristotle (cf. the passages from *De Anima* and *De Sensu* cited below, notes 2 and 3).

2. See ch. iv *passim*, and especially 429b23–26. The whole discussion in this chapter seems to presuppose the mind's unity. Ch. vi is similar in this regard. Note in particular 430b6 and 430b15–16. In ch. vii see 431a14–431b2.

3. Note the references to "white and sweet": 447b23, 448a16–17 ff., and 449all ff.

4. The classical statement of the common sensorium is in *On Sleep and Waking*, 455a13–455b2. For an interpretation different from the one I am offering in this essay, see Charles H. Kahn, "Sensation and Consciousness in Aristotle's Psychology," in, *Articles on Aristotle: 4. Psychology and Aesthetics,* eds., Jonathan Barnes *et al.*(New York: St. Martin's Press, 1978). Kahn asserts: "In terms of fullness of treatment there can be no doubt: Aristotle's work on the Soul is primarily a treatise on Sensation. This fact underlines the close relationship between this work and the zoological studies; the sense faculty is for Aristotle the essential principle of the animal as such." (p. 5) But what if *aísthesis* (sense-perception) is really a lower level of *noûs* (mind)?

5. *De Anima* III, ii, 426b8–30.

6. *De Interpretatione*, ch. i, 16a4–9.

7. *De Anima* III, vii, 431a24–26. See also III, ix 432a16–17, and III, iv, 429b23–24.

8. *Ibid.,* III, vi, 430b6.

9. *Ibid.,* III, ii, 427a16–17.

10. Cf. *De Partibus Animalium* III, v, particularly 667b15–31.

11. De Anima III, viii, 432a1–3.

12. *Ibid.*, III, iv, 429b32–430a3.

13. *Ibid.*, III, viii, 432a3–11.

14. *Ibid.*, III, vii, 431b3.

15. *De Memoria* 449b32–450a6.

16. *De Anima*, III, iv, 429a30–429b6.

17. *Ibid.*, III, iii, 427b17 *et passim.*

18. *Ibid.*, III, xi, 434a6–7.

19. *Nicomachean Ethics*, IX, ix, 1170a16–20.

20. Cf. *Nicomachean Ethics* X, vii, especially 1177a11–18, 1177b27–32, and 1178a5–8.

21. De Anima II, iv, 415a27–415b8.

22. *Metaphysics* X, i, 1052a35–36.

23. *Ibid.*, 1052a23–26.

24. *Ibid.*, 1054a13.

25. *Ibid.*, IV, ii, 1003b26–35.

26. *De Anima* II, i, 412a20–29.

27. Descartes, *Meditations*, "Sixth Meditation" (85–86), [68], tr. Lawrence J. Lafleur in *Discourse on Method. Meditations* (Indianapolis: Bobbs-Merrill, 1960), p. 139.

28. Hume, *Treatise of Human Nature*, I, iv, 6.

29. Immanuel Kant, *Critique of Pure Reason*, A 106–7.

30. Kant, *Prolegomena to Any Future Metaphysics*, tr. Lewis W. Beck (Indianapolis: Bobbs-Merrill, 1960), p. 52.

31. *Ibid.*

32. See Aristotle, *Physics* II, i, 192b13–15.

Bibliography

Ahumada, Rodolfo. *A History of Western Ontology: From Thales to Heidegger*. Washington, D.C.: University Press of America, 1978.

Alighieri, Dante. *The Divine Comedy of Dante Alighieri: Inferno*, tr., Allen Mandelbaum. Quality Paperback Book Club, 1980.

Allen, Woody. *Getting Even*. New York: Warner Paperback Library, 1972.

The American Heritage Dictionary. 2nd College Edition. 1985.

Aristotle. *Aristotle's De Motu Animalium*, tr., Martha Craven Nussbaum. Princeton: Princeton University Press, 1978.

Aristotle. *The Basic Works of Aristotle*, ed., Richard McKeon. New York: Random House, 1941.

Aristotle. *The Categories. On Interpretation. Prior Analytics*, trs., Harold P. Cook and Hugh Tredennick. Loeb Classical Library. Cambridge and London: Harvard University Press & William Heinemann, 1962.

Aristotle. *The Metaphysics: Books I-IX*, tr., Hugh Tredennick. Loeb Classical Library. Cambridge and London: Harvard University Press & William Heinemann, 1961.

Aristotle. *Metaphysics: Books X-XIV*. Oeconomica and Magna Moralia, trs., Hugh Tredennick and G. Cyril Armstrong. Loeb Classical Library. Cambridge and London: Harvard University Press & William Heinemann, 1962.

Aristotle. *Nicomachean Ethics*, tr., Martin Ostwald. Indianapolis: Bobbs-Merrill, 1962.

Aristotle. *The Nichomachean Ethics*, tr., H. Rackham. Loeb Classical Library. Cambridge and London: Harvard University Press & William Heinemann, 1956.

Aristotle. *On the Soul. Parva Naturalia. On Breath*, tr., W. S. Hett. Loeb Classical Library. Cambridge and London: Harvard University Press & William Heinemann, 1964.

Aristotle. *The Physics*. Two volumes. Vol. I, trs., Philip H. Wicksteed and Francis M. Cornford. Vol. II, tr., Francis M. Cornford. Loeb Classical

Library. Cambridge and London: Harvard University Press & William Heinemann, 1963 and 1952.

Aristotle. *Politics*, tr., H. Rackham. Loeb Classical Library. Cambridge and London: Harvard University Press, 1932.

Aristotle. *Posterior Analytics. Topica*, trs., Hugh Tredennick and E. S. Forster. Loeb Classical Library. Cambridge and London: Harvard University Press & William Heinemann, 1966.

Augustine, Saint. *St. Augustine's Confessions*. With an English translation by William Watts, 1631. Vol. I. Loeb Classical Library. Cambridge and London: Harvard University Press & William Heinemann, 1989.

Augustine, Saint. *Of True Religion*, tr., J. H. S. Burleigh; intro., Louis O. Mink. Chicago: Henry Regnery, 1959.

Austin, J. L. *How to Do Things with Words*. New York: Oxford University Press, 1965.

Austin, J. L. *Philosophical Papers*, 2nd ed., eds., J. O. Urmson and G. J. Warnock. London: Oxford University Press, 1970.

Boethius. *The Consolation of Philosophy*, tr., Richard Green. Indianapolis: Bobbs-Merrill, 1962.

Buchler, Justus. *Nature and Judgment*. New York: Grosset & Dunlap, 1966.

Burtt, Edwin A., ed. *The English Philosophers from Bacon to Mill*. New York: Random House, 1939.

Cassell's The New Cassell's German Dictionary. 1965.

Chomsky, Noam. *Reflections on Language*. New York: Pantheon Books. Random House, 1975.

Copleston, Frederick. *A History of Philosophy*. Volume IV. Descartes to Leibniz. Garden City, N.Y.: Image Books. Doubleday, 1963.

Copleston, Frederick. *A History of Philosophy*. Volume V. Modern Philosophy: The British Philosophers. Part I. Hobbes to Paley. Garden City, N.Y.: Image Books. Doubleday, 1964.

Copleston, Frederick. *A History of Philosophy*. Volume 6. Modern Philosophy. Part II. Kant. Garden City, N.Y.: Image Books. Doubleday, 1964.

Dennett, Daniel C. *Consciousness Explained*. Boston: Little, Brown, 1991.

Descartes, René. *Discourse on Method. Meditations*, tr., Lawrence J. Lafleur. Indianapolis: Bobbs-Merrill, 1960.

Dewey, John. *Human Nature and Conduct. An Introduction to Social Psychology*. New York: Random House, 1950.

Franklin, Allan. *The Principle of Inertia in the Middle Ages.* Boulder: Colorado Associated University Press, 1976.

Ghiselin, Brewster, ed. *The Creative Process: A Symposium.* New York: The New American Library, 1952.

Greene, Robert. *The Categorical-Mnemonic Method of Language Learning.* 1997. Unpublished manuscript.

Greene, Robert. *New Linguistics Report.* 1998. Unpublished manuscript.

Greene, Robert. *Substance, Mind and the Categories: An Aristotelian Theory of Language.* Dissertation. University of Colorado, 1974.

Greene, Robert. *The Unity of Philosophy and Science. Introduction: Dualism and Overspecialization.* Unpublished ms., 1993.

Guyton, Arthur C. *Basic Human Neurophysiology*, 3rd ed. Philadelphia: W. B. Saunders, 1981.

David Hall. "On Putting Philosophy in Its Place: And What Do *You* Do?" *Nova* 20, No. 2 (Dec. 1984): 3–5.

Hegel, Georg Wilhelm Friedrich. *Hegel. Selections*, ed., J. Loewenberg. New York: Scribner, 1929.

Hegel, Georg Wilhelm Friedrich. *Einleitung in die Geschichte der Philosophie.* Ed. Johannes Hoffmeister. Philosophische Bibliothek. Hamburg: Felix Meiner, 1940.

Hegel, Georg Wilhelm Friedrich. *Enzyklopaedie der philosophischen Wissenschaften.* Eds. Friedhelm Nicolin and Otto Pöggeler. Philosophische Bibliothek. Hamburg: Felix Meiner, 1959.

Heidegger, Martin. *Being and Time*, trs., John Macquarrie and Edward Robinson. New York: Harper & Row, 1962.

Heidegger, Martin. *Die Grundbegriffe der antiken Philosophie.* Gesamtausgabe, Vol. 22, ed., Franz-Karl Blust. Frankfurt am Main: Vittorio Klostermann, 1993.

Hobbes, Thomas. *Elements of Philosophy concerning Body.*

Housman, A(lfred) E(dward). *The Collected Poems of A.E. Housman.* New York: Henry Holt, 1940.

Hume, David. *Treatise of Human Nature.*

Kahn, Charles H. "Sensation and Consciousness in Aristotle's Psychology." In *Articles on Aristotle: 4. Psychology and Aesthetics*, eds., Jonathan Barnes *et al.* New York: St. Martin's Press, 1978.

Kant, Immanuel. *Critique of Pure Reason*, tr., Norman Kemp Smith. New York: St. Martin's Press, 1965.

Kant, Immanuel. *Kritik der reinen Vernunft*, ed., Raymund Schmidt. Hamburg: Felix Meiner, 1956.

Kant, Immanuel. *Prolegomena to any Future Metaphysics*, tr., Lewis White Beck. Indianapolis: Bobbs-Merrill, 1950.

Keats, John. "On First Looking into Chapman's Homer."

Kimball, Bruce A. *Orators and Philosophers: A History of the Idea of Liberal Education*. Expanded ed. New York: College Entrance Examination Board, 1995.

Kramers' Engels Woordenboek. 1960.

Kristeller, Paul Oskar. "Stoic and Neoplatonic Sources of Spinoza's *Ethics*." *History of European Ideas* 5, No. 1 (1984): 1–15.

Kuhn, Thomas S. *The Copernican Revolution*. New York: Random House, 1957.

Kuhn, Thomas S. *The Structure of Scientific Revolutions*, 2nd ed. enlarged. Chicago and London: University of Chicago Press, 1970.

Lakoff, George. *Women, Fire, and Dangerous Things: What Categories Reveal about the Mind*. Chicago and London: University of Chicago Press, 1987.

Larousse Unabridged French-English/English-French Dictionary. 1993.

Larousse Diccionario General español-ingles. 1983.

Leibniz, Gottfried Wilhelm. *Leibniz. Selections*, ed., Philip P. Wiener. New York: Scribner, 1951.

Locke, John. *An Essay Concerning Human Understanding*, ed., Alexander Campbell Fraser in two volumes. New York: Dover, 1959.

Mansion's Shorter French and English Dictionary.

Matthews, Gary G. *Cellular Physiology of Nerve and Muscle*. 3rd ed. Malden, Mass.: Blackwell Science, 1998.

Modrak, Deborah K.W. *Aristotle: The Power of Perception*. Chicago and London: University of Chicago Press, 1987.

Muller, V. K.. *English-Russian Dictionary*. 17th rev. and enlarged ed. New York: Dutton, 1981.

Olomucki, Martin. *The Chemistry of Life*, tr., Isabel A. Leonard from *La Chimie du Vivant*. New York, McGraw-Hill, 1993.

Oxford English Dictionary. 1971.

Oxford English Dictionary. Supplement. 1987.

Plato. *Platonis Opera*, ed., John Burnet. Oxford: The Clarendon Press.

Plato. *Plato: The Collected Dialogues*, eds., Edith Hamilton and Huntington Cairns. Bollingen Series LXXI. Princeton, N.J.: Princeton University Press, 1961.

Pope, Alexander. *The Poems of Alexander Pope*, ed., John Butt. New Haven: Yale University Press, 1963.

Prisma's English-Swedish Dictionary. 1988.

Rabelais, François. *Gargantua and Pantagruel.* Volume I, tr., Sir Thomas Urquhart. London and New York: Dent & Dutton, 1962.

Randall, J. H. Jr. *Aristotle.* New York: Columbia University Press, 1960.

Randall, J. H. Jr. *The Career of Philosophy*, Volume I, From the Middle Ages to the Enlightenment. New York and London: Columbia University Press, 1962

Randall, J. H. Jr. *The Career of Philosophy*, Volume II, From the Enlightenment to the Age of Darwin. New York and London: Columbia University Press, 1965.

Rorty, Richard. *Philosophy and the Mirror of Nature.* Princeton, N.J.: Princeton University Press, 1979.

Spinoza, Benedict de. *Ethics*, ed., James Gutmann. New York: Hafner Press. Macmillan, 1949.

The Statistical Abstract of the United States 1995.

The Statistical Abstract of the United States 1996.

The Statistical Abstract of the United States 1997.

Sullivan, Walter. "Of Aristotle, Atoms and a Retiring Sage." *The New York Times*, 12 Oct. 1974, sec.1, p.1 *et seq.*

Swift, Jonathan. *A Full and True Account of the Battel Fought last Friday, Between the Antient and the Modern Books in St. James's Library.*

Taylor, Charles. *Hegel.* Cambridge: Cambridge University Press, 1975.

Tortora, Gerard J. and Anagnostakos, Nicholas P. *Principles of Anatomy and Physiology*, 3rd ed. *New York: Harper & Row, 1981.*

Wedin, Michael V. *Mind and Imagination in Aristotle.* New Haven and London: Yale University Press, 1988.

Whitehead, Alfred North. *Process and Reality. An Essay in Cosmology.* New York: Harper, 1960.

Whitman, Walt. *Leaves of Grass.*

Wittgenstein, Ludwig. *Philosophische Untersuchungen. Philosophical Investigations*, 3rd ed., tr., G. E. M. Anscombe. New York: Macmillan, 1969.

Index